Other Books by Anthony Louis

Horary Astrology Plain and Simple (Llewellyn Publications, 2002)

Tarot Plain and Simple (Llewellyn Publications, 2002)

The Art of Forecasting Using Solar Returns (The Wessex Astrologer, 2008)

Tarot Beyond the Basics (Llewellyn Publications, 2014)

LLEWELLYN'S

COMPLETE BOOK OF

TAROT

About the Author

Anthony Louis (Conn.) is a physician and psychiatrist. Astrology has been his avocation for more than thirty years. He has lectured internationally on horary astrology and has published numerous articles in magazines such as *American Astrology*, *The Mountain Astrologer*, and *The Horary Practitioner*.

To Write to the Author

If you wish to contact the author or would like more information about this book, please write to the author in care of Llewellyn Worldwide, and we will forward your request. Both author and publisher appreciate hearing from you and learning of your enjoyment of this book and how it has helped you. Llewellyn Worldwide cannot guarantee that every letter written to the author can be answered, but all will be forwarded. Please write to:

Anthony Louis
%o Llewellyn Worldwide
2143 Wooddale Drive
Woodbury, MN 55125-2989

Please enclose a self-addressed stamped envelope for reply or $1.00 to cover costs.
If outside the USA, enclose an international postal reply coupon.

Many of Llewellyn's authors have websites with additional information and resources. For more information, please visit us at: www.llewellyn.com.

LLEWELLYN'S

COMPLETE BOOK OF

TAROT

A COMPREHENSIVE GUIDE

ANTHONY LOUIS

Llewellyn Publications
Woodbury, Minnesota

FIRST EDITION
First Printing, 2016

Book design by Bob Gaul
Interior card images: Classic Tarot © 2014 by Llewellyn Publications with art by Eugene Smith and text by Barbara Moore
Cover design by Lisa Novak
Cover images: iStockphoto.com/64726409/©PeterHermesFurian; iStockphoto.com/10620241/©narcisa; iStockphoto.com/56232750/©Digimann; The Magician, The Fool, The High Priestess and The Hermit cards from the Rider-Waite Tarot Deck®, known also as the Rider Tarot and the Waite Tarot, reproduced by permission of U.S. Games Systems, Inc., Stamford, CT 06902 USA. Copyright ©1971 by U.S. Games Systems, Inc. Further reproduction prohibited. The Rider-Waite Tarot Deck® is a registered trademark of U.S. Games Systems, Inc.; The 6 of Cups, 3 of Wands and 2 of Discs cards from the Thoth Tarot reproduced by permission of Ordo Templi Orientis; The Tower and 10 of Swords cards from Ancient Tarot of Marseilles reproduced by permission of Lo Scarabeo.
Editing by Laura Graves
Interior illustrations by Llewellyn Art Department

Llewellyn Publications is a registered trademark of Llewellyn Worldwide Ltd.

Library of Congress Cataloging-in-Publication Data
Names: Louis, Anthony, 1945– author.
Title: Llewellyn's complete book of tarot : a comprehensive resource / Anthony Louis.
Description: first edition. | Woodbury : Llewellyn Worldwide, Ltd, 2016. | Includes bibliographical references.
Identifiers: LCCN 2016008864 (print) | LCCN 2016013038 (ebook) | ISBN 9780738749082 | ISBN 9780738750033
Subjects: LCSH: Tarot.
Classification: LCC BF1879.T2 L6825 2016 (print) | LCC BF1879.T2 (ebook)| DDC 133.3/2424—dc23
LC record available at http://lccn.loc.gov/2016008864

Llewellyn Publications
A Division of Llewellyn Worldwide Ltd.
2143 Wooddale Drive
Woodbury, MN 55125-2989
www.llewellyn.com

Printed in the United States of America

Dedication

In New York City a young man carrying a musical instrument stops an elderly woman and asks, "Excuse me, ma'am, how do I get to Carnegie Hall?"

The lady looks him straight in the eye and responds, "Practice, practice, practice!"

This book is dedicated to all who are seeking a way to Carnegie Hall.

Contents

Contents

Contents

Preface

When Llewellyn first contacted me about writing this book, I was delighted and a bit daunted. The acquisitions editor, Barbara Moore, explained that her company had a series entitled *The Complete Book of …* and was seeking an author for their *Complete Book of Tarot*. The word "complete" provoked a twinge of anxiety. Over the years I have run into tarot enthusiasts who have amassed more than a thousand books and an equally stunning number of tarot decks for their collections! How could a single book call itself "complete" when measured against such a vast landscape? Clearly, some decisions about content had to be made.

After mulling the issue over, I came to the following resolution. This book would follow certain principles to offer a "complete" and even-handed approach in the space of a single volume. To achieve this goal, I established the following guidelines:

- The book would cover the essential topics that someone new to tarot should know. The focus would be on a tarot "core curriculum"—a term that has become both popular and reviled in contemporary news about American education.

- The material covered would be based on established traditions in tarot literature. To this end, I would cite the works of such tarot giants as Etteilla (Jean-Baptiste Alliette), the French occultist whose writings first popularized tarot in Europe; S. L. MacGregor Mathers of the Hermetic Order of the Golden Dawn; Arthur Edward Waite, intellectual father of the influential Rider-Waite-Smith deck; and Aleister Crowley of the Thoth tarot deck.

- For easy reference, the text would be concise and to the point and would include a detailed table of contents to enable readers to search easily for topics of interest.

- More obscure and esoteric aspects of tarot would be mentioned only in passing. Readers would be referred to other texts to pursue specialized topics in further detail.

- To avoid rehashing what can be found in currently available texts, this book would present the core material in a fresh and interesting manner.

- Because the tarot is the product of the Italian Renaissance, this book would include the Christian cultural influences on tarot symbolism that many authors omit. In addition, it would discuss the symbolic use of the Hebrew alphabet, which was crucial to the Golden Dawn's method of delineating the major arcana (the twenty-two allegorical picture cards of the traditional tarot deck).

- Because the Hermetic Order of the Golden Dawn had such an overwhelming influence on modern tarot interpretation at the end of the nineteenth century, this book would follow the Golden Dawn's astrological correspondences for the cards.

- Tarot readers come from many different backgrounds and have diverse worldviews, so this book would seek to be as objective and nonjudgmental as possible.

- Because it can be difficult for a sole author to remain objective, I would label my personal opinions as such. For example, I regard the modern use of the tarot as a form of divination (an attempt to "communicate with the gods") but with the important caveat that *the gods help those who help themselves.* Readers should be aware that I am assuming this point of view.

- A major focus of the book would be the use of the art of tarot as a tool for insight, empowerment, clarification, and self-understanding rather than its older use as a method of fortune-telling, popularized in Hollywood movies.

- The book would avoid dogmatic pronouncements and instead serve as a tarot travelogue, much like a guidebook to a foreign country. In it, I would describe things I had seen and done in tarot land, but it would be up to readers to explore the territory, do their own experimentation, and come to their own conclusions.

My hope as an author is that I have succeeded in presenting a useful and comprehensive guide to tarot for the twenty-first century. It will be up to the reader to decide whether this book has lived up to these aspirations.

One

Why Learn the Tarot?

On Divination

The tarot offers a tool for gaining perspective on complicated situations. As you lay out the cards, their images resonate with your question and shed light on the nuances of your circumstances. As you reflect on these images, you can gain clarity into the pros and cons of a decision you need to make. In this sense, reading the tarot is similar to the process of brainstorming, which can generate new ideas and help to solve problems.

Although the tarot originated as a deck of playing cards, it is commonly used today for divination, which we might define as "brainstorming with the help of the gods." Some people may be put off by the idea of divination, so it is worthwhile to explore the meaning of this term. In Latin, *divinus* is a word referring to the gods. In ancient times, people believed that certain information, such as knowledge of the future, belonged exclusively to divine beings. Mortals, for their part, developed various methods to petition the gods to share their divine knowledge with humankind, and such methods were called divination.

Over the years the term *divination* has broadened to include any method that "attempts to foretell the future or to discern unknown matters, as though by supernatural means." [1] In this definition, the word "supernatural" refers to methods that cannot be proved by the scientific method—that is, methods hard science cannot yet or perhaps never will be able to explain. Scientists regard such techniques

---

1. This definition is a compilation and paraphrase of standard definitions of "divination" found in several different dictionaries.

as "pseudoscience" because they fall outside the area of knowledge the scientific method is designed to explain. There can be little doubt that, together with practices like Freudian psychoanalysis, divination with tarot cards is one such pseudo-science. On the other hand, many individuals testify that they have benefited greatly from tarot readings as well as from sessions with a psychoanalyst.

The other part of the proposed definition states that *divination* attempts to discern occult information *as though by supernatural means*. Not infrequently, the knowledge gained during a tarot reading feels eerily as if it were a form of extra-ordinary knowing or as if it had a supernatural origin. Various dictionarie define *divination* as an inspired guess (where does the inspiration come from?), a presentiment, an intuitive perception, a prophecy, an instinctive foresight, or simply as the interpretation of signs and omens.

Given that the tarot can be used as a form of divination, let's plunge right in and ask the tarot a question. A logical place to start is to inquire of our tarot deck what it can do for us, but first let me mention some customary terminology. In tarot literature, we call the person who consults (queries) the cards the *querent* (client, seeker) and the person who interprets the cards the *reader*. If you interpret your own cards, you are acting as both the querent who queries and the reader who deciphers the message in the cards.

What Can the Tarot Do for You?

To answer this question, I shuffled the tarot deck carefully and randomly drew four cards (four is the number of structure and organization) while focusing in a relaxed and open state of mind on the intention of receiving an answer to my question. Intention, as we shall see, plays a critical role in tarot reading. Shuffling the cards with sincere intention and expectation of receiving a helpful response is essential to the process. Insincere or frivolous questions result in a meaningless, random set of cards.

Here is what the tarot had to say about what it can do for us:

1. The Two of Swords

In this card, a woman sits blindfolded on the shore of a body of water. She holds aloft two swords, evenly balanced. Above her hangs a crescent moon, symbolizing her changing emotional state. She may be trying to resolve conflicting feelings or attempting to choose between evenly matched options, represented by the dual swords. The tarot appears to be saying that it can help us to sort out our feelings, clarify our choices, and assist us in making more reasoned decisions. The eighteenth-century French occultist who popularized tarot, Etteilla, considered the Two of Swords as a card of rapport and affection, so the tarot may be also saying that it can bring new friendships into our lives.

2. The Seven of Pentacles

The gardener in the Seven of Coins is tending a bush sprouting seven Pentacle-fruits. Some of the fruit looks healthy and delicious, others look discolored and unappetizing. The man seems to be taking a break, perhaps to contemplate his work and decide upon a next move. With this card, the tarot is suggesting that it can help us to reflect on our labors, enabling us to make prudent choices that lead to a productive outcome. A. E. Waite, author of the Rider-Waite-Smith deck, described the young man on this card as viewing the fruits "as if they were his treasures and that his heart was there," so maybe the tarot is also saying that it can help us to clarify our heart's desires.

3. The Devil

Tarot expert Paul Huson wrote a book called *The Devil's Picturebook,* so named because during unenlightened times the divinatory power of the cards was attributed to Satan. The Devil card sometimes frightens readers from a strongly religious upbringing. Most tarot readers view this card as a warning to avoid becoming a slave to materialistic desires, such as the lust for fame, power, sex, pleasure, wealth, or self-aggrandizement. On the positive side, this card can represent the determination to accomplish a valued goal in the material world. With the Devil card, the tarot is suggesting that it can help us to explore our most primitive desires and confront the shadow side of our personalities. Carl Jung would be very pleased with this advice.

4. *The Ten of Cups*

The Ten of Cups shows a happy family enjoying life in secure circumstances. Unlike the Devil card (which focuses almost exclusively on self-interest and material lusts), the Ten of Cups displays the joy of sharing in close personal relationships. As the last card in the spread, the Ten of Cups suggests that, in the end, the tarot can help us to establish more loving relationships. The Golden Dawn associated this card with the warlike planet Mars, suggesting that the support of close personal relationships can help us weather the stresses and conflicts of daily life.

As you read the above interpretations, keep in mind that these comments represent merely my own impressions in the context of the question. If you have other insights or gut feelings about how these cards may answer the question, your views are equally as valid as mine and deserve respect for the wisdom that they contain. Sir Francis Bacon (1561–1626) advised us always to pay attention to thoughts that come unbidden, for they are often the most valuable.

Additional Insight: The High Priestess

Finally, I should mention that for many contemporary tarot readers, the High Priestess is a symbol of the wisdom of the tarot. Originally called the Female Pope (*La Papessa*), this priestess represents an unorthodox, nonpatriarchal approach to knowing. In the Rider-Waite-Smith tradition, she sits in front of a body of water, signifying our emotions and the unconscious. Behind her stretches a veil that obscures the entryway to the inner world of hidden knowledge. Either side of the priestess stand light and dark pillars, suggesting that she can help us to reconcile apparently conflicting dualities. As an unorthodox wisdom figure, *La Papessa* offers us access to extraordinary ways of knowing, including the various occult and esoteric sciences. Her astrological symbol is the Moon, a feminine planet linked to cycles, sleep, dreams, intuition, goddesses, spellcasting, shapeshifting, and ceremonial magic.

My Story

For as long as I can remember, I have been fascinated by divination. It must have to do with attending a Catholic school run by well-meaning but rather superstitious nuns. The good sisters told us fascinating stories about a host of divine miracles, the prophecies of Fatima the Pope was keeping secret, spirits who returned from the dead to warn mortals about the dangers of sin, guardian angels who never took their eyes off you even when you were sitting on the toilet, and saints with special powers to foresee the future and "bi-locate," to be in two places at once. I thought it would be really neat to be able to bi-locate.

The fantastical nature of such stories prompted me to become a skeptic at a young age. In each successive grade in Catholic school, we studied the *Baltimore Catechism* with its images of white milk in glass bottles being stained with "evil" black spots every time we sinned. The white milk represented our immortal souls and the black spots all the bad things we had done. The only way to remove these evil spots was to pray and do penance. The alternative was to burn eternally in the fires of hell. Each year the catechism began with the same questions and answers, which we had to memorize verbatim:

"Who made you?" "God made me."

"Why did God make you?" "God made me to know, love, and serve him in this world."

Having learned the party line, I began looking for the evidence that God made me. I could recall that before my younger brother was born my mother's belly got very large. She told me that a baby was growing inside. I suspected that my father had something to do with it, but I wasn't sure. Then one day my mother went to the hospital and came home with a much smaller belly and a new baby brother. She never mentioned God taking part in the process.

I grew up in a small town in Connecticut and attended the local parochial school. Some kids in my neighborhood were Protestants; they belonged to the YMCA with its indoor basketball court and swimming pool. The nuns, however, warned us of the evils of Protestantism. It would be a sin to join the YMCA because Protestantism is based on a false reading of the Bible, and the YMCA would lure us away from the one true faith, endangering our immortal souls.

This last admonition confused me because I spent a lot of time playing with two of the Protestant kids in my neighborhood. Neither seemed very much interested in religion. As far as I could tell, they never tried to corrupt my immortal soul; they just wanted to ride their bikes, go for hikes, and play ball. The mismatch between the nuns' teachings and the evidence of my senses only served to deepen my skepticism.

One day in a classroom discussion I mentioned that I was impressed by something I had read about astrology. The nun's ears perked up, and a look of alarm spread across her face. Hadn't the good sisters warned us that true prophecy comes from God and any other form of future casting is the work of the devil? Whatever is forbidden, however, becomes more appealing. It wasn't long before I began to study astrology in earnest.

My interest in astrology was sparked in the late 1950s when my father put a dime into a machine at an amusement park to purchase his sun sign horoscope. The accuracy of the report was astounding. How could a machine know so much about my father? I had to find out, so I went to the library and began to read every book I could find about astrology. Before long I was casting charts and making predictions for family and friends. Astrology appeared to have some validity, but I couldn't explain how it worked scientifically. I was also a budding scientist at the time and loved reading books about the natural sciences.

A brief example of an accurate prediction might be useful. In my teens, I did not know my exact time of birth. It was not recorded on my birth certificate, and my father could only recall that I was born in the morning. My mother died when I was eight years old, so I could not ask her. Using a technique I found in an astrology book, I calculated that I must have been born around 9:04 in the morning. Years later I found my father's notebook in the attic and discovered that he had written: "Anthony, born 9:05 AM." I was astounded that the astrological calculation was only a minute off from the time recorded in my father's journal! Either this was an amazing coincidence, or there was some truth to all this astrology stuff.

In my late teens, I started reading Freud and Jung and became fascinated with dream symbols and psychological archetypes. My study of the celestial science resonated with what these two great psychologists had to say. In my own experience, Jung's writings made sense regarding the contents of the collective unconscious. The same images that populated mythology, religion, and world literature cropped up in astrology and tarot. The symbolism shared by psychology, psychoanalysis, and astrology held my attention throughout my studies.

In the late 1960s, an astrologer friend introduced me to the tarot. At first I was put off by the cards' ambiguity. Unlike astrology, whose predictions were mathematically precise, tarot interpretations seemed very subjective and less rule-bound. In the early 1970s, I read a book by Eden Gray (now a classic) that made the cards more understandable, but their interpretation remained vague and imprecise in my hands.

About a decade after reading Eden Gray's book, I made a decision to master the tarot. My method was to read everything I could about the cards and do hundreds of readings, taking careful notes and following up on the outcomes. It dawned on me (I'm a slow learner) that although reading books about tarot is helpful, the best way to learn is to use the cards often and review consistently how the symbols in the cards play out in real life.

A friend suggested I compile my tarot notes in book form, which resulted in *Tarot Plain and Simple* (1996). My continued interest in the shared symbolism of astrology and tarot eventually led to a second book, *Tarot Beyond the Basics* (2014). Because of the popularity of the first two books, Llewellyn asked me to write this one, my third about the tarot. The reader will notice the influence of Freud and Jung as well as my background in psychiatry and psychology in the way I approach the cards.

Two

Where Did the
Tarot Come From?

A Capsule History of the Tarot

Before we can address the question of where the tarot originated, we must clarify what we mean by the tarot. The *Oxford Dictionary* gives the following definition of tarot: "playing cards, traditionally a pack of 78 with five suits, used for fortune-telling and (especially in Europe) in certain games. The suits are typically swords, cups, coins (or pentacles), batons (or wands), and a permanent suit of trump."[2] We will examine this definition more carefully in the next chapter. For now, let's focus on where these seventy-eight cards came from.

Playing cards could only exist after the invention of paper, which historians attribute to the Chinese roughly a hundred years before the birth of Christ. Many historians believe that the ancient Chinese invented playing cards as well as games such as dominos and mahjong. Playing cards eventually made their way eastward along trade routes and became popular among Arab countries in the Middle East. The Mamluk playing cards of fourteenth-century Egypt are strikingly similar to modern playing cards as well as the pip cards of tarot decks.

Most likely the Arabs who came to Spain during the second half of the fourteenth century carried the Mamluk deck with them so they could continue to play the Egyptian game of *na'ibs* or "deputies."

---

2. "Tarot," *Oxford Dictionary*, www.oxforddictionaries.com/us/definition/american_english/tarot, accessed 12 January 2015.

The Arabic *na'ib* means someone who is second in command. The Spanish called the playing cards *naipes* after the game, and the word *naipe* eventually became an official part of the Spanish language.

Early in the fifteenth century, artisans in northern Italy added a fifth trump suit to the four standard suits of the Mamluk-inspired cards, creating a deck to play the game of *trionfi*, or triumphs, similar to the modern game of bridge. The word *tarot* may derive from the Italian name for the deck, *tarrochi*. Renaissance artists drew their inspiration for the allegorical images on the trump cards from the Bible as well as from ancient Greek and Roman manuscripts, which were all the rage in Renaissance Italy. Each trump in the card sequence outranks the one that comes before it.

Much of the imagery of early tarot decks derives from the influence of the Roman Catholic Church on the culture of the time. Daily life was structured around religious feasts and the pantheon of Catholic saints, each of whom had a special day on the calendar. Because the common people could not read and write, the Church relied on images, allegories, and the spoken word to guide the faithful toward salvation. Together with the images of Greek and Roman mythology, these Christian allegories made their way onto the trump cards of the tarot.

From Italy, the tarot deck traveled to France where it found safe haven in the city of Marseille, a major center for the production of tarot decks in the following centuries. In Italy this deck was originally called the *carte da trionfi*, that is, the trump or "triumph cards"—a reference to the allegorical cards numbered I to XXI (with or without the inclusion of the Fool.)Historian Gertrude Moakley noted that the fifteenth-century tarot deck painted by Bonifacio Bembo followed the pattern of ancient Roman triumphal marches (*trionfi*) celebrated in Petrarch's famous fourteenth-century poem "I Trionfi." Images of triumphal marches can still be seen on the triumphal arches of the Forum in Rome.

A commentary from Yale's Beineke Library states that "I Trionfi" reflects Plutarch's "contemplation of the successive victories of Love, Chastity, Death, Fame, Time, and Eternity. The poet becomes the moralist and philosopher who searches for meaning, as life passes from one stage to the next."[3] Similarly, the tarot's major arcana reflect the triumph of love over secular powers and religious authorities as well as the struggles between vice and virtue on the journey toward the "promised land" depicted on the final trump card.

Although tarot originated as a card game and work of art for wealthy Italian families, it may have been used for a rudimentary form of divination as early as the sixteenth century. The Italian nobility of the 1500s played a game called *tarrochi appropriati* in which players drew cards at random, using the images on those cards to inspire the writing of poetic verses about each other's destiny. These cards were called *sortes*, an Italian word meaning fate, lot, destiny, or chance. Over time the tarot became a tool for divination.

Throughout history, any sort of random occurrence served as a ready vehicle for divining the future, including the pattern of stars in the sky, the appearance of clouds, the arrangement of tea

---

3. "I Trionfi," Yale Beineke Library, brbl-archive.library.yale.edu/exhibitions/petrarch/about.html, accessed 15 January 2015.

leaves in a cup, the entrails of dead animals, and so on. By the early 1700s, the card readers of northern Italy developed a system for divining with playing cards, and around 1750 the French cartomancer Etteilla noted that he learned to tell fortunes by means of playing cards from three cartomancers, one of whom hailed from northern Italy's Piedmont region. Etteilla's publications spurred a contagious interest in the use of tarot for fortune-telling throughout Europe, an interest that has continued to modern times.

Myths about the Tarot

In tarot literature, you will find dozens of not-so-factual claims about the cards. This section will examine some of the common myths about tarot. By "myths" I mean assertions which are neither verifiable nor grounded in firm evidence. The following tarot myths appear in no particular order.

Myth 1: The tarot is a picture book written by priests of the Egyptian god Thoth Hermes Trismegistus that was later brought to Europe by the gypsies. A concise statement of this myth appears in *The Secret Teachings of All Ages* by Manly P. Hall:

> It has been asserted that the Book of Thoth is, in reality, the mysterious
> *Tarot of the Bohemians*—a strange emblematic book of seventy-eight leaves which has been
> in possession of the gypsies since the time when they were driven from their ancient temple. [4]

Fact 1: The tarot was invented as a card game during the Renaissance by Italian artists who incorporated images and ideas from ancient Greek and Roman mythology, which probably included themes derived from the cult of Thoth Hermes Trismegistus. The gypsies, who originated in India, were not ancient Egyptian priests and did not arrive in Europe until well after the Italians produced the first tarot decks.

Myth 2: The tarot is evil and owes its accuracy to the workings of the devil.

Fact 2: The tarot is simply a deck of sevety-eight cards with imaginative images printed on them. The accuracy of the tarot depends on the intuitive faculties of the reader. Evil does not reside in pieces of cardboard; it is a distinctly human trait. Those who are old enough may recall the introduction to the classic radio program *The Shadow:* "Who knows what evil lurks in the hearts of men? The Shadow knows!"

Myth 3: You must never make a major decision without first consulting the cards.

---

4. Manly P. Hall, "The Life and Teachings of Thoth Hermes Trismegistus," in *The Secret Teachings of All Ages* (San Francisco: H.S. Crocker, 1928), 38, available at www.sacred-texts.com/eso/sta/sta08.htm, accessed 20 January 2015.

Fact 3: The tarot is simply a tool that can help us to clarify our thinking. It's up to us whether or not we use the cards. Some people find the tarot helpful, others do not. Occultist Hajo Banzhaf has cautioned that tarot is a good servant but a bad master. We should consult the tarot only if we find it helpful.

Myth 4: To use tarot effectively, you must first have a working knowledge of other disciplines such as astrology, Kabbalah, alchemy, and numerology.

Fact 4: The tarot is an independent symbolic system. It has much in common with the symbolism of astrology, alchemy, Kabbalah, and so on, but you don't need to know these other systems to make use of the cards. As Arthur E. Waite noted, "True tarot is symbolism; it speaks no other language and offers no other signs." [5] That said, there are certain basic symbols that appear commonly in most modern tarot decks. These include the symbolism of numbers and the use of the four classical elements: Fire, Water, Air, and Earth. In addition, certain decks are grounded in the Kabbalah or astrology, for example, and they are dedicated to devotees of these esoteric disciplines. When deciding on a deck to use, it is useful to become familiar with the symbolism the artist has employed in illustrating the cards.

Myth 5: The Catholic Church banned tarot as a form of heresy and as dangerous black magic.

Fact 5: In the 1400s, the original tarot decks were used for card games in northern Italy. Around this time, the church was preaching against all games of chance (playing cards, dice, board games, and so on) as forms of gambling and frivolous activity that distracted the faithful from the road to salvation. In modern times, Pope Francis (2014) has said: "In order to solve their problems many people resort to fortune tellers and tarot cards. But only Jesus saves, and we must bear witness to this! He is the only one." [6] Interestingly, the modern use of the tarot for self-exploration is more consistent with the ideas of the Protestant Reformation than with traditional Catholicism because tarot assumes that individuals can discover truth on their own without the intermediacy of a hierarchical religious organization.

Myth 6: You must be psychic to read the tarot.

Fact 6: The *Oxford Dictionary* defines *psychic* as "relating to or denoting faculties or phenomena that are apparently inexplicable by natural laws, especially involving telepathy or clairvoyance." [7] In my view, the tarot is a tool that allows us to tap into our intuition, the results of which often appear "inexplicable by natural laws" because we tend to ignore intuitive hunches as we grow into adulthood. The tarot helps restore the balance between rational analysis and listening to our gut. With continued practice, you may be surprised at how often unexpected yet verifiable impressions seem to leap from the cards.

---

5. A. E. Waite, *The Pictorial Key to the Tarot* (Secaucus, NJ: Citadel Press, 1959), 4.

6. "Tarot Readers and Fortune Tellers Cannot Save You, Says Pope Francis," *The Catholic Herald*, 5 April 2013, www.catholicherald.co.uk/news/2013/04/05/tarot-readers-and-fortune-tellers-cannot-save-you-says-pope-francis/, accessed 14 February 2015.

7. "Psychic," *Oxford Dictionary*, www.oxforddictionaries.com/us/definition/american_english/psychic, accessed 2 February 2015.

Myth 7: The tarot is always right (fate), and there is nothing you can do to change the future revealed in the cards (free will).

Fact 7: Nothing is infallible. The tarot can provide clarification and guidance, but what you do with your life is up to you. The noted occultist Dion Fortune viewed the tarot as an intuitive compass: "A divination should be regarded as a weather vane which shows which way the winds of the invisible forces are blowing, but it should be always remembered that a weather-vane was not meant to determine the course that a ship is to take; it merely indicates how best to trim the sails." [8]

Myth 8: The Death card means that you or someone close to you is about to die.

Fact 8: Hollywood movies suggest that the Death card almost inevitably foreshadows some character's imminent demise. In real life, however, the Death card indicates an important transition, the closing of one chapter and the opening of another. Only rarely does it indicate a physical death. For example, a friend once asked me to read his cards, and the central card of his layout was Death. It made sense because he was in the midst of deciding whether to retire from his job and begin a new phase of his life as a retired person. Now, many years later, he is still alive and enjoying his retirement.

Myth(s) 9: One must follow certain rules and rituals regarding the acquisition, handling, and storage of the cards. Various myths fall under this heading, including admonitions such as:

- The freeloader myth: never buy your own cards; they must be given to you as a gift.

- The silk cloth myth: always wrap your cards in silk cloth and store them in an oak box with crystals like quartz or amethyst.

- The OCD or spiritual cooties myth: only *you* are allowed to touch your cards because others will contaminate them with bad vibrations.

- The sleep-with-your-cards myth: you must sleep with a new deck of cards under your pillow to become properly attuned to them.

- The spiteful cards myth: you can only own one deck, the one you use for reading. Keeping other decks in the house will make your preferred deck jealous, and out of spite, it won't give you good readings anymore.

- The split-brain myth: cut the deck only with your left hand because the left side of your body is more attuned to your unconscious mind, which resides in the right side of the brain.

- The evil kitty myth: keep the cards away from cats because felines act as a drain on psychic ability.

---

8.   Dion Fortune, *Practical Occultism in Daily Life* (Wellingborough, UK: Aquarian Press, 1935), 39.

- The bad vibrations myth: you must cleanse your cards of negative energies by smudging them (passing each card through the smoke of a burning plant such as white sage or lavender).

- The lunar energy myth: you must leave your cards overnight in the moonlight so they can absorb psychic lunar vibrations.

- The incantation myth: you must say a special prayer or perform an incantation before reading with the cards.

Fact(s) 9: A good tarot deck is something to care for and cherish just as you would any object of beauty. Cards that get sticky with jam are hard to shuffle. Although it's nice to receive the cards as a gift, most tarot readers buy their own decks and have more than one. If any of the above practices appeal to you, by all means engage in them but don't feel obliged to do so. A useful discussion of this topic can be found in the article "Caring for Your Tarot Cards" by Catherine Chapman.[9]

Myth(s) 10: There are certain rules you must obey when doing tarot readings. Some of these are:

- Never read for yourself, but…

- If you do read for yourself, don't do so more than twice a year.

- It's bad luck to charge money to read the cards for others, but…

- It's a sign that you don't respect the value of the tarot if you don't charge for your readings.

- You must get certified by an "official" tarot organization to become a legitimate reader (as far as I know, the tarot community has not yet elected a Pope or Papess).

- The tarot always gives a correct answer, and any errors in a tarot reading are due to the practitioner's failure to understand what the cards are saying, but…

- You should abandon a divination if the cards do not clearly address the querent's concerns.

- Each tarot card has a specific and timeless archetypal meaning, but…

- The meaning of a tarot card depends entirely on the intuition and sensitivity of the reader.

- There is a correct and established way to read the cards, and you must follow these rules if you wish to make an accurate interpretation, but let your intuition be your guide.

---

9. Catherine Chapman, "Caring for Your Tarot Cards," 3 July 2010, http://tarotelements.com/2010/07/03/caring-for-your-tarot-cards/, accessed 12 November 2014.

Fact(s) 10: Every reader develops his or her own method of interpreting the cards on the basis of experience and intuition. The Golden Dawn routinely abandoned a divination if the querent's significator failed to appear in a spread in a way that clearly addressed the client's concerns. It's hard to be objective when reading for yourself or for people you care about. Remember that the doctor who treats himself has a fool for a patient. When in doubt, it is wise to get a second opinion from an experienced tarot reader. As you become more skilled, your readings will become valuable resources others are willing to pay for, just as they would compensate any valued consultant.

Myth 11: Tarot readers are charlatans and con artists.

Fact 11: The majority of tarot readers are honest, well-intentioned individuals who use the cards for personal development and spiritual understanding. Unfortunately, in every profession there is a small group of dishonest individuals who seek to scam the public. You should avoid readers who insist on telling you how to live your life. Also, run quickly from those who warn you of a dire fate or an evil spell only *they* can remove for an appropriately large sum of money. Send me the money instead—it will do you as much good!

Myth 12: You must learn the history of the tarot to become a good reader.

Fact 12: The history of the tarot is fascinating, but you don't need to know it to read the cards effectively. On the other hand, learning about the origins of the ideas and symbols artists used to illustrate the cards can give you a greater sense of their meaning and place in Western culture. I enjoy understanding the evolution of ideas and historical trends, so I have included numerous comments about history throughout this text. Knowing a little about the history can keep you from falling prey to many of the false ideas about the cards that have been perpetrated over the course of time. Tarot is a fanciful and imaginative process, so it's nice to keep at least one foot planted on the ground.

Myth 13: Some tarot cards are really very "good" and others are really very "evil."

Fact 13: All tarot cards are neutral; they merely present universal archetypal images that are part of the human experience. The "goodness" or "badness" of a card depends entirely on what we choose to do with the energy represented. Yin is balanced by yang; every positive in life has its shadow side, and vice versa. A knife in the hands of a surgeon can save a life, but the same knife wielded by a terrorist can wreak havoc. A Zen Buddhist proverb illustrates this idea: A farmer's horse ran off, prompting the neighbors to lament, "That's bad." The next day the horse returned along with three wild horses, and the neighbors declared, "That's good." When the farmer's son broke his leg trying to tame the wild horses, the neighbors commented, "That's bad." The next day, the army came to draft the farmer's son for an impending battle but because of his broken leg, they didn't draft him. It so happened that all the soldiers who fought in the battle died, but the son survived because of his fractured limb. This time the neighbors kept silent. They had learned the futility of judging situations in terms of black and white, good and bad.

Three

Will the Real Tarot
Please Stand Up?

The Structure of the Tarot Deck

We saw in the last chapter that the modern tarot deck consists of seventy-eight playing cards in five suits: Wands (batons), Swords, Cups, Pentacles (coins, disks), and trumps (keys, major arcana). Tarot cards today are used to play card games but more commonly are used as tools for divination. The structure of the current tarot deck derives from the ordinary playing cards (*na'ibs, naipes*) the Arabs brought to Spain some seven hundred years ago. The practice of playing games with cards was well-established on the Iberian Peninsula by the year 1375 CE.

The Mamluk Deck

The Mamluk Sultanate of Egypt (1250–1517 CE) consisted of a ruling class of soldiers who loved to play card games in their free time. A beautiful example of the Mamluk playing cards can be seen at the Topkapu Museum in Istanbul, Turkey. The pack consists of four suits of thirteen cards each, just as can be found in modern playing card decks. Each suit consists of ten pip (numbered) cards and three court cards: a *malik* (king), a *nā'ib malik* (viceroy or deputy king), and a *thānī nā'ib* (second or under-deputy). The four suits of the Mamluk deck include:

- *Polo sticks*, which became the active energetic Wands of the tarot.

- *Cups* or chalices, which remained the convivial Cups of the modern tarot.

- *Scimitars*, which became the incisive Swords of tarot. Scimitars are short swords with curved blades that broaden toward the point. They are most devastating when used to slash an enemy from atop a moving horse.

- *Dinars* (gold coins), which became the pragmatic Pentacles, Disks, or Coins of today's tarot.

The Standard Tarot Deck

The Mamluk deck entered Europe via Spain and gradually spread to other countries. It was not long before the Europeans, upon noticing that the Mamluk court cards consisted of three men and no women, decided to add one to the court. This feminine touch resulted in a deck with a king, queen, cavalier, and knave. The inclusion of a queen in the European playing card deck may have been motivated by the actual dynasties and rulership in a culture where queens held positions of authority.

The Italian artists who painted the first tarot decks added a fifth, or trump, suit to the four standard suits to create a deck for playing a game similar to modern bridge. The early tarot decks varied in the total number of cards contained. As the tarot deck continued to evolve, the total number of cards eventually settled at seventy-eight.

At the end of the fifteenth century, the French conquered Milan and the Piedmont region of Italy. One of the spoils of this war was the Italian tarot deck, which the French brought back to their homeland. The city of Marseille on France's Mediterranean coast became a center for the production of tarot cards and the origin of the Tarot of Marseille, which set the standard pattern for all subsequent tarot decks. As a result, today's tarot consists of:

- A trump suit of twenty-two cards consisting of an unnumbered Fool and twenty-one numbered trump cards, often called the major arcana ("greater secrets").

- Four standard suits, usually called Wands, Cups, Swords, and Pentacles, each consisting of ten pip cards in each suit. Occultists call the tarot's non-trump suits the minor arcana ("lesser secrets").

- Four court cards in each suit, modeled after the European royal court consisting of a King, Queen, Knight, and Page.

The Main Types of Tarot Decks

Three main types of decks currently dominate the tarot landscape:

- The Tarot of Marseille, the oldest known of which is by Jean Noblet in Paris around 1650.

- The Rider-Waite-Smith Tarot, published in 1909, undoubtedly the most popular deck of the last century. It has been cloned many, many times.

- The Crowley-Harris Thoth Tarot, created between 1938 and 1943 but first published as a tarot deck in 1969.

The following section will review these three decks in some detail along with other significant tarot decks that are part of tarot history.

Visconti-Sforza Decks

The earliest Italian tarot decks varied in the number and arrangement of cards. The so-called Visconti-Sforza decks contained images of members of the wealthy Milanese Visconti and Sforza families dressed in their finest attire. The cards themselves are beautiful works of art; more than a dozen such decks can be found in various museums, libraries, and private collections around the world. These card decks may have been used to play the trick-taking game of *trionfi* (trumps).

Unfortunately, complete sets of these early tarot cards no longer exist. The Pierpont-Morgan Bergamo deck, produced in 1451, originally consisted of seventy-eight cards. The Cary-Yale deck, which may be the oldest extant set of tarot, probably contained eighty-six cards in all. At some point, card makers decided to limit the "standard" tarot deck to seventy-eight cards comprised of twenty-two trumps, forty numbered pip cards, and sixteen court cards, as we have today.

The Sola-Busca Deck

This exquisite deck was owned by the Venier family of Venice. Most likely produced around 1491 by artist Nicola di Maestro Antonio, the Sola-Busca deck consists of seventy-eight cards and is unique in that each card is illustrated with characters based on figures of classical antiquity. Some authors believe that the symbolism of this deck derives from alchemical theories about transforming base metals into gold. The practice of illustrating each of the seventy-eight tarot cards with a unique scene or character would not be repeated until Pamela Colman Smith painted the now famous Rider-Waite-Smith deck in 1909.

The Tarot of Marseille

When the French conquered Milan and the Piedmont of northern Italy in 1499, they brought the Italian game of *trionfi* back with them to southern France. The tarot became popular in the city of Marseille, which grew into a major center of playing card manufacture in Europe. The tarot decks produced there, for obvious reasons, became known as the Tarot of Marseille. The pattern and arrangement of the Marseille's seventy-eight cards became the standard against which later decks would be measured. The Tarot of Marseille became the most widely used deck in non-English-speaking countries.

The Marseille deck consists of twenty-two trumps, forty pip cards, and sixteen court cards. The trumps are in the same arrangement as most modern decks with the exception of Justice (*La Justice*) falling in position VIII whereas Strength (*La Force*) falls in position XI. The Fool (*Le Mat*) is unnumbered. Today's Magician, trump I, was called *Le Bateleur* (the Juggler, Mountebank, Showman, Buffoon). Trump II was *La Papesse*, the Female Pope, whereas trump V was *Le Pape*, the Pope of the Catholic Church. In addition, today's Tower, trump XVI, was labeled *Le Maison Dieu*, the House of God. Finally, Trump XIII, the modern Death card, was without name and was referred to as *L'Arcane sans nom* (the unnamed trump).

The pip cards of the Marseille deck do not contain scenes like the Rider-Waite-Smith deck. Instead the symbols of each suit are simply repeated on the pip cards the requisite number of times. For example, the Five of Cups displays five cups, the Six of Swords shows six swords, and so on. The court cards consist of a king, queen, knight, and page (*roy, reine, chevalier, valet*).

In recent years, the Tarot of Marseille has enjoyed increasing popularity, spurred on by the writings of authors like Alejandro Jodorowsy and Yoav Ben-Dov, who offer beautiful modern reproductions of antique tarot decks in the Marseille tradition. The influential tarot teacher Caitlín Matthews has endorsed the use of the Marseille deck, as can be seen in this article about tarot mythology (italics mine):

> "…*the meaning of divination cards changes over time, shaped by each era's culture and the needs of individual users.* This is partly why these decks can be so puzzling to outsiders, as most of them reference allegories or events familiar to people many centuries ago. Caitlín Matthews, who teaches courses on cartomancy, or divination with cards, says that before the eighteenth century, the imagery on these cards was accessible to a much broader population. But in contrast to these historic decks, Matthews finds most modern decks harder to engage with." [10]

Esoteric Decks

Divination has always been part of human history, and it is not surprising that tarot cards would be enlisted for this purpose. In the sixteenth century, people used the cards to select random passages from an oracular textbook, much as dinner guests at Chinese restaurants do when they select fortune cookies to read oracular statements about their future. Early in the eighteenth century, European manuscripts began appearing that detailed basic divinatory meanings and systems for laying out the cards.

10. Hunter Oatman-Stanford, "Tarot Mythology: The Surprising Origins of the World's Most Misunderstood Cards," 18 June 2014, www.collectorsweekly.com/articles/the-surprising-origins-of-tarot-most-misunderstood-cards/, accessed 10 April 2015.

In the latter half of the eighteenth century, amidst the burgeoning interest in ancient Egypt, French occultists began to publish wild speculations about the influence of Egyptian mythology on the tarot's development. In 1773, the French pastor Antoine Court de Gébelin claimed (without a shred of evidence except his vivid imagination) that Egyptian priests coded the *Book of Thoth* into the images of the tarot. Occultists took this fanciful theory and ran with it as if this unsubstantiated conjecture were established fact.

While de Gébelin was fabricating his Egyptian fantasies, another French occultist, Jean-Baptiste Alliette, known as Etteilla (his surname spelled backwards), began to write about divining with playing cards. His book, entitled *Enjoying the Playing Cards Called Tarot* (1783), became an immense success and served to popularize tarot divination throughout France and much of Europe. Unfortunately, Etteilla swallowed de Gébelin's fanciful theories hook, line, and sinker, and his popular text did much to promulgate the false idea that ancient Egypt was the origin of the tarot. [11] Nonetheless, tarot divination established a firm foothold in Europe that would last to the present century.

The Hermetic Order of the Golden Dawn

Late in the nineteenth century arose in England an occult society devoted to ritual magic and esotericism: the Hermetic Order of the Golden Dawn. Among the many members of the Golden Dawn were notables such as poet William Butler Yeats, author Bram Stoker of *Dracula* fame, and occultists Dion Fortune, Israel Regardie, Aleister Crowley, A. E. Waite, and Pamela Colman Smith.

The study of the tarot became a core element in the Golden Dawn teachings as an attempt to synthesize many occult traditions into a coherent philosophy, much like the unified field theory scientists aspired to develop in modern physics. Central to the Golden Dawn system was the idea that the Kabbalah, a school of Jewish mysticism, contains the secret to understanding the meaning and purpose of the universe. The Golden Dawn assigned meanings to tarot cards based on associations with the letters of the Hebrew alphabet, the Kabbalah, the decans (ten-degree divisions of zodiac signs) of astrology, and other esoteric disciplines.

The Golden Dawn's influence on the development of tarot in the twentieth century cannot be underestimated. Several modern authors have produced tarot decks rooted in the notebooks and records of the Golden Dawn. Among these are Robert Wang's Golden Dawn Tarot and Godfrey Dowson's Hermetic Tarot. The two most influential decks of the twentieth century, those of Waite-Smith and Crowley-Harris, were brainchildren of former Golden Dawn members.

Rider-Waite-Smith Tarot

Without a doubt, the Waite-Smith deck, published originally by the Rider Company in 1909, has been the most popular modern deck in the English-speaking world. After leaving the Order of the Golden

---

11. This idea has a shred of truth in it because the Mamluk cards from which the tarot evolved were products of medieval Egypt.

Dawn, A. E. Waite set out to publish a deck of his own. Working with artist Pamela Colman Smith (known as "Pixie"), Waite produced a unique deck that, unlike the Marseille pattern decks, illustrated each of the forty pip cards with a scene evocative of the card's divinatory meaning. It was the first deck since the Sola-Busca of 1491 to be illustrated in this fashion. The presence of scenes and characters on each card rendered this deck one of the easiest to learn and made tarot reading accessible to the masses. Many modern decks, including the Llewellyn Classic Tarot used to illustrate this text, are clones of the Waite-Smith images.

Crowley-Harris Thoth Tarot

The eccentric and brilliant occultist Aleister Crowley (whom the press called "the worst man in the world") also broke with the Golden Dawn. [12] Toward the end of his life, Crowley decided to produce a tarot deck that reflected his years of study and practice of esotericism. Enlisting the aid of the artist Lady Freida Harris, Crowley collaborated with her from 1938 to 1943 to transform his ideas into reality. He wrote a companion book for the deck called *The Book of Thoth* to explain the intricate symbolism of the cards. Crowley's encyclopedic knowledge of occult disciplines is reflected in Lady Harris's paintings; the Thoth deck has become a favorite among scholarly occultists who enjoy the philosophy, mythology, occultism, and metaphysics underlying this magnum opus.

Theme-Based Tarot Decks

A tarot enthusiast I know has collected more than a thousand different decks, and there are countless others on the market. Many tarot decks focus on a particular theme and appeal to a specific audience. For example, there is an Herbal Tarot for those interested in the healing properties of herbs, a Tarot of the Cat People that combines science fiction and fantasy, a Ghosts & Spirits Tarot for those interested in the supernatural, a Halloween Tarot that follows the adventures of a black cat on Halloween, not to mention a Jungian Tarot, a Housewives Tarot, a Kama Sutra Tarot (rated X), a Steampunk Tarot, a Zombie Tarot, and even a Quantum Tarot for people interested in modern physics. Whatever tickles your fancy, there is probably a tarot deck designed with you in mind.

Nonstandard "Tarot" Decks

Sometimes the term "tarot" is applied loosely to any deck used for divination. Technically speaking, most dictionaries define *tarot* as a set of seventy-eight cards consisting of twenty-two trump cards, forty pip cards, and sixteen court cards. Nonetheless, several decks have appeared under the rubric of "tarot" without the classical structure of the standard Marseille deck. Such decks can be considered nonstandard tarots.

For example, the Deva Tarot, published in Austria in 1986, consists of ninety-three cards instead of the standard seventy-eight. The cards of the Deva deck are square, and their illustrations and symbolism

---

12.   "The Worst Man in the World," *The Sunday Dispatch* (2 July 1933).

are patterned after the Crowley-Harris Thoth images. The major arcana of this deck include an additional card called "the Separator," and the minor arcana include an extra suit called "triax" to symbolize the Aether or the Spirit.

Fortune-telling and Oracle Decks

In addition to nonstandard tarots, there are many sets of cards devoted to fortune-telling and divination that do not claim to be variations of tarot. These include "oracle decks" such as angel cards, goddess guidance decks, rune cards, I Ching cards, and so on. Oracle decks, sometimes called wisdom decks, vary in the number of cards they contain. Typically, oracle decks center on a theme from religion, mythology, or an esoteric tradition, with each card representing a spiritual principle for reflection and meditation. Hay House, a major publisher of oracle decks, says the following on its website (italics mine): "*Oracle cards* are useful for anyone looking for answers and meaning. They differ from tarot cards in that they do not necessarily follow the traditional suits of tarot cards. *Wisdom cards* provide powerful messages to encourage positive thinking." [13]

Fortune-telling cards differ from oracle cards in that they are designed specifically to reveal the future. Reading fortune-telling cards requires a different mindset than reading the tarot. Fortune-telling card interpretations are suggestive of the stereotypical Hollywood scenes in which a mysterious reader looks at the cards and utters in a knowing tone of voice: "You will meet a tall dark stranger on a cruise this summer but he will be mainly interested in your money, so be careful." Currently the most popular fortune-telling deck is the thirty-six-card Petit Lenormand.

---

13. Hay House, "What are Oracle Cards?" oracle-cards-hayhouse.tumblr.com/about-oracle-cards, accessed 17 March 2015.

Four

<figure>ornamental flourish</figure>

Deciding How
to Use the Cards

The Many Uses of the Tarot

Tarot began as a game of cards and, in some places, is still used for this purpose. Over the years, however, the deck became a tool for occultists seeking an esoteric understanding of the universe. In the 1700s, card readers, especially in France, began to use the tarot to make predictions about the future. During the past half-century, fortune-telling with the cards has fallen out of favor and instead the deck has become a tool for brainstorming, idea clarification, and self-discovery. Some modern-day counselors and psychotherapists utilize tarot decks to help clients deal with traumatic events and explore psychological issues.

A very common modern use of the tarot is to help clarify issues that are on your mind. The most common areas of concern by far are love and romance. Other common topics are career changes, education, travel, money, financial matters, and health issues. With the recent worldwide recession and associated slump in the housing market, questions about selling houses and relocating have become more common.

Some clients use the tarot regularly for meditation and spiritual enlightenment. When a querent has no specific question in mind, one can do a general reading to suggest issues that are currently important for the querent to ponder. General readings often highlight concerns that warrant further exploration. For example, the Chariot might indicate plans to buy or sell a car, the Hierophant might presage a church wedding, Justice might refer to a court case or legal matter, and so on.

Tarot and Journaling

The ancient Greek philosopher Socrates advised that "an unexamined life is not worth living." Philosophy literally means "love of wisdom," and journaling is a way to record our pursuit of wisdom, with Socrates as our guide.

The offspring of a sculptor father and a midwife mother, Socrates developed what we now call the Socratic method of leading his students to wisdom. Instead of imparting information, Socrates asked penetrating questions that provoked his students to come up with their own answers. Following his mother's lead, Socrates viewed himself as a midwife of the mind, opening passages through which the knowledge inherent in the human soul could emerge into the light of day. As we follow his lead in seeking wisdom, it is useful to record thoughts and reflections in a journal.

In the dialogue *Phaedrus*, Plato, the most famous student of Socrates, called his teacher the wisest, most just, and best of all men he had ever known. According to Robert Place, the Renaissance artists who designed the Chariot card were inspired by Plato's metaphor of the human soul as a rational charioteer trying to control the unruly horses of appetite and will. In this metaphor, Plato represented Socrates's idea that being truly human implies "the capacity to transcend instinct and desire and to make conscious, ethical choices." [14]

In the Middle Ages, theologian Thomas Aquinas used Plato's metaphor of the charioteer to represent the cardinal virtue of Prudence, a card which seemed mysteriously absent from the major arcana of the Marseille tarot. The other cardinal virtues—Justice, Fortitude (Strength), and Temperance—each had a card devoted to them. It may be that the Chariot trump of the tarot was intended to represent Prudence, as the ideas of Aquinas were widely known at the time the tarot was created.

In any case, journaling with the tarot has many advantages. These include:

- Examining your life in the pursuit of wisdom

- Getting to know yourself better

- Slowing down to reflect on life

- Managing stress

- Strengthening immunity and improving health

- Understanding how you feel on the inside

---

14. Simon Longstaff, "The Unexamined Life Is Not Worth Living," 2 June 2013, www.newphilosopher.com/articles /being-fully-human/

- Clarifying your understanding of relationships and situations

- Healing emotional wounds

- Reducing anxiety

- Enhancing your sense of serenity and self-acceptance

- Keeping a record of personal growth

- Reviewing the course of your life

- Stimulating creativity

How can tarot help in this process? Because the cards depict archetypal images universal to the human condition, you can use your daily draw as a starting point for self-examination and reflection in your journal. For example, a card may bring to mind memories that you would like to explore further. The images on a card might remind you of a relationship you'd like to understand more deeply. If you have suffered emotional trauma (and who hasn't at some point in their life?), the research of psychologist James Pennebaker suggests that journaling just twenty minutes a day for a few days can have a remarkably healing effect. This healing appears to be the result of exploring without inhibition, and in a safe environment, your deepest feelings about the emotional upheaval. [15]

Tarot and Creativity

As the saying goes, a picture is worth a thousand words. The images that appear on modern tarot cards are evocative of archetypal human conundrums, complex feeling states, and common life situations. Because the tarot is so effective at stimulating our intuition, it is a wonderful tool for brainstorming, shifting perspective, generating novel ideas, and developing creative solutions. If you are interested in using the tarot as a tool to enhance creativity, the following three books are highly recommended:

- *Strategic Intuition for the 21st Century: Tarot for Business* by James Wanless

- *Tarot for Writers* by Corrine Kenner

- *What's in the Cards for You?* by Mark McElroy

---

15. James W. Pennebaker, "Writing about Emotional Experiences as a Therapeutic Process," *Psychological Science* 8.3 (May 1997): 162–166 ; also available at homepage.psy.utexas.edu/homepage/faculty/Pennebaker/Reprints /P1997.pdf

Tarot as a Spiritual Practice

My longstanding interest in astrology has prompted me to study the attributions of the Golden Dawn and their tarot associations to supplement my understanding of an astrological birth chart. The natal horoscope is simply a map of the heavens centered around one's birthplace on Earth and calculated for the exact moment when you emerge as a separate individual from your mother's womb.

Each planet and significant point in the horoscope can be associated with three distinct tarot card types: the major arcana cards, the people or court cards, and the numbered pip cards. Many tarot enthusiasts believe the major arcana signify important spiritual lessons to be learned. The court cards often represent personality traits or attitudes that may help or hinder the querent on his or her path in life. The pip cards depict everyday situations and mundane areas of life the querent will experience.

Using these ideas, we can reflect on the spiritual significance of any point in our natal horoscope. For example, President Barack Obama was born with the planet Mars at 22° 34′ Virgo. The red planet is the god of war and bloodshed. The position of Mars in a chart helps us to understand our aggressive instincts and how we act with courage, assertiveness, and confidence. If President Obama wished to understand his natal Mars more fully, an astrologically informed tarot reader could lay out the following cards, which are associated with Obama's Mars in the third decan of Virgo:

- *Major arcana cards*: the Hermit (Virgo), the Magician (third decan of Virgo).

- *Court card*: Queen of Swords.

- *Pip card*: Ten of Pentacles.

The major arcana (the Hermit and the Magician) suggest that President Obama's spiritual lessons include learning how to deal with aggression in a contemplative, well-reasoned and skillful manner. The Queen of Swords is a model for the type of cool rationality that might help in situations of conflict related to warlike Mars. The Ten of Pentacles indicates that the president is likely to learn this lesson in his material affairs and in efforts to pass on his legacy to the next generation.

If astrology is not your cup of tea, Carolyn Cushing of the Art of Change Tarot website offers a weekly three-card "Path-Practice-Posture" layout along similar lines. [16] Carolyn calls her layout the "Soul Practices" or "Sacred Practices" spread. Her preferred deck for this spread is the Gaian Tarot by Joanna Powell Colbert.

The Sacred Practices spread is usually performed once weekly by separating the deck into major arcana, court cards, and numbered pip cards. You select one card at random from each grouping. The major arcana card represents the week's spiritual *path*. The pip card signifies a contemplative *practice* that will guide you along that sacred path. Finally, the court card indicates a personality *posture*, that is, the attitudes and behaviors that will assist you in your spiritual practice. The combination of these three cards offers a spiritual lesson to contemplate during the week ahead.

---

16.   Carolyn Cushing, artofchangetarot.com/.

If you apply Carolyn's method to your birth horoscope, the spiritual lessons connected with each planet and significant point can be viewed as affecting your entire lifetime. For those who believe in reincarnation, such lessons may signify the spiritual reasons for which you chose to reincarnate in your present lifetime and under your current circumstances.

Tarot as an Adjunct to Psychotherapy

Tarot has become increasingly popular in consulting rooms of counselors and psychotherapists. Books such as Sallie Nichols's *Jung and Tarot: An Archetypal Journey* and Arthur Rosengarten's *Tarot and Psychology: Spectrums of Possibility* have done much to integrate the Jungian archetypes found in the tarot with modern psychotherapy. In addition to these books, New York therapist Elinor Greenberg has offered workshops on the use of tarot as a projective technique in psychotherapy.

In Israel, Dr. Ofra Ayalon has developed the Therapy Cards Reading (TCR) technique to help people work through trauma with the aid of the images on the cards. TCR functions by "interpreting a card image as a visual metaphor referring to the person's life issues. But unlike divination or Tarot reading, an important principle of TCR is that *the one who holds the card holds the message.* There are no fixed interpretations for the cards, no professional 'reader' who interprets them for you. Instead, a guide or a partner is there to help you focus on an issue, and explore what the image means for you." [17] In my experience, the most helpful tarot readings are those done in in a manner similar to TCR: the reader serves as a guide to help the querent focus on the issues reflected in the cards and to understand what they mean in his or her life.

The Importance of a Tarot Diary or Notebook

Virtually every tarot teacher recommends keeping a tarot journal to record your impressions of the cards and the readings you do. Some people use a spiral-bound notebook, others prefer a looseleaf binder that makes it easy to add pages and rearrange notes. If you prefer working at a computer, you can use a program like Evernote or Scrivener to keep track of your tarot information. If you want to go public, you might consider posting your notes on a tarot-oriented blog.

Everyone has a unique learning style, and there is no one right way to journal in your tarot diary. It's probably a good idea to devote a separate page to each card on which you can note your impressions, the details that stand out to you, and your experiences with the card. You will also want to keep a record of your readings, when and with whom you did them, what you said, how you arrived at your conclusions, and how matters eventually turned out. In this way you can review your work and learn from your successes and well as your mistakes. Experience is the best teacher.

---

17. Yoav Ben-Dov, "Therapy Cards Reading" at www.cbdtarot.com/2014/06/30/therapy-cards-reading/, accessed 17 April 2015.

If you enjoy Carolyn Cushing's Sacred Practices spread described earlier in this chapter, you can journal weekly about the three questions of this layout. Some people find that asking a specific question of the tarot helps them to focus on the particular images in the card and to write more meaningfully about their significance. Others prefer to meditate on a card and record their general insights and impressions. You will need to experiment to see which method works best for your learning style.

No matter how you decide to keep your tarot journal, it is an invaluable tool in the learning process. When you review what you have written, you will be impressed by the progress you have made and will almost always gain new insights as you reflect on past readings. Some readers eventually use the material in their tarot notebooks as the foundation for writing a book about tarot.

Tarot Ethics

My background in medicine and psychotherapy has prompted me to apply the same ethical standards to tarot readings that I use when seeing patients in the consulting room. Perhaps the most famous set of ethical guidelines was elaborated by Hippocrates late in the fifth century BCE. These standards have become a cornerstone of medical practice. Paraphrasing Copland's 1825 translation of Hippocrates's original Greek text, I have adapted the Oath of Hippocrates for modern tarot readers: [18]

A Hippocratic Oath for Tarot Readers

I swear by Apollo the physician, and Aesculapius the surgeon, likewise Hygeia and Panacea, and summon all the gods and goddesses to witness that I will observe and keep this oath to the utmost of my power and judgment.

I will revere those who taught me the art of tarot; and I will impart all my acquirement, instructions, and whatever I know to all my pupils, who likewise shall bind and tie themselves by a professional oath.

With regard to reading the cards, I will devise and order for my clients the best tarot consultations, according to my judgment and means; and I will take care that they suffer no hurt or damage. Nor shall any person's entreaty prevail upon me to read the cards in a manner that brings hurt or damage to anyone; neither will I counsel any tarot reader to do so.

Further, I will comport myself and use my knowledge in a godly manner. I will offer no advice about matters of which I lack expert knowledge, but shall commit such affairs entirely to an appropriately trained professional.

Whatsoever house I may enter, my visit shall be solely for the benefit and advantage of the querent; and I will willingly refrain from doing any injury or wrong from falsehood, and (in an especial manner) from acts of an amorous nature, whatever be the rank of those for whom I consult the cards, whether mistress or servant, bond or free.

---

18.   James Copland, "The Hippocratic Oath," *The London Medical Repository* 23 (135): 258 (1 March 1825).

Whatever, in the course of my practice, I may see or hear (even when not invited) and whatever I may happen to obtain knowledge of, if it be not proper to repeat, I will keep it sacred and secret within my own breast.

If I faithfully observe this oath, may I thrive and prosper in my fortune and profession, and live in the estimation of posterity; or on breach thereof, may the reverse be my fate!

Special Ethical Considerations

- *Reading for children.* Minors have special legal protections that need to be respected. In some cases, tarot may be regarded with suspicion because of the family's cultural background or religious beliefs. In offering readings for children, the tarot consultant must be especially careful to respect the laws of the state and the rights of the parents. Sensitive issues such as bullying or abuse may come up in readings; the consultant should be prepared to take appropriate measures to protect the child. The choice of a tarot deck is also important. Some modern decks have adult themes, including frontal nudity or depictions of violence that may be inappropriate for children or objectionable to their parents. Several whimsical decks geared especially toward children are available, such as the Snowland Deck by Ron and Janet Boyer and the Halloween Tarot by Karin Lee and Kipling West.

- *Third-party readings.* A querent may ask you to consult the cards for someone who is not present. Most readers believe you should only do a reading for the querent and avoid consulting the cards to garner information about someone who has not given permission, as it is tantamount to spying. The tarot is not a granny cam. In the words of Hippocrates, "Whatever I may happen to obtain knowledge of, if it be not proper to repeat, I will keep it sacred and secret within my own breast."

- *Offering professional advice.* Tarot readers should stick to reading the cards with the intention of empowering clients to clarify their thinking and make their own well-informed decisions. Tarot consultants should *not* offer advice about matters requiring professional expertise such as medical treatment, legal matters, financial planning, investment counseling, psychotherapy, etc. Such issues must be taken to an appropriately trained professional. Even if the tarot reader happens also to be a doctor or lawyer, the tarot reader should stick to interpreting the cards in an ethical matter. The act of offering professional advice changes the relationship so that the querent becomes the doctor's patient, the lawyer's client, and so on; then the tarot reader is subject to the ethical standards of his or her profession.

- *Charging money for readings.* A tarot reader provides a service and deserves to be paid a reasonable fee for a job well done. It is important to be upfront about the nature of the service you are offering and inform clients what a card reading can and cannot do. It is unethical to use the cards to frighten clients into giving you large sums of money for which you promise to "remove a curse" or "cast a spell" to change their lives. Your job is to empower clients to make their own decisions and to change their own lives. Whatever you say or do as a tarot reader should be, first and foremost, for the benefit of the querent rather than for personal gain.

- *Proselytizing during readings.* We live in a diverse society. Those who seek guidance from the cards come from a variety of religious, cultural, and philosophical backgrounds. Tarot readers should not try to impose their own belief systems on their clients. It is imperative to show respect for people even if you don't share their worldview. The tarot can shine light on the querent's issues and concerns, but the cards do not tell the querent what to believe or what to do. Stick to saying what you see in the cards and insist that querents make their own decisions and live their own lives.

Five

Associations and Correspondences

Joseph and the Dream of the Pharaoh

Even though the tarot originated as a card game in Renaissance Italy, it eventually became used throughout Europe as a tool for divination. The word "divination" comes from the Latin *divinare*, meaning to foresee or to be divinely inspired. Divination as a practice has occured throughout recorded history. An early example of divination can be found in the Book of Genesis of the Bible, in which the Hebrew Joseph interprets the dream of the Egyptian Pharaoh as a message from God:

And Joseph said unto Pharaoh, The dream of Pharaoh is one: God hath shewed Pharaoh what he is about to do. The seven good kine [cattle] are seven years; and the seven good ears [of grain or corn] are seven years: the dream is one. And the seven thin and ill-favored kine that came up after them are seven years; and the seven empty ears blasted with the east wind shall be seven years of famine. This is the thing which I have spoken unto Pharaoh: what God is about to do He sheweth unto Pharaoh (Genesis 41:25–28, King James Version).

Throughout history, all cultures have sought messages from the divine in the random happenings of daily life. Apparently, the gods communicate with us mortals through chance happenings and haphazard patterns in the mundane world. Just as Joseph could read God's intentions in the Pharaoh's dream, the practice of divination with cards is part of a long tradition whose roots extend at least as far back as the early days recorded in the Bible.

In the following sections, we will look at some of the connections tarot readers have made between the cards and other popular methods of divination.

Tarot and Number Symbolism

The symbolism of numbers plays an important role in many forms of divination, including the tarot. In Western philosophy, the belief in the spiritual significance of numbers dates at least as far back as ancient Greece, especially the time of Pythagoras. Often described as the first pure mathematician, Pythagoras of Samos (c. 570 BCE–c. 495 BCE) is credited with the Pythagorean theorem that we learned in high school. Pythagoras was a major proponent of the symbolic significance of numbers. According to his biographer Iamblichus (c. 300 CE), Pythagoras taught that number is the ruler of forms and ideas, and the cause of gods and daemons.

Tarot Birth Cards (Mary K. Greer's Method)

One way in which tarot readers use number symbolism is to select cards from the major arcana corresponding to the numerologically reduced numbers in one's birth date. This calculation is made by adding together the day, month, and year of birth and continuing to add the individual digits in that sum, a method suggested by Mary K. Greer in her book *Tarot for Your Self*.[19] An example will make the process clear:

Consider Mother Teresa, born on August 26, 1910:

Day of birth =   26
Month of birth =   8
Year of birth =   1910
_____

We add the day, month, and year of her birth: 26 + 8 + 1910 = 1944.

We next add the digits in the above sum, 1 + 9 + 4 + 4 = 18, which corresponds to the Moon card (XVIII) of the major arcana.

We can reduce 18 even further: 1 + 8 = 9, which corresponds to the Hermit (IX).

Thus, the Moon and the Hermit cards are believed to have lifelong symbolic importance for a person born on this date. If we consider that the Moon card is linked to Pisces, the sign of selfless service, and the Hermit card to someone seeking spiritual truth, these two cards appear to be relevant to the life of Mother Teresa.

---

19.   A birth card calculator can be found online at The Tarot School site: www.tarotschool.com/Calculator.html

Mary Greer would call the Moon Mother Teresa's "personality card" and its further reduction to 9 (1 + 8), her "soul card." If the sum of the birth digits happens to be a number between 1 to 9, then the personality and soul cards are the same.

When calculating the birth card, if the sum of the digits is greater than 22, you must reduce that number again until you obtain a number between 1 to 22. Each number corresponds to an associated tarot trump, with 22 representing the Fool because the sum of birth numbers cannot equal 0.

Tarot Year Card (Mary K. Greer's Method)

Just as you can calculate cards that are symbolically important for your year of birth, you can also identify cards that are significant for any given year of your life (a year being measured from one birthday to the next). Let's look at an example.

Former president Bill Clinton was born on August 19, 1946. Thus, his birth cards are found by adding 8 + 19 + 1946 = 1973, and then reducing 1973: 1 + 9 + 7 + 3 = 20. Clinton's personality card is 20, Judgment (XX), and his soul card is 20 reduced: 2 + 0 = 2, the High Priestess (II).

To calculate his cards for the year in which Clinton was impeached (1998), we would add the month and day of his birth (August 19) to the year in question, 1988: 8 + 19 + 1998 = 2007. Then, reducing 2007, we get 2 + 0 + 0 + 7 = 9, the Hermit (IX). Thus, the year measured from Clinton's birthday in August of 1998 until August of 1999 was a time of withdrawal and turning inward to seek spiritual wisdom. Themes of introspection and personal integrity are typical of a Hermit year.

An Alternate Method for Calculating Birth Year Cards

An alternate method for calculating birth cards also appears in the literature. Unlike Mary Greer's method, this alternate technique involves simply adding together all the single digits in your birth date rather than adding the day plus the month plus the year.

In the case of Mother Teresa, we would proceed as follows:

August 26, 1910 → 8 + 2 + 6 + 1 + 9 + 1 + 0 = 27, which reduces to 2 + 7 = 9, or the Hermit (IX). In this method, Mother Teresa's personality and soul cards are both the Hermit (IX).

In the case of Bill Clinton, his birthday August 19, 1946 reduces as follows: 8 + 1 + 9 + 1 + 9 + 4 + 6 = 38, which reduces to 3 + 8 = 11 (Strength or Justice, his personality card). The number 11 then reduces to 1 + 1 = 2, the High Priestess (his soul card). Note that in the traditional tarot of Marseille, card XI was Strength (which Crowley renamed Lust). In the Rider-Waite-Smith deck, card XI became Justice. One could argue that themes of strength, lust, and justice have characterized the life and personality of President Clinton.

Number	Symbolism
0	Pure potential without form
1	The initial spark, will, creation, inspiration, beginnings, new life, birth, the first manifestation of potential
2	Duality, partnership, relationships, choice, decision, balance, gestation, more than one option, in between, on the fence
3	Fertility, the first fruits of a joint venture, cooperative endeavors, triadic relationships, creating something new, the offspring of combining complementary pairs
4	Structure, stability, order, logic, foundation, manifestation, matter, the ability to endure
5	Instability, disruption, struggle, conflict, strife, upset, crisis, a downswing, tension, uncertainty, purging, disequilibrium
6	Equilibrium reestablished, harmony, fairness, equity, communication, sharing, compassion
7	Assessment, reflection, reevaluation, standing at a threshold, seeking advantage
8	Movement, action, power, determination, the beginning of the end
9	The final single digit, the end of the cycle of single digits, culmination, fruition, attainment
10	One more than the final single digit, one too many, more than enough, full completion of a cycle, readiness to move on and begin anew

Table of Number Symbolism

Another way in which numbers contribute to tarot symbolism is through the link between the symbolic properties of numbers and the cards corresponding to those numbers. Some of these properties are summarized in the accompanying table. As you become more familiar with the tarot, you may wish to add your own meanings to this list.

Primum Non Nocere

A word of caution about number symbolism is in order. In my opinion, the use of number symbols to interpret the tarot should empower the querent to choose his or her own path in life. The best tarot interpretations are those that empower and liberate the client, in the sense of the biblical passage: "And ye shall know the truth, and the truth shall make you free" (John 8:32, KJV). Comments that provoke fear or induce dependency may be hurtful to the querent. Just as a physician takes the oath *primum non nocere*—first, do no harm—so too must the tarot reader focus on benefiting the client and avoiding deleterious consequences. If tarot reading devolves into a superstitious practice, hurt is likely to follow.

A case in point occurred in Burma in 1987 during the dictatorship of Ne Win, a superstitious leader who was overly dependent on the advice of numerologists. Ne Win was convinced that his lucky number was nine. As a result, on September 5 of that year, the Burmese government announced (without warning or compensation) that it was demonetizing the 25-, 35- and 75-kyat notes because these denominations were not divisible by nine and were thus unlucky. In addition, 45- and 90-kyat notes were introduced because they were divisible by nine. The effect of this sudden change in the currency was devastating. In the blink of an eye, 75 percent of the country's currency became worthless, causing families to lose their life savings. Riots followed, and a military coup overthrew Ne Win in 1988. When all was said and done, nine did not turn out to be such a lucky number for the superstitious dictator!

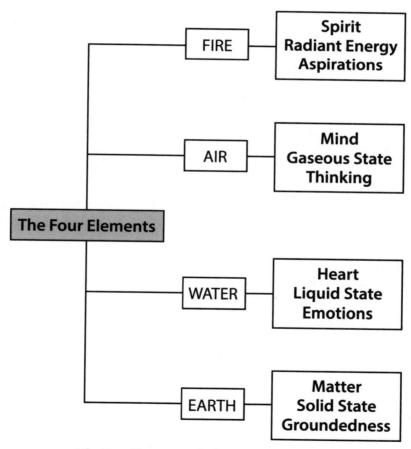

The Four Elements and Their Correspondences

Tarot and the Four Elements

The ancient Greeks developed a theory of four basic elements to explain the nature of reality. The idea that everything in nature can be explained in terms of four elemental principles held sway for more than two thousand years and has had a major impact on philosophy, medicine, art, science and divination. Modern physics, for example, speaks of four fundamental forces of nature. In the field of psychology, Carl Jung made use of the theory of four elements to develop his ideas about the functioning of the human mind. The popular Myers-Briggs personality types are based on this ancient theory of four elements.

Much of the symbolism of modern astrology and tarot derives from the four elements of ancient Greece: Fire, Air, Water, and Earth. It is important to keep in mind that the four elements are abstract philosophical principles rather than concrete objects in the material world. One might think of the four elements metaphorically as varieties of energy, types of consciousness, or differing ways of approaching the world.

A glance at the four elements reveals that two of the elements, Fire and Air, tend to rise *above* the surface of the Earth while the other two, Water and Earth, tend to sink *below* the surface of the Earth. Thus, Fire and Air are considered to be more phallic, centrifugal (thrusting away from a center), and outer directed, whereas Water and Earth are regarded as more receptive, centripetal (pulling toward a center), and inner directed.

Being gaseous, Air rises. The element Fire also rises, as it represents radiant energy that can escape the Earth's atmosphere. The light (fire) from the sun travels through space to reach our planet. The two upward- and outer-directed elements, Fire and Air, are considered *active masculine* principles. In the tarot, the suit of Wands is commonly associated with Fire and the suit of Swords with Air. The pip cards of the Wands and Swords typically represent circumstances and emotional situations with an upward outward movement (excitement, adventure, conflict, travel, expansion, relocation, departure, etc.).

Water sinks and is held up by a container formed from Earth, the heaviest of the four elements. Thus, Water and Earth trend *downward* and are considered inner-directed *receptive feminine* elements. In the tarot, the suit of Cups is usually associated with Water and the suit of Coins or Pentacles, Earth. The pip cards of the Cups and Pentacles suits typically represent circumstances and emotional situations with a downward or inward movement (reflection, contemplation, joy, grief, healing, celebration, family happiness, arrival, etc.).

Keywords for the Four Elements

Since most modern tarot decks rely heavily on this symbolism, we will be referring to the four elements throughout this text. The following list summarizes some of the key meanings and associations of each of the elements:

Fire: energy, impulse, enthusiasm, initiative, power, action, directness, inspiration, spontaneity, dynamism, expansion, adventure, exploration, generativity, self-sufficiency, freedom; the suit of Wands; the Fire signs Aries, Leo, and Sagittarius.

Earth: material goods, resources, money, work, sensual pleasure, building, tangible results, security, stability; goal-orientated, practical, analytical, organized, patient, persistent, grounded, deliberate, resourceful; the suit of Pentacles (Coins); the Earth signs Taurus, Virgo, and Capricorn.

Air: communication, sharing ideas, inquisitiveness, mental agility, interrelationships, connecting the dots, logic, wit, cool objectivity, quickness, cunning, persuasion, strategy, thoughts, words, intellect; the suit of Swords; the Air signs Gemini, Libra, and Aquarius.

Water: emotions, moods, feelings, sensitivity, intuition, receptivity, empathy, nurturing, intimacy, compassion, intuition, occult matters, hidden depths, oneness, spirituality; the suit of Cups; the Water signs Cancer, Scorpio, and Pisces.

Tarot and Astrology

Late in the nineteenth century, the Hermetic Order of the Golden Dawn incorporated astrology into its understanding of tarot symbolism. Arthur Edward Waite, a member of the Golden Dawn, instructed artist Pamela Colman Smith ("Pixie") to illustrate the numbered or pip cards of the Waite-Smith deck according to her understanding of the influence of the signs of the zodiac on each of the four suits of the tarot. Thus, anyone who uses the Waite-Smith deck is relying on astrological symbolism, often without being aware of it. First published in 1909, the Waite-Smith deck became the most popular tarot of the past hundred years in the English-speaking world. Due to the widespread influence of the Golden Dawn, astrology has played a major role in defining the meanings of today's tarot cards.

The Zodiac: A Dozen Parts of a Circle

The zodiac consists of a dozen signs, each 30 degrees wide. By definition, an astrological sign is a mathematical division of the 360-degree circle into twelve parts. Every so often an ignorant science reporter claims that astronomers have discovered a thirteenth sign, when in reality they are referring to a thirteenth constellation. The claim that there are thirteen signs is patent nonsense because by definition a sign is one-twelfth of a circle. There cannot be thirteen parts in a dozen, except in the world of science writers who pontificate about matters of which they are ignorant.

The zodiac signs derive their names from the constellations (star groupings) of the ancient zodiac. The Golden Dawn assigned the signs of the zodiac to twelve of the major arcana cards. Note that the following dates are approximate. As you read the list of characteristics, try to think of people you know who are born under that sun sign. How accurate do you find the zodiac signs to be in describing your acquaintances?

1. Fiery Aries (Mar. 21–Apr. 19), the Emperor

Ruled by the warrior god Mars, Aries comes first in the zodiac. An enterprising cardinal sign, Aries the Ram marks the start of spring in the Northern Hemisphere, which in many cultures is the beginning of the new year. As the first sign of the annual cycle of seasons, Aries is associated with the Emperor, trump IV, a card often depicted in fiery red tones. The Queen of Wands falls largely under Aries, a sign whose natives are characterized by these traits:

Assertive	Independent	Enjoy a good fight
Fiery	Active	Like to start something new
Bold	Energetic	Seek to establish a separate identity
Pioneering	Outgoing	Not always good on the follow-through
Direct	Competitive	Eager to take action
Forthright	Combative	Have leadership ability
Courageous	Ambitious	Good at selling others on their ideas
Straightforward	Impatient	Dislike dependency
Charismatic	Impulsive	Want to be number one
Enterprising	Fond of challenge	Prefer battle over appeasement for resolving conflict
Confident	Headstrong (like to butt heads)	Winning isn't everything, it's the *only* thing
Pioneering	Love to use their bodies	

2. Earthy Taurus (Apr. 20–May 20), the Pope

Ruled by the goddess of love Venus, Taurus comes second in the zodiac. Taurus the Bull, a persistent and slow-to-change fixed sign, is associated with the Hierophant (the High Priest or Pope), trump V. The King of Pentacles falls largely under Taurus, a sign whose natives are characterized by these traits:

Sensual	Security-conscious	Fond of good food and bodily comfort
Grounded	Determined	Like to build
Solid	Stable	Love nature
Reliable	Dependable	Enjoy peace and serenity
Firm	Faithful	Have a well-developed sense of touch
Practical	Stubborn (bull-headed)	Like creature comforts
Realistic	Hard-working	Do not like to be rushed
Steady	Sensible	Seek value
Calm	Family-oriented	Predictable
Unruffled except when roused to anger	Mellow	Prefer simplicity and functionality to gaudy frills
Persistent	Self-indulgent	Possessive
Pragmatic		

3. Airy Gemini (May 21–Jun. 30), the Lovers

Ruled by fleet-footed Mercury, the messenger of the gods, Gemini comes third in the zodiac. Gemini the Twins is an adaptable mutable sign associated with the Lovers, trump VI. In Greek mythology, the Gemini twins were the mortal and immortal sons of Zeus who so loved each other that the divine member of the pair made the choice to forsake his immortality so he could remain with his mortal sibling for eternity, joined together as the constellation of the Twins of the zodiac. The Knight of Swords falls largely under Gemini, a sign whose natives are characterized by these traits:

Inquisitive	Mental	Always on the go
Talkative	Communicative	Love variety
Verbal	Adaptable	Often autodidacts

Perceptive	Clever	Like to gather and share information
Restless	Ingenious	Value being well-informed
Mentally agile	Youthful	Enjoy the expression of ideas
Versatile	Witty	Love to read and are constantly learning
Intellectual	Scattered	Hate being bored
Good story tellers	Fleet of foot	Like to keep busy
Have the gift of gab	In perpetual motion	Can get lost in details
Sociable	Easily distracted	Can be fickle or superficial
Friendly	Changeable	Prone to inconstancy
Curious	Easily bored	Have too many irons in the fire
Observant	Good with words	

4. *Watery Cancer (Jun. 21–Jul. 22), the Chariot*

Ruled by the Moon, the sign Cancer comes fourth in the zodiac. Cancer the Crab, an initiatory cardinal sign, is associated with the Chariot, trump VII. In the philosophy of Thomas Aquinas, which was popular at the time of the creation of the earliest tarot decks in northern Italy, the chariot and its driver were symbols of the cardinal virtue of Prudence. The three other cardinal virtues—Justice, Strength, and Temperance—all have a specific trump card named after them. The Queen of Cups falls largely under Cancer, a sign whose natives are characterized by these traits:

Sensitive	Defensive	Have good memories
Empathic	Cautious	Devoted to home and family
Intuitive	Indirect	Enjoy mentoring others
Emotional	Quiet	Like to feel needed by others

Moody	Shy	Enjoy learning about history and traditions
Gentle	Timid	Thrive on emotional contact with others
Protective	Protective of self and others	Readily sense and respond to the moods of others
Caring	Easily hurt	Dislike being told what to do
Kind	Security-conscious	Tend to avoid direct confrontation
Giving	Domestic	Hide their feelings under a facade of composure
Mothering	Tribal	Tough on the outside, tender on the inside
Healing	Care-giving	Nostalgic
Nurturing		

5. Fiery Leo (Jul. 23–Aug. 22), Fortitude

Ruled by the Sun, Leo comes fifth in the zodiac. Leo the Lion, a consolidating fixed sign, is associated with Strength, trump VIII. (Note that in older decks Strength is trump XI, but the Golden Dawn changed the numbering to make the tarot cards match the order of the astrological signs.) The King of Wands falls largely under Leo, a sign whose natives are characterized by these traits:

Commanding	Radiant	Like being the center of attention
Confident	Buoyant	Need to feel appreciated
Dramatic	Proud	Natural showmen
Expressive	Arrogant	Enjoy the limelight
Creative	Regal	Crave admiration and social recognition
Like to perform before an audience	Loyal	Prefer being the top dog (or lion)

Authoritative	Generous	Enjoy leadership positions
Dynamic	Open	Seek wholeness
Charismatic	Ambitious	Dislike pettiness
Theatrical	Warm-hearted	Enjoy working with children
Bossy, pushy at times	Generative	Desire admiration for their creative self-expression
Active	Jump right in	May take offense at being criticized
Energetic	Like being in charge	Willing to take risks
Passionate		

6. Earthy Virgo (Aug. 23–Sep. 22), the Hermit

Ruled by communicative Mercury the messenger of the gods, Virgo comes sixth in the zodiac. Virgo the Virgin, an adaptable mutable sign, is associated with the Hermit, trump IX. The Knight of Pentacles falls largely under Virgo, a sign whose natives are characterized by these traits:

Methodical	Shy	Health-conscious
Analytical	Introverted	Tend to worry
Discriminating	Humble	Fond of animals
Conscientious	Careful	Good with words
Discerning	Prudent	Enjoy rendering service to others
Observant	Organized	Seek meaning though their work
Perfectionist	Adaptable	Value time alone (like the Hermit)
Always seeking self-improvement	Helpful	Dislike spending time unproductively
Hard-working	Attentive	Capable of self-sacrifice

Intelligent	Critical	Do not enjoy the limelight
Skeptical	Orderly	Often prefer to work behind the scenes
Cautious	Detail-oriented	Hide their light under a bushel basket
Reserved	Meticulous	Want always to be right
Modest	Curious	May fail to see the forest for the trees
Frugal	Thrifty	"You can't be too careful."

7. Airy Libra (Sep. 23–Oct. 22), Justice

Ruled by Venus the goddess of love, Libra comes seventh in the zodiac. Libra the Scales of Justice, an active initiatory cardinal sign, is associated with Justice, trump XI. (Note that in older decks Justice is trump VIII, but the Golden Dawn changed the numbering to make the tarot trumps match the order of the astrological zodiac.) The Queen of Swords falls largely under Libra, a sign whose natives are characterized by these traits:

Graceful	Impartial	Try to reconcile opposing viewpoints
Elegant	Respectful	Have a good sense of beauty and proportion
Diplomatic	Accommodating	Seek equilibrium and harmony
Peaceable	Fashionable	Always engaged in a balancing act
Refined	Artistic	Want to be liked by others
Esthetically sensitive	Indecisive	Value one-on-one relationships
Thoughtful	Intellectually inclined	Seek completion in a soul mate
Objective	Tend to sit on the fence	Peace at any price
Balanced	Able to see all sides of an issue	Concerned with justice and human rights

Charming	Weigh all options before making a decision	Share with others
Sociable	Enjoy the interplay of ideas	Prefer to negotiate rather than do battle to resolve conflict
Fair		

8. *Watery Scorpio (Oct. 23–Nov. 21), Death*

Ruled by warlike Mars the warrior god and in modern astrology by Pluto, Scorpio is the eighth sign. Scorpio the Scorpion, a fixed sign of concentrated energy, is associated with the Death card, trump XIII. The King of Cups falls largely under Scorpio, a sign whose natives are characterized by these traits:

Intense	Probing	Make good psychologists and psychoanalysts
Determined	Hypnotic	Devoted to bringing about transformation
Intelligent	Mysterious	Seek to understand in depth
Keenly perceptive	Penetrating	Can cut to the chase of an argument
Analytical	Cunning	May have a talent for healing others
Insightful	Purging	Interested in unconscious motivations
Resolute	Investigative	Appreciate human sexuality
Passionate	Private	Like to uncover whatever is hidden or occult
Magnetic	Introspective	May sting like a scorpion
Powerful	Moody	Make good researchers and detectives
Intuitive	Brooding	Like to get to the bottom of things
Engaging	Want to live life intensely	May hold a grudge

Loyal	Love ferreting out the truth	Have powerful emotions that may erupt forcefully
Resourceful	Tune in to the emotions of others	

9. Fiery Sagittarius (Nov. 22–Dec. 21), Temperance

Ruled by expansive Jupiter, Sagittarius comes ninth in the zodiac. Sagittarius the Centaur Archer, a flexible mutable sign, is associated with Temperance, trump XIV. The Knight of Wands falls largely under Sagittarius, a sign whose natives are characterized by these traits:

Adventurous	Gregarious	Seek truth and wisdom
Expansive	Fun-loving	Perpetually learning something new
Sincere	Enthusiastic	Enjoy the transmission of ideas
Energetic	Impulsive	Idealistic
Idealistic	Inspirational	Fight to preserve their rights
Optimistic	Good humored	Willing to take risks
Independent	May find it hard to commit to a relationship	Love to explore foreign ideas and philosophies
Future-oriented	Dislike restriction	Prone to wanderlust
Straight-shooting	Enjoy risk	Always seeking to expand their horizons
Restless	Fond of travel and foreign cultures	Dislike criticism
Adaptable	Like the outdoors	"Don't fence me in."
Energetic	Enjoy sports and physical activities	Value personal freedom
Frank		

10. *Earthy Capricorn (Dec. 22–Jan. 19), the Devil*

Ruled by taskmaster Saturn, Capricorn comes tenth in the zodiac. Capricorn the Mountain Goat or Seagoat, an active initiatory cardinal sign, is associated with the Devil, trump XV. The Queen of Pentacles falls largely under Capricorn, a sign whose natives are characterized by these traits:

Ambitious	Sure-footed	Hardworking
Goal-oriented	Industrious	Slow but sure
Practical	Strategic	Want to climb to the top
Disciplined	Resourceful	Seek professional recognition and approbation
Cautious	Determined	Plan for the long term
Skeptical	Patient	Commit to achieving a demonstrable goal
Sensible	Self-sufficient	Respect experience and wisdom
Efficient	Traditional	Seek the respect of others
Prudent	Conservative	Fond of music
Responsible	Status-conscious	Have a strong sex drive (like the lusty Greek god Pan)
Authoritative	Introverted	Can be capricious
Grounded	Disciplined	Do not suffer fools gladly

11. *Airy Aquarius (Jan. 20–Feb. 18), the Star*

Ruled by taskmaster Saturn and in modern astrology by Uranus, Aquarius is the eleventh sign. Aquarius the Water Bearer, a consolidating fixed sign, is associated with the Star, trump XVII. The King of Swords falls largely under Aquarius, a sign whose natives are characterized by these traits:

Offbeat	Opinionated	May be eccentric or iconoclastic
Individualistic	Assertive	Like to experiment with new ways of doing things
Ahead of their time	Revolutionary	Defender of human rights
Original	Rebellious	Enjoy time with acquaintances but have few close friends
Creative	Advanced	Fond of modern technology
Inventive	Libertarian	Like to debate and to have intellectual discussions
Intelligent	Innovative	Willing to champion causes
Curious	Forward-looking	Refuse to be bound by convention
Maverick	Vulnerable	Have a strong sense of their own individuality
Friendly	Sensitive	Convinced that their way of seeing things is the correct way
Unique	Coolly logical	Easily dissatisfied in others who fail to live up to their ideals
Eccentric	Objective	Dislike taking orders
Independent	Cerebral (head over heart)	Tend to blame others for their own failures
Nonconformist	Humanitarian	March to the beat of their own drummer
Stubborn	Utopian	"To thine own self be true."
Willful	Idealistic	Emotionally detached
Uncompromising		

12. Watery Pisces (Feb. 19–Mar. 20), the Moon

Ruled by expansive Jupiter and in modern astrology by Neptune, mystical Pisces is the twelfth and final sign. Pisces the Fishes, an adaptable mutable sign, is associated with the Moon card, trump XVIII. The Knight of Cups falls largely under Pisces, a sign whose natives are characterized by these traits:

Sensitive	Creative	Moved by human suffering
Kind	Artistic	Easily connect with the feelings of others
Empathic	Psychic	Enjoy helping others, especially those less fortunate
Adaptable	Intuitive	Aware of the interconnectedness of all living things
Imaginative	Mysterious	Interested in the unconscious
Intuitive	Tender	Understand the role of illusion in creating a worldview
Compassionate	Meditative	Value peace and tranquility
Helpful	Gullible	Fascinated by the mysteries of the universe
Receptive	Vulnerable	Seek to understand the oneness of all creation
Dreamy	Interested in religion and spirituality	Like to spend time alone or in quiet places
Mellow	Capable of great self-sacrifice	May play the martyr in relationships
Poetic	Fond of music and dance	Drawn to thinking globally or in terms of universal principles
Romantic	Defend the underdog	

The Planets

Ancient astrology dealt with the seven planets ("wanderers") visible to the naked eye. The awareness of these seven wandering "stars" gave rise to the seven-day week, each day being named after one of the visible planets: Sunday (Sun day), Monday (Moon day), Tuesday (Mars day), Wednesday (Mercury day), Thursday (Jupiter day), Friday (Venus day), and Saturday (Saturn day). The ancients included the Sun and the Moon among the planets because they wandered across the heavens. The Golden Dawn assigned seven of the major arcana cards to the seven visible "planets" of antiquity.

Sun (the Vital Center)

The Sun, the center of the solar system and the giver of life, is assigned to the Sun card, trump XIX. The Sun is a "planet" of brilliance, clarity, vital energy, music, and athleticism.

Moon (Emotions and Inner Life)

The Moon is the queen of the night who reflects the light of the Sun. She is assigned to the High Priestess or Female Pope, trump II. The Moon is a "planet" of moods, emotions, mothering, the unconscious, inner life, cycles, water (the tides), and travel.

Mercury (Communication and Dexterity)

Mercury is the messenger of the gods, assigned to the Magician, trump I. Mercury is a planet of communication, travel, commerce, dexterity, sleight of hand, trade, writing, theft, and magic.

Venus (Love and Affiliation)

Venus is the goddess of love, pleasure, and beauty. She is assigned to the Empress, trump IV. Venus is a planet of amorousness, love, affection, reconciliation, peace, and harmony.

Mars (Strife and Conflict)

Mars, the red planet, is the god of war, bloodshed, and macho masculinity. He is assigned to the Tower, trump XVI. Mars is a planet of assertiveness, strife, conflict, aggression, force, warfare, and domination.

Jupiter (Expansion and Good Fortune)

Jupiter is the king of the gods who bestows good luck. He is assigned to the Wheel of Fortune, trump X. Jupiter is the planet of expansion, abundance, broadening horizons, and good fortune.

Saturn (Contraction and Hard Knocks)

Saturn is Father Time and the outermost visible planet. Representing duty and the reality principle, he is assigned to the World, trump XXI, the final card of the major arcana. Saturn is a planet of duty, contraction, structure, limits, boundaries, obstacles, heaviness, and melancholy.

The Golden Dawn did not make use of the so-called modern planets: Uranus, Neptune, and Pluto. Instead, they associated the three unassigned major arcana (the Fool, the Hanged Man, Judgment) with the classical four elements as follows.

The Four Elements and the Major Arcana

Air: The Fool

The element Air is assigned to the Fool, a card without a number but sometimes labeled "0" in modern decks. Modern astrologers often assign Uranus to Aquarius and to the Fool.

Water: The Hanged Man

The element Water is assigned to the Hanged Man, trump XII. Modern astrologers sometimes assign Neptune to Pisces and to the Hanged Man.

Fire: Judgment

The element Fire is assigned to Judgment, trump XX, perhaps because during the Last Judgment God will decide who enters heaven and who will burn eternally in the fires of hell. Modern astrologers often assign Pluto to Scorpio and to Judgment.

Earth

The element Earth has no major arcana card assigned to it, perhaps because it represents the entire material universe in which we learn the lessons of the major arcana.

The Golden Dawn, the Decans, and Number Symbolism

The Golden Dawn used number associations in various ways to assign meanings to the tarot cards. One of their fundamental ideas was to pair the thirty-six pip cards numbered two through ten with the thirty-six decans of the zodiac. What is a decan?

The decanate system divides the 360-degree circle of zodiac signs into thirty-six equal parts of 10 degrees each. Each sign consists of three decans. There are twelve signs, so there are 12 x 3 = 36 decans. For thousands of years, astrologers have assigned the visible planets to these decans. Thus, each tarot card numbered from two through ten is associated with a decan as well as with the planet ruling the decan. In his book *Mystical Origins of the Tarot*, author Paul Huson shows how the decans' esoteric meanings influenced the Golden Dawn's interpretations of the cards.

The Golden Dawn's idea was straightforward. In Western astrology, the zodiac is based on the seasons of the year. Working with the cards numbered two through ten in each of the four suits, the Golden Dawn assigned:

- 2, 3, 4 to the first month of a season

- 5, 6, 7 to the second month of a season

- 8, 9, 10 to the third or final month of a season

Let's look at this Golden Dawn tarot scheme in more detail:

Spring: Wands—Pentacles—Swords

- First month: Aries (Fire)—Two, Three, and Four of Wands

- Second month: Taurus (Earth)—Five, Six, and Seven of Pentacles

- Third month: Gemini (Air)—Eight, Nine, and Ten of Swords

Summer: Cups—Wands—Pentacles

- First month: Cancer (Water)—Two, Three, and Four of Cups

- Second month: Leo (Fire)—Five, Six, and Seven of Wands

- Third month: Virgo (Earth)—Eight, Nine, and Ten of Pentacles

Fall: Swords—Pentacles—Wands

- First month: Libra (Air)—Two, Three, and Four of Swords

- Second month: Scorpio (Water)—Five, Six, and Seven of Cups

- Third month: Sagittarius (Fire)—Eight, Nine, and Ten of Wands

Winter: Pentacles—Swords—Cups

- First month: Capricorn (Earth)—Two, Three, and Four of Pentacles

- Second month: Aquarius (Air)—Five, Six, and Seven of Swords

- Third month: Pisces (Water)—Eight, Nine, and Ten of Cups

Golden Dawn Assignment of Planets to Tarot Pips

The accompanying table shows the Golden Dawn's scheme of zodiac signs and planetary rulers for the pip cards. Some tarot readers use the range of dates assigned to each card as an aid to judging the timing of events in a spread. (In this table: W = Wands, P = Pentacles, S = Swords, and C = Cups.)

Sign	Ruler	Decan Rulers	Pip Card	Tropical Sun Sign Dates (approximate)	Court Card
Leo (Strength) *Fixed*	**Sun** (Sun)	Saturn Jupiter Mars	5 W 6 W 7 W	Jul 22–Aug 1 Aug 2–Aug 11 Aug 12–Aug 22	King W King W Knight P
Virgo (Hermit) *Mutable*	**Mercury** (Magician)	Sun Venus Mercury	8 P 9 P 10 P	Aug 23–Sep 1 Sep 2–Sep 11 Sep 12–Sep 22	Knight P Knight P Queen S
Libra (Justice) *Cardinal*	**Venus** (Empress)	Moon Saturn Jupiter	2 S 3 S 4 S	Sep 23–Oct 2 Oct 3–Oct 12 Oct 13–Oct 22	Queen S Queen S King C
Scorpio (Death) *Fixed*	**Mars** (Tower)	Mars Sun Venus	5 C 6 C 7 C	Oct 23–Nov 1 Nov 2–Nov 12 Nov 13–Nov 22	King C King C Knight W
Sagittarius (Temperance) *Mutable*	**Jupiter** (Wheel of Fortune)	Mercury Moon Saturn	8 W 9 W 10 W	Nov 23–Dec 2 Dec 3–Dec 12 Dec 13–Dec 21	Knight W Knight W Queen P
Capricorn (Devil) *Cardinal*	**Saturn** (World)	Jupiter Mars Sun	2 P 3 P 4 P	Dec 22–Dec 30 Dec 31–Jan 9 Jan 10–Jan 19	Queen P Queen P King S
Aquarius (Star) *Fixed*	**Saturn** (World)	Venus Mercury Moon	5 S 6 S 7 S	Jan 20–Jan 29 Jan 30–Feb 8 Feb 9–Feb 18	King S King S Knight C
Pisces (Moon) *Mutable*	**Jupiter** (Wheel of Fortune)	Saturn Jupiter Mars	8 C 9 C 10 C	Feb 19–Feb 29 Mar 1–Mar 10 Mar 11–Mar 20	Knight C Knight C Queen W
Aries (Emperor) *Cardinal*	**Mars** (Tower)	Mars Sun Venus	2 W 3 W 4 W	Mar 21–Mar 30 Mar 31–Apr 10 Apr 11–Apr 20	Queen W Queen W King P
Taurus (High Priest) *Fixed*	**Venus** (Empress)	Mercury Moon Saturn	5 P 6 P 7 P	Apr 21–Apr 30 May 1–May 10 May 11–May 20	King P King P Knight S

Sign	Ruler	Decan Rulers	Pip Card	Tropical Sun Sign Dates (approximate)	Court Card
Gemini (Lovers) *Mutable*	**Mercury** (Magician)	Jupiter Mars Sun	8 S 9 S 10 S	May 21–May 31 Jun 1–Jun 10 Jun 11–Jun 20	Knight S Knight S Queen C
Cancer (Chariot) *Cardinal*	**Moon** (High Priestess)	Venus Mercury Moon	2 C 3 C 4 C	Jun 21–Jul 1 Jul 2–Jul 11 Jul 11–Jul 21	Queen C Queen C King W
Fool Hanged Man Judgment	**Air** (Uranus) **Water** (Neptune) **Fire** (Pluto)	Note the Chaldean order above		The above dates are only for the position of the **Sun**	W = Wands P = Pentacles S = Swords C = Cups

The Kabbalah and the Tree of Life

In addition to using astrology to understand the cards, the Golden Dawn included the Kabbalah to explain tarot symbolism. The interpretations of the numbered pip cards reflect the meaning of the corresponding number on the Tree of Life. That idea, of connecting the tarot with the Hebrew alphabet and the Kabbalah, can be traced back to Athanasius Kircher, a German Jesuit scholar of encyclopedic interests. Born around 1601, Kircher displayed an early interest in science, medicine, philosophy, and ancient cultures. He learned Hebrew from a rabbi and became fascinated by ancient Egyptian culture, eventually speculating that Egypt was the source of ancient mysteries. Kircher's adaptation of the Tree of Life is still used by modern ceremonial magicians and tarot practitioners.

As mentioned, the Golden Dawn occultists made use of Kabbalah to assign meanings to tarot cards. In particular, they paired the meanings of the numbered Sephiroth (emanations) of the Tree of Life with cards of the same number. The Tree of Life is oriented in space like the Hanged Man, growing upside-down. The initial spark of creation takes place at the top of the tree in the Sephirah Kether ("the Crown"), numbered one. The roots of the tree lie in heaven, and its ultimate fruit manifests at the bottom in Malkuth ("the Kingdom of Earth"), numbered ten. Keywords for the Tree of Life include:

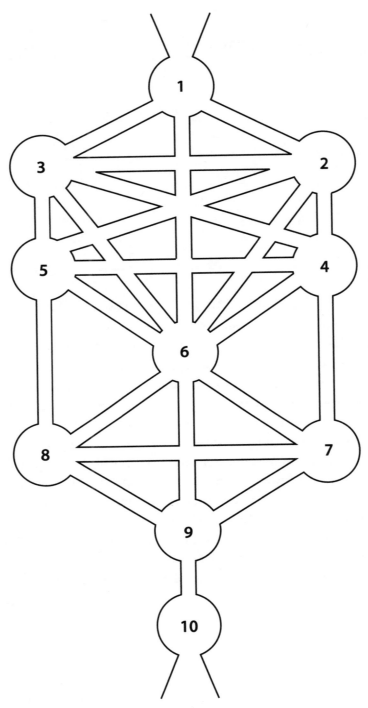

The Tree of Life

1. Kether (Crown)

The Crown—the initial spark of creation. Kether is associated with the *primum mobile,* and according to some modern astrologers, the planet Pluto. The tarot cards related to the number one are the Magician (I), the Wheel of Fortune (X, $1 + 0 = 1$), the Sun (XIX, $1 + 9 = 10 \rightarrow 1 + 0 = 1$), and the four Aces, representing the pure potential and initial spark of the four elements.

2. Chokmah (Wisdom)

Wisdom—the Great Father. Chokmah is associated with the entire zodiac circle and, by some modern astrologers, with the planet Neptune. The tarot cards related to the number two are the High Priestess (II), Strength or Justice (XI, $1 + 1 = 2$), Judgment (XX, $2 + 0 = 2$), and all the pip cards numbered two. Chokmah represents the four elements in their purest form.

3. Binah (Understanding)

Understanding—the Great Mother. Binah is associated with the planet Saturn. The tarot cards related to the number three are the Empress (III), the Hanged Man (XII, $1 + 2 = 3$), the Universe (XXI, $2 + 1 = 3$), and all pip cards numbered three.

4. Chesed (Mercy)

Mercy/Peace. Chesed is associated with Jupiter, the planet of generosity, mind-expanding journeys, and good fortune. Tarot cards related to the number four are the Emperor (IV), Death (XIII, $1 + 3 = 4$), the Fool (0 or XXII, $2 + 2 = 4$), and all pip cards numbered four.

5. Geburah (Severity)

Severity/Strength/Justice—Necessary purging. Geburah is related to the destructive forces that eliminate what is no longer useful. Geburah is associated with Mars, the planet of conflict and strife. The tarot cards related to the number five are the High Priest (V), Temperance (XIV, $1 + 4 = 5$), and all the pip cards numbered five.

6. Tiphareth (Harmony)

Harmony/Beauty—the Son. Tiphareth is associated with the life-giving Sun, which "dies" at sunset only to be reborn at the next sunrise. The tarot cards related to the number six are the Lovers (VI), the Devil (XV, $1 + 5 = 6$), and all pip cards numbered six.

7. Netzach (Victory)

Victory/Eternity. Netzach is associated with Venus, the planet of love, beauty, creative intuition, art, and tender emotions. The tarot cards related to the number seven are the Chariot (VII), the Tower (XVI, $1 + 6 = 7$), and all pip cards numbered seven.

8. Hod (Splendor)

Glory / Splendor. Hod is associated with the planet Mercury and thus with rational thought and the orderliness of the universe. The tarot cards related to the number eight are Strength or Justice (VIII), the Star (XVII, $1 + 7 = 8$), and all the pip cards numbered eight.

9. Yesod (Foundation)

Foundation. Yesod is associated with the Moon and thus with dreams, imagination, introspection, natural cycles, and fertility. The tarot cards related to the number nine are the Hermit (IX), the Moon (XVIII, $1 + 8 = 9$), and all the pip cards numbered nine.

10. Malkuth (Manifestation)

Manifestation—the Kingdom—Earth—the Daughter. Malkuth is associated with the Earth, with tangible reality and all living things. The tarot cards related to the number ten are the Wheel of Fortune (X), the Magician (I, $1 = 1 + 0$), the Sun (XIX, $1 + 9 = 10$), and all the pip cards numbered ten.

Runes and Tarot

Many tarot readers are familiar with the Nordic or Futhark runes that can be used for divination. Some historians believe that the runes originated with the ancient Etruscans and spread to northern Europe via trade routes. According to one theory, knowledge of the runes may have played a role in the development of the tarot, though there is scant evidence to support this conjecture. The runes and the tarot are distinct divinatory systems, and there is no one-to-one correspondence between them. Nonetheless, the runes and tarot cards have some archetypal images in common, the most compelling of which is tarot's Hanged Man, suspended upside-down like Odin on Yggdrasil, the World Tree of Norse mythology.

Six

Reversals and Dignities

Tarot Inversions

If you shuffle a deck to randomly mix the cards, some of them will appear upside down when you lay them out in a spread. Entire books have been written about how to interpret reversed or inverted cards. Mary K. Greer's *Complete Book of Tarot Reversals* is an excellent resource. Some readers simply ignore card reversals and read all cards upright. Others find inverted cards to be indispensable. This chapter presents some viewpoints about card reversals, and you will need to experiment to decide whether or not you want to use them.

A fundamental principle is that a card's essential meaning does not change simply because it appears upside down. What does change is the way in which you perceive the card as opposed to what the card essentially signifies. If you stand on your head, the room you occupy is still the same room. Your perception of your surroundings, however, becomes altered in the process. In other words, the room stays the same but *you* experience it differently.

Is It Undignified for a Tarot Card to Stand on Its Head?

With tongue in cheek, in my book *Tarot Beyond the Basics* I compared reversed cards to reversed rolls of toilet paper. Some people prefer toilet tissue to emerge over the top of the roll and others prefer to draw it from the bottom. [20] Regardless of whether you pull your paper from the top or the bottom, each roll of toilet paper serves the same function. With tarot cards, however, being upside-down can make it harder for you to see what's going on, so you may need to adjust the card to appreciate its meaning more fully. In a similar way, a reversed tarot card in a reading may imply a need to adjust to a situation or expend extra effort to appreciate what's happening.

Let's do an experiment. Take the Tower (trump XVI) from your tarot deck. In Llewellyn's Classic Tarot, the scene depicts a tower struck and shattered by lightning. Two occupants of the tower fall headfirst toward the rocks below. In mythology, the thunderbolt is a favorite weapon of the gods who evidence their displeasure by hurling bolts of lightning at mortals below. The Greek philosopher Heraclitus believed that the sky god Zeus represented the ordaining pattern of the universe and that Zeus' thunderbolt symbolized divine force steering the course of events.

Given this mythology, we can construct a meaning for the upright version of this card. The occupants of the Tower have built their edifice without regard to spiritual principles or divine law. As a result, the deity (Zeus in the case of ancient Greece) has decided to teach them a lesson by destroying their tower, thus forcing them to reevaluate their spiritual lives and start anew.

If we invert the Tower card, we get a different view of the situation. Now the rocky terrain is located above the two individuals, and the thunderbolt emerges from the left-hand corner of the card beneath their feet. They do not see the dangerous lightning because they are "looking up" at the rocks at the top of the reversed card. They are not cognizant of the divine displeasure represented by the thunderbolt beneath them. Thus, they have ignored an important spiritual message and have failed to learn from their difficult circumstances.

These are my impressions of the upright and inverted tower displayed on this card. As an exercise, try turning the Tower card upright and then inverting it. Note how your perception of the card changes as you alter its orientation in space. Over time, do the same experiment with each card in the deck and jot down your impressions in your tarot notebook. If you use inverted cards in your readings, record how the meanings of the reversed cards play out in the life of the querent. Eventually you will amass a useful collection of upright and reversed meanings for each card.

---

20. According to the U.S. patent No. 465,588 filed on December 22, 1891, the inventor of toilet paper intended it to be used as "over" rather than "under." (For a diagram of its intended use, see www.today.com/home/toilet-paper -over-or-under-debate-resolved-1891-patent-t9776.)

The Tower Reversed

Tarot literature is full of ideas about what reversed cards can mean. Many authors suggest that you decide in advance what you want reversal cards to mean before you do a reading. In this way, there will be no confusion about the meaning of a card that appears inverted in the spread. Here are some of the common ideas about what upside-down cards might signify:

- The exact opposite of the upright position.

- A delay, blockage, or hindrance.

- Struggling to appreciate what's going on.

- Needing to make an adjustment to come to terms with the situation.

- A decrease in the intensity or effectiveness of the upright card.

- A release from the influence of the upright card.

- A need to return to the lesson of the previous card in the sequence (an idea of Paul Fenton-Smith).

- Hidden or unconscious factors as opposed to the overt or conscious meanings of the upright card.

- Specific meanings such as those given in classical texts by Etteilla or A. E. Waite, for example. (In the discussion of the individual cards in this book I have quoted some classical meanings for easy reference.)

For many years I used reversed cards in my tarot practice. More recently, however, I have taken to keeping all the cards upright. In doing so, I consider all the potential meanings of a card in a reading, both positive and negative. We can use the energy represented by any card in a constructive or a harmful manner. Commenting on the full range of meanings, including the potentially negative uses of an upright card, has the potential to empower clients to take responsibility for what is happening in their lives.

Caveat about Reversed Card Meanings

In the chapters detailing the meanings of the individual cards, I have included possible interpretations for the upright and reversed orientations of each card. Please take these delineations with a grain of salt. One of the reasons I stopped using reversed cards was that often the alleged reversed meaning was carried by the upright card, and vice versa. When you read the delineations offered in this text, consider that either the upright or the reversed "meaning" of any card may apply, regardless of whether the card appears upright or inverted.

On Tarot Dignity

The idea of a tarot card having "dignity" comes from the Order of the Golden Dawn and is based on the philosophy of the four elements. When we speak of a card having dignity, we are referring to the card's rank or relative importance with respect to the other cards in a spread. This topic can be a bit complicated, and beginners may wish to skim this section and return to it later when they have a better grasp of the cards.

As we have seen, each tarot card can be assigned to one of the classical four elements of antiquity. As will be explained further on, the combination of elements determines how the cards in question affect each other's dignity. By way of review:

- Fire = Wands

- Water = Cups

- Air = Swords

- Earth = Pentacles

Each major arcana card is assigned to one of the four elements. These assignments can be found in the individual descriptions of the cards in chapter on the major arcana. To interpret tarot layouts, the Golden Dawn used a combination of card counting together with a method of assessing the interactions of the four elements to judge the dignity or relative importance of each card in the spread. Let's begin by taking a look at card counting.

Card Counting

Unlike modern tarot readers who use reversals and complex spreads, the Golden Dawn kept all the tarot cards upright and laid them out in a row. They began by reading the sequence of cards starting from the querent's significator, using a method called card counting in the direction toward which the significator was facing. This was done by assigning each card a numerical value as follows:

- Aces count as 5 (Crowley counted Aces as 11).

- Kings, Queens, and Knights count as 4.

- Pages count as 7.

- Pip cards count as the number of the card.

- Major arcana count as 12 for cards assigned to signs of the zodiac, 9 for the ones assigned to planets, and 3 for those assigned to the elements.

- The card from which the count started was considered the first card in the counting sequence.

Let's look at an example of card counting. Suppose the querent's significator is the Knight of Wands. In the Llewellyn Classic Tarot this Knight faces left, so the count is done in a leftward direction. Because the card is a Knight (assigned a count of 4) looking to the left, we would count four cards to the left, beginning with the Knight of Wands as card number 1.

For instance, consider this sequence of seven cards:

9 Cups	2 Cups	5 Swords	Tower	Knight of Wands	Ace Pentacles	3 Swords
(Water)	(Water)	(Air)	(Fire)	(Fire)	(Earth)	(Air)
	4	3	2	1		

Starting with the significator Knight as number 1, we count four to the left and arrive at the Two of Cups, which suggests that the querent may have a love relationship or close partnership on his mind.

Elemental Dignities

To determine how two cards interact, the Golden Dawn used the system of elemental dignities to determine how two adjacent cards affected each other and also to judge how two flanking cards of a three-card sequence interacted to affect the dignity of the central card. The basic principles are:

- Two cards of the same element greatly enhance each other's influence.

- Fire (Wands) and Water (Cups) are inimical and greatly weaken each other's influence. (In Greek philosophy, Fire is hot and dry, whereas as Water is cold and wet. Fire and Water thus have no qualities in common and are contrary to one another.)

- Earth (Pentacles) and Air (Swords) are inimical and greatly diminish each other's influence. (In Greek philosophy, Earth is cold and dry, whereas as Air is hot and wet. Earth and Air thus have no qualities in common and are contrary to one another.)

- Combinations of nonconflicting elements mildly enhance each other's influence because they have one of the basic qualities (hot, cold, wet, dry) in common.

Qualities of the Elements

The basic qualities of the elements are as follows:

- Fire = hot + dry
- Water = cold + wet (fluid)
- Air = hot + wet (fluid)
- Earth = cold + dry

The table below illustrates these relationships.

- Hot is opposed to cold
- Wet is opposed to dry
- Fire (Wands) is contrary to Water (Cups)
- Air (Swords) is contrary to Earth (Pentacles)
- Air (Swords) and Fire (Wands) have "hot" in common
- Air (Swords) and Water (Cups) have "wet" in common
- Earth (Pentacles) and Fire (Wands) have "dry" in common
- Earth (Pentacles) and Water (Cups) have "cold" in common

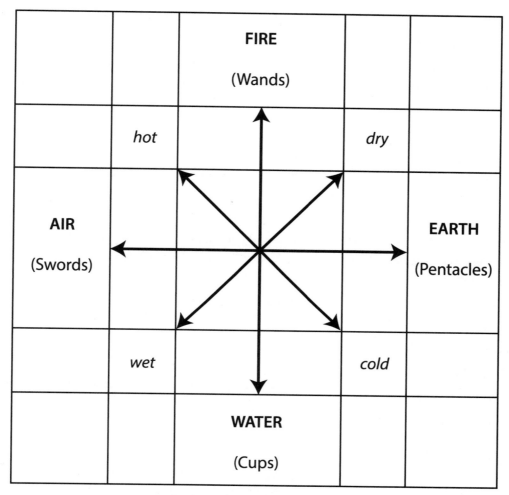

Basic Qualities of the Elements

In the Golden Dawn method, each card is modified by the cards that lie immediately on either side of it. Thus, if a card is flanked by cards of the same suit, it is greatly strengthened for good or evil depending on the nature of the card. If a card is flanked by cards of the contrary suit, it is greatly weakened for good or evil. Other combinations of flanking cards have an intermediate effect as they share one of the essential qualities of their element. The nature of the effect is reflected in the quality receiving the emphasis:

- Hot rises, expands, quickens, excites, animates, and moves upward and outward.
- Cold sinks, contracts, slows, delays, calms, cools, and moves downward and inward.

- Wet flows, merges, adapts, associates, is flexible, and has indistinct permeable boundaries.

- Dry hardens, resists change, makes distinctions, reduces to essentials, is rigid, and has fixed, well-defined boundaries.

Determining Dignity: An Example

9 Cups — *2 Cups* — *5 Swords* — *Tower* — *Knight of Wands* — *Ace Pentacles* — *3 Swords*
(Water) *(Water)* *(Air)* *(Fire)* *(Fire)* *(Earth)* *(Air)*

In the seven-card layout discussed previously, one might ask what effect the Tower (a Fire card) has in the reading. Since the Tower (Fire, hot + dry) lies between a Sword (Air, hot + wet) and a Wand (Fire, hot + dry), the Tower's influence is enhanced but not overwhelmingly so, as would be the case if the Tower were flanked by Fire cards on each side. The "wet" of the Air card to the Tower's left cancels the "dry" of the Fire card to the Tower's right, leaving some "hot" from the Air card to enhance the Fire of the Tower. In this reading, the querent might expect some sort of moderately disruptive unexpected occurrence, symbolized by a slightly strengthened or "hotter" Tower card.

Determining Dignity: A Second Example

9 Cups — *2 Cups* — *5 Swords* — *Tower* — *Knight of Wands* — *Ace Pentacles* — *3 Swords*
(Water) *(Water)* *(Air)* *(Fire)* *(Fire)* *(Earth)* *(Air)*
  4 3 2 1

As a second illustration, consider the Two of Cups, which was the first card to which the counting method guided us from the querent's significator, the Knight of Wands. In this spread, the Two of Cups (Water, cold + wet) lies between a Cup (Water, cold + wet) and a Sword (Air, hot + wet). The "cold" of the Cup on its left cancels the "hot" of the Sword on its right, leaving an extra amount of the quality of "wet" to enhance the already "wet" property of the Two of Cups. Thus, we might expect the Knight of Wands to go with the "wet" flow and lose himself in the relationship suggested by the "wetter" Two of Cups.

An Example of Dignity from the Golden Dawn

Finally, let's consider an example from the annals of the Golden Dawn, which regarded the normally favorable Ten of Cups as having a negative influence when it appeared in this three-card sequence: 10 Wands—10 Cups—5 Swords. The cards surrounding the Ten of Cups in this case have the effect of converting the pleasure signified by this card into something not worth the pain and trouble it would take to attain. How did the Golden Dawn arrive at this conclusion?

10 Wands — 10 Cups — 5 Swords
(hot + dry) (cold + wet) (hot + wet)

The Ten of Cups (Water, cold + wet) is flanked by a Wand (Fire, hot + dry) on the left and a Sword (Air, hot + wet) on the right. The "dry" of the Wand cancels the "wet" of the Sword, leaving two excess "hots" surrounding the central card. These two excess "hots" cancel the "cold" of the Ten of Cups, leaving "hot + wet" in the center of the triplet. The result is that the Ten of Cups now behaves more like the Ten of Swords (hot + wet) so that the normal pleasure of the Ten of Cups becomes painful to achieve (Ten of Swords). In other words, the Ten of Cups retains its essential happy meaning but the pain and suffering of Swords (hot + wet) modifies that happiness.

The decision to use elemental dignities depends on the personality of the tarot reader. Some enjoy this kind of systematic quasi-mathematical reasoning when reading the cards; others find it burdensome and prefer to read intuitively. It's a matter of taste and preference.

It is possible to arrive at a similar interpretation without taking into account the elemental dignities, thus avoiding the mental gymnastics of the Golden Dawn approach. Looking at the same three-card spread, an intuitive reader might reason that the Ten of Wands indicates an oppressive burden and the Five of Swords a painfully humiliating situation. Because the Ten of Cups is sandwiched between these two difficult cards, the pleasure promised by the Cups is likely to be compromised by the surrounding stressful situations.

Seven

How to Ask a
Question of the Tarot

Garbage In, Garbage Out

There is a well-known saying in computer science: garbage in, garbage out. The same holds true when asking questions of the tarot. A thoughtful, open-ended question is a prerequisite for obtaining a useful reading from the cards. In this chapter, we will look at various ways to phrase questions, some of which are productive and others of which are likely to result in ambiguous or less than helpful readings.

The Oracle at Delphi

Long before the tarot existed, the people of the Mediterranean sought guidance from the Oracle at Delphi. Generals of armies and heads of state would not take major decisions without first consulting the Oracle, Apollo's representative on Earth. In ancient Greece, the god Apollo had the power to foresee the future, an ability he bestowed upon the priestess of the temple at Delphi.

Dignitaries and common people alike would flock to the sanctuary at Delphi and pay large sums of money for an audience with Apollo's priestess. After collecting her fee, the oracle would enter the inner chamber of the temple, sit on a tripod, and inhale the mind-altering fumes that rose from a chasm in the earth. Soon thereafter she would fall into a trance (today we would say she was tripping) and begin to utter comments that were unintelligible to the human mind. Presumably these utterances described visions of the future, channeled directly from the mind of Apollo. Fortunately the priests in attendance were able to translate the oracle's mutterings into everyday language, but there was always a catch.

The mind of a god behaves in ways beyond human understanding. To the human mind the prophecies at Delphi appeared ambiguous, full of double meanings and capable of contradictory interpretation. Nonetheless, the Oracle at Delphi gained a reputation for 100 percent accuracy. If an army general inquired about an impending battle, the Oracle might respond: "A great general will emerge triumphant." The military leader would then depart, muster his resources, plan a strategy, and enter the fray confident that a great general was assured victory. The Oracle, however, did not specify which great general would win the battle.

A skeptic might conclude that the Delphic Oracle was simply a con artist who extracted money from gullible clients in return for little of value. A more sophisticated critic might regard this story as proof of the wisdom of Apollo, a god who knew that providing an unambiguous vision of the future would prevent his devotees from assuming responsibility for their actions, rendering them unable to grow spiritually as they chose their own destinies.

The Wisdom of Modern Physics

Our view of the nature of reality has changed dramatically since the time of the Delphic Oracle. Modern physics talks about subatomic realms and multiple universes. The scientific method implies that our theories about reality are provisional; they are likely to change as we grow in experience and garner additional knowledge.

The noted physicist Werner Heisenberg once said (italics mine): *"What we observe is not nature itself but nature exposed to our method of questioning ... asking questions about nature in the language that we possess and trying to get an answer from experiment by the means that are at our disposal."* [21] If we consider the tarot in light of Heisenberg's statement, reading the cards is our method of questioning, and the answer we receive depends on the language that we possess and the means that are at our disposal. Let's look at these three ingredients of inquiry described by Heisenberg.

1) The Method of Questioning

Both practical and intangible factors go into our method of questioning. Obviously, we need a tarot deck to shuffle and mix thoroughly to randomize the sequence of cards. We cut the deck and lay out a number of cards in a predetermined pattern. Next we attempt to interpret the cards and their interrelationships to arrive at a divinatory insight. An essential intangible component consists of asking our question with the sincere expectation of receiving an answer from the cards. If the querent and the

---

21.   Werner Heisenberg, *Physics and Philosophy: The Revolution in Modern Science* (1958), 78, at www.todayinsci.com/H /Heisenberg_Werner/HeisenbergWerner-Quotations.htm, accessed 10 April 2015.

reader lack sincerity in their intention to obtain a helpful response, tarot divination will turn into a mere parlor game. Sincerity of intention is essential. Garbage in, garbage out. It's not nice to fool with Mother Nature.

2) The Language We Possess

Tarot readers possess the language of symbolism. The language of tarot is rooted in the symbols of mythology, dreams, biblical stories, religion, poetry, literature, music, depth psychology, personal experience, the collective unconscious, and various esoteric traditions (astrology, Kabbalah, numerology, alchemy, ceremonial magic, etc.). Arthur E. Waite, the intellectual father of the Waite-Smith deck, commented that "the true Tarot is symbolism; it speaks no other language and offers no other signs." [22] In this sense, questioning by means of the tarot differs from the questioning done by science, which relies on the language of mathematics to make its inquiries. The bulk of this text is devoted to exploring the symbolic language of tarot.

3) The Means at Our Disposal

The means at our disposal consist of sincerity of intention, a deck of tarot cards, a quiet meditative environment, and an understanding of the archetypal symbolism underlying mythology, literature, psychology, and the world's religions. The capacity of human beings to utilize symbols to give meaning to their lives is what distinguishes the human animal from other species. In short, the tarot connects us with that part of our minds which makes us truly human.

What Kinds of Questions are Best and Least Suited to the Tarot?

Not long ago I attended a weekend workshop by Rachel Pollack, whose 1980 book *78 Degrees of Wisdom, A Psychological Approach to the Tarot* was highly influential in changing the way tarot is practiced in the English-speaking world. At one point during the conference, Rachel commented that she and Mary K. Greer are credited with "rescuing tarot from fortune-telling" in the 1980s. Prior to that time, the use of the tarot focused primarily on telling the future.

During tarot's fortune-telling days, clients used to ask yes-no questions (Will I pass the exam?), seek to have the cards make decisions for them (Should I take the job with Edsel?), inquire about the exact timing of events (When will I get married?), spy on other people (Is my girlfriend/boyfriend cheating on me?), find out specifically what the future has in store (What will be the name of my future spouse?), or ask for medical, legal, or investment advice (Is stock in Apple Computer worth buying?). Nowadays such questions are better asked of a dedicated fortune-telling deck such as the Petit Lenormand.

---

22.   A. E. Waite, *The Pictorial Key to the Tarot* (Secaucus, NJ: Citadel Press, 1959), 4.

Tarot, on the other hand, has evolved to become a tool to tap into one's intuition, understand one's motivations, gain insight, and brainstorm. The modern focus on the use of the tarot has changed from fortune-telling to gaining perspective, clarifying issues, and taking responsibility for one's life. The older fortune-telling aspects of tarot do not fit well with the current approach of empowering clients to make informed decisions. In fact, the majority of modern tarot readers prefer not to be viewed as fortune tellers.

From a modern perspective, the most useful questions are open-ended inquiries that help a client to flesh out a situation and lead to fresh insights into the issues involved in making a decision. The cards act as tools that enable us (the reader and the querent) to tap into our intuition and access our inner wisdom. We, and not the cards, provide the answers. To paraphrase President John F. Kennedy, a fortune-telling focus asks "what will the future do for me?" whereas a modern focus on empowerment asks "what can I do to affect my future?"

Productive tarot questions might be worded as follows:

- What do I need to know about this situation to make a wise decision?

- Are there any issues I should pay special attention to? What might I be ignoring?

- What can I do in this situation to increase the chances of a favorable outcome?

- How might I be working against my own best interests?

- What role do I play in what is happening?

- What is the best strategy if I wish to accomplish such and such, and what is best for me to avoid?

- How can I improve my chances in this situation? What would be a good next step?

- What obstacles do I need to confront to achieve my goals?

- What do I most need to know about this situation? What am I not seeing clearly?

- What can I learn from this situation or from my past mistakes?

- Help me to understand my motivations so that I can see my way more clearly.

- If I follow this particular path, how is the situation likely to evolve?

- For general readings: what issues do I need to focus on in my life at this time?

Eight

How to Read What Is Written in the Cards

Tarot as an Art

Like medicine, tarot is an art. To master any of the arts, the student must learn the basic science and essential skills of the field and put them into practice. Essentially, the tarot cards present a series of images the reader interprets to tell a story. A basic assumption is that the stories we tell ourselves shape our self-image and influence how we conduct out lives. By giving voice to the images on the cards, the tarot reader offers to the querent a narrative to ponder. The importance of giving verbal expression to the sequence of tarot images can be seen in the ideas of the noted linguist Saussure regarding the role of words in everyday life:

> "Words are not mere vocal labels or communicational adjuncts superimposed upon an already given order of things. They are collective products of social interaction, essential instruments through which human beings constitute and articulate their world." [23]

---

23.   Roy Harris, *Language, Saussure and Wittgenstein* (London: Routledge, 1988), ix.

God Loves a Good Story

Long ago in a remote village of Eastern Europe, the members of a small Jewish community turned to their rabbi for help with a vexing problem. A devout man, the rabbi went to a consecrated spot in the forest, lit a sacred fire, recited a special prayer and, speaking aloud, told the village's story to the Lord. Soon thereafter he had a clear insight into how to resolve the problem.

Generations passed and the village again found itself beset by difficulties. As was their custom, the villagers turned to their rabbi who went to the woods to say the special prayer, but quickly realized that the traditional method of lighting the sacred fire had been lost to history. Nonetheless, speaking aloud, he told the village's story to the Lord and received guidance about how to fix the situation.

Centuries passed and the village again turned to their rabbi for help. The new rabbi went to the woods but no longer knew the location of the consecrated spot, nor did he know how to light the sacred fire. He had even forgotten the words of the special prayer. Nonetheless, speaking aloud, the rabbi told the village's story to the Lord and was soon filled with wisdom about how to remedy the situation. The very act of speaking aloud to tell the village's story to the Lord with the sincere expectation of receiving divine guidance was the essential ingredient of this healing ritual.

Author Rami M. Sharpiro, who recounts such Hasidic tales, explains: "Humans are storytelling animals…Our stories define us, instruct us, create us. Without our stories we do not exist…[f]or us our story is our self…[a]nd the story you tell determines the meaning you derive from the events of your life."[24] The tarot too is a storytelling ritual that allows us to retell and even change our stories in ways that can heal us. Jane Stern's book *Confessions of a Tarot Reader* illustrates this storytelling approach; she tells real-life tales of a number of her tarot clients to illustrate the archetypal meanings of each of the cards of the major arcana.

The Secret to Reading the Cards

Reading what is written in the cards is an art that can be mastered with a combination of sufficient study and practice. Divination with the tarot uses the card's images to tell a story that has relevance for the querent. Essentially, reading the tarot is a form of myth-making, which functions like the stories of antiquity, allowing access to thoughts, feelings, and images by which we can make sense of our experiences and lend meaning to our lives. Facilitating access to these archetypal images is the core of the process.

A critic might object that the tarot reader is simply making up stories that coincidentally connect with the querent's concerns. To some extent this objection is valid, but most readers soon discover that especially relevant cards often do appear in ways that can feel quite uncanny.

---

24.   Rami M. Shapiro, *Hasidic Tales* (Woodstock, VT: SkyLight Paths Publishing, 2003), xxii.

The power of the tarot lies in the fact that each card represents an archetypal situation all of us may have experienced at some point in our lives. By creating a forum that allows the reader and querent to meditate jointly on these archetypes, a good tarot reading almost always touches on issues of great personal significance, and, just as in the story of the Hasidic rabbi, has the potential to heal.

Critics might also object that the theory of archetypes is merely a fanciful speculation with little scientific support. Interestingly, recent studies at Emory University have demonstrated that memories of experiences shared by our ancestors may be transmitted through our DNA. For example, scientists were able to show that mice trained to fear a specific odor would pass these emotions down through generations, presumably enabling future mice to be better prepared to deal with a similar situation. As Dr. Brian Dias of Emory University has explained, "Our results allow us to appreciate how the experiences of a parent, before even conceiving offspring, markedly influence both structure and function in the nervous system of subsequent generations." [25]

How, then, does one master the art of story-telling with the cards? Paul Huson, a recognized expert on the history of tarot, believes that the secret to reading the tarot *resides in the person who divines* rather than in the cards themselves: "As I see it, cartomantic rules and regulations have been cobbled together from a variety of sources, and I hold to the school of thought that the secret of successful divination lies within the diviner. Actually, I believe anyone who wants to read the cards is not only free to, but must evolve a personal method for himself or herself …" [26]

A Storytelling Example

To illustrate the storytelling technique, consider the following reading. It was done for a college student who asked about pursuing graduate studies in psychology, her university major. An advisor had cautioned her that the field of psychology was becoming increasingly competitive, and she was worried about obtaining an advanced degree for which there might be little demand in the future. We decided on a three-card spread; she drew the Five of Wands, the Seven of Pentacles, and the Page of Swords.

---

25. Dr. Brian Dias, quoted in "Science Is Proving Some Memories Are Passed Down From Our Ancestors," *The Galactic Free Press*, 05 April 2015, at soundofheart.org/galacticfreepress/content/science-proving-some-memories-are-passed -down-our-ancestors, accessed 5 May, 2015.

26. Paul Huson, quoted from his website: www.paulhuson.com/

Five of Wands, Seven of Pentacles, and Page of Swords (left to right)

The first card shows five youths engaging in spirited competition, mirroring quite closely the situation that prompted her to ask for a reading. The second card depicts a young farmer pausing to reflect on his crops (the seven pentacles) and making plans for the future direction of his efforts. The third card, the Page of Swords, sometimes appears when the querent is expecting or dealing with unwelcome news or advice. This Page is highly intelligent, clever, and resourceful. The tarot seemed to be saying that this student was indeed confronting stiff competition and would need to plan her future moves carefully, using all her intelligence and mental resources. After pondering this interpretation, she asked to draw another card to clarify the implications of the Page of Swords, and she selected the Three of Pentacles.

This card shows a young artisan working diligently to create an object of beauty in cooperation with two individuals who respect his work and are willing to pay him well for his skilled labor. Here the tarot seems to be advising the student to master an area of her craft and establish a reputation for doing her work with diligence and expertise.

Three of Pentacles

The Cards as Living Entities

The notorious occultist Aleister Crowley compared learning the tarot to making a new set of friends. Viewing the cards as living individuals, Crowley suggested methods that enable students to form personal relationships with the entities of the tarot. The view of the individual cards as living beings may seem a bit far-fetched, but it is not so different from the Jungian view that the tarot signifies universal archetypes of the collective unconscious.

Crowley believed that newcomers to the tarot could truly appreciate the cards only if they observed closely how the tarot behaves over a substantial period of time. In other words, an understanding of the tarot comes only through extensive experience with the cards, treating them as if they were sentient beings. How do you get to Carnegie Hall? Practice, practice, practice!

Crowley cautions that merely intensifying one's study of the cards as objective things rather than as living individuals is not sufficient. The student must live with the cards, and the cards in turn must live with the student. The tarot novice and the living cards must take time to get to know one another. How else can a relationship form and grow?

To quote Crowley: "A card is not isolated from its fellows. The reactions of the cards, their interplay with each other, must be built into the very life of the student … How is he to blend their life with his? The ideal way is that of contemplation … The practical every-day commonplace way is divination." [27]

Occultist Dion Fortune carried Crowley's cards-as-living-entities metaphor even further, suggesting that students sleep with their cards, much like young lovers who spend nights together exploring every nook and cranny of each other's bodies.

Shuffling and Selecting the Cards

If reading the tarot involves using the cards to prime your intuition so you are able to tell a coherent story, then mastering the art of tarot divination requires practice in storytelling. As the saying goes, a picture is worth a thousand words. The art of tarot involves translating the images on the cards into a mythological tale that can be of benefit to the querent. When you read the cards for someone, you collaborate with the person to create a story that puts some aspect of their life into meaningful perspective. In this process, the reader and the querent are spurred on by the images on the cards.

The following suggestions may help beginning tarot students to develop this skill:

- Trust your intuition and pay special attention to the first thoughts and impressions that come to mind as you look at the cards.

- Practice making up a story about each card in your deck and speak it out loud. What is the emotional climate of the card? What do the colors on the card evoke in your imagination? What kind of situation might the card represent? What are the characters thinking and feeling? Where have they come from to get to this point on the card? Where are they headed after the scene on the card has run its course? What do their postures and facial expressions suggest? If they could speak, what might they be saying? If you were in their situation, how would you be feeling? What would you do about it?

- Do the same exercise with groups of two or more cards. How does each card connect to the others? What do they have in common? How do they contrast with one another? What would need to happen for the situation on one card to develop into the scene depicted on the next? Which characters are looking at each other? Which are looking away from one another? How might the characters on different cards interact?

- Do this exercise with each card for each position of a tarot layout or spread. Common spread positions include past, present, future, obstacles, assistance, advice, pros,

---

27. Aleister Crowley, *The Book of Thoth* (San Francisco: Weiser, 1969), 249.

cons, hidden issues, one's environment, hope and fears, likely outcome, and so on. A detailed example of this exercise can be found in the book *Tarot Decoder* by Kathleen McCormack, in which the author gives her impressions of the meaning of each card in each of the ten positions of the Celtic Cross spread.

- Lay out all the cards of a particular suit in sequential order and make up a story that links each card to the next. Let your imagination run wild.

- Take your time and be patient. Rome wasn't built in a day.

Reading over the Internet

Traditionally people have consulted tarot readers in person. Although some tarot authorities feel that only the reader (and not the querent) should be allowed to handle the deck, most readers believe it is important for the querent to participate in shuffling and cutting the deck as part of the process of selecting the cards. This personal involvement by the querent allows the deck to resonate more effectively with the inquirer's concerns.

In this age of the Internet, tarot readings can now be done online with the querent residing quite some distance in space from the reader and thus unable to have physical contact with the cards. To allow the querent active participation, I have evolved the following method for reading online. After discussing the querent's concerns and the type of reading that might be appropriate, I ask the querent to reflect on the question while I shuffle the cards. I instruct the querent to tell me to stop shuffling when the time feels right. I then cut the cards and reassemble the deck, placing the bottom cut on top.

Next, I ask the querent to think of a number from one to ten, and I count down from the top of the deck to the card corresponding to the number chosen. I repeat the process of shuffling, cutting, and selecting a number from one to ten until the querent and I have jointly chosen all the cards in the layout. In this way the querent has actively participated in shuffling, cutting, and selecting all the cards for the reading with me acting in a surrogate capacity. Querents are usually impressed by how well the cards they choose by "randomly" selecting a number from one to ten fit the nature of their concerns. I put the word "randomly" in quotes because the choice of each card is likely an example of Jungian synchronicity.

Telling Time with the Tarot

Is Telling Time Possible?

Opinion is divided about whether one can predict the timing of events with the tarot. My own view based on experience is that the cards do *not* pinpoint exact times when a specific event is likely to occur. Astrology is more useful for this purpose. Instead, I view the tarot as a technique that empowers querents to clarify situations and effectively make decisions that will influence their future. What will happen in the future depends on how we think, feel, act, and decide in the present. If we change our pattern of thinking and our belief systems, the future will change with them. Let's review some of the timing techniques suggested in the literature.

The Most Simple Timing Technique

A simple and effective timing technique is to include a specific time frame in your inquiry. For example, instead of asking a general question about a new relationship, you can word the question as follows: "How will this new relationship evolve *over the next three months?*" Other examples of inquires with a time limit include asking, "What do I need to learn from you *today?*" or "What do I need to focus on *this week/month/in the coming year?*" and so on. In short, if you have a question about a specific period of time, simply include the time frame in the question.

Seasons of the Year Correspondences

There are four suits in the tarot and four seasons of the year; thus, you can pair each tarot suit with one of the seasons. These associations will guide your intuition to judge a likely time of occurrence. A commonly used set of associations comes from astrology:

- Wands—Fire—Spring
- Cups—Water—Summer
- Swords—Air—Autumn
- Pentacles—Earth—Winter

If you prefer a system of associations other than the astrological one, by all means use it.

The following method is a simple way to answer the question, "When (in what season of the year) will such and such occur?" Shuffle the deck while you focus on your concern with the sincere intention of obtaining an answer. When the time feels right, cut and reassemble the deck. Now turn over the cards in order, one at a time. The first Ace to appear will indicate the answer according to its suit. For example, if the first Ace belongs to the suit of Pentacles, the answer is "wintertime."

How Fast Will Matters Evolve?

Rather than give a specific time period, this method suggests how fast a matter will develop depending on the suit of the outcome card or on the predominance of a particular suit in a spread. Wands, being hot and fiery, suggest rapid action. Swords, being hot and airy, are quick but not as fast as Wands. Cups, being cold and watery, are somewhat slow. Finally, Pentacles, being cold and earthen, are the slowest of all. To summarize:

- Wands—hot and fiery—very fast (hours to days)
- Swords—hot and airy—moderately fast (days to weeks)

- Cups—cold and watery—moderately slow (weeks to months)

- Pentacles—cold and earthy—very slow (months to years)

Finally, I should mention that the Golden Dawn associated each tarot card with a specific time period. These associations are included in the individual descriptions of the cards in subsequent chapters. I suggest experimenting with the above methods, and you can also Google tarot timing techniques to see if any of the suggestions for timing events are of use in your tarot practice.

Nine

Laying Out the Cards to Do a Reading

What Is a Tarot Spread?

Tarot readers typically lay out the cards in a predetermined pattern called a spread. Each position in the spread is assigned a particular meaning, and the card falling in that location is interpreted in the context of the meaning attributed to that spot in the layout. For example, in a three-card past-present-future spread, the card in the first position refers to the past, the central card gives information about the present, and the final card indicates future trends.

The tarot literature is replete with spreads for every occasion. Several books are available detailing a large variety of ways to lay out the cards. Perhaps the most popular spread of the last century is the Celtic Cross layout, popularized by A. E. Waite in his influential 1910 book on the tarot. The Celtic Cross was Waite's attempt to present a simple alternative to the intricately complex Opening of the Key method he learned from the Golden Dawn.

Today, many readers prefer to invent their own spreads to suit the question at hand and thereby provide the specific information desired by the querent. In 2013, Llewellyn published a "toolkit" for constructing spreads entitled *The Deck of 1000 Spreads*, authored by Tierney Sadler. The back cover of this toolkit says that users can "mix and match these 59 labeled and 6 blank cards to customize any tarot reading imaginable. Each one features a color-coded theme, the name of a commonly used spread position, and a written description of that position." The color-coded themes include the focus of the question, the influences to which the querent must attend, the characters involved in the situation, the time frame, and issues related to the outcome including relevant advice, the potential resolution, and any lessons to be learned.

The Daily Draw

Many readers pull a daily card at random as a focus for contemplation. There is nothing special about drawing a new card each day. If your "daily" card seems particularly meaningful, feel free to ponder it for several days before moving on to another card. If it feels irrelevant, you are free to choose a different card for the day. My own practice is to keep a tarot deck on my desk so that I can shuffle the cards and draw one whenever the spirit moves me. The following suggestions may be helpful for your daily draw:

- Shuffle the deck in a relaxed and meditative state with the sincere intent of pulling a card that will be meaningful to you at this moment.

- When the time feels right, draw a card at random.

- Speaking out loud, describe the card as if you were talking to a friend. Remember the tale of the rabbi who told the story of his village to the Lord. Don't try to analyze the meaning of the card at this stage. Simply say aloud what you see on the card.

- If you gain any insights as you are speaking about the card, record them in your tarot journal.

- Next think about possible interpretations of the card. Do any of these meanings relate to your current life? If so, make a note in your journal. Feel free to read what tarot authors have written about the card, keeping in mind that no one has a stranglehold on the truth.

- Later in the day, reflect on the card and ask yourself the same questions. In what ways has the archetypal significance of the card manifested in your daily life? Perhaps you noticed a theme of the card in an interaction with a friend or in a news story, a TV show, and so on. What lessons have you learned from the card? Again, note any such insights and experiences in your journal.

- If a card feels particularly significant, feel free to ponder it for several days before moving on to another card.

- If pulling just a single card for the day does not appeal to you, try drawing several cards on a regular basis. Remember that practice is key.

One-Card Readings

Just as in the daily draw, you can pull a single card at random to clarify a situation. As usual, shuffle the cards in a meditative state with the sincere intention of drawing a card to shed light on the matter. The following is an example of a one-card reading. Before reading the details of the situation, look at the image on the Ten of Swords and say what you see. What kind of situation might this card represent?

Ten of Swords

The Situation

Before reading on, be sure you have looked at the image of the Ten of Swords and considered what type of situation it might represent. Here's the story. I belong to a weekly group to practice exchanging languages online. On one occasion the leader of the group left a message that she could not attend because her husband had suddenly taken ill and she needed to accompany him to the hospital. Concerned about her husband's illness, I drew a single card from the deck: the Ten of Swords.

This ominous looking card depicts a man lying on the ground with ten swords piercing his body. The card seemed to suggest that her husband's condition was fairly serious. No one in the group heard any news from her during the following week, and she did not appear for the next group. We were all a bit worried.

At the end of the second week, she sent an e-mail explaining that her husband had been taken by ambulance to the hospital and admitted to the Intensive Care Unit. She had remained with him at the hospital and did not have access to a computer to get in touch with the group. Her life had been totally turned upside down. She was not sure when she could return to the group because she and her husband were facing nonstop visits with doctors, nurses, and therapists, and she didn't know how long it would last. The image on the Ten of Swords card captured quite well her experience of her husband's illness. Fortunately he was eventually released from the hospital and made a slow recovery, perhaps symbolized by the bright sunlight in the distant background on this card.

Two-Card Readings

One-card readings are limited in scope because a single card does not give a sense of the flow of events. To get an inkling of how matters will progress, it is usually necessary to pull two or more cards. The following is an example of a two-card reading.

The question was asked by a woman whose son had recently been arrested for a DUI (driving under the influence). The penalties in her state were quite harsh for such an offense and she feared her son might go to prison. Because our time was limited, I had her draw only two cards with the intention of understanding the likely outcome of her son's day in court. She pulled the Six of Swords and the Ten of Cups, in that order.

The sequence of cards implies movement away from a difficult situation toward a period of family tranquility. The first card, the Six of Swords, shows a ferryman propelling a woman and child (the querent and her son?) away from troubled waters. The ferryman could well stand for the lawyer whom her son had consulted to handle his case. She and her son felt confident in the lawyer's ability. The outcome was that her son did not go to jail. Instead, he received a suspended sentence with a requirement to do community service and attend alcohol counseling. A little further on, we will see another reading for the same situation, this time asked by the woman's husband.

Six of Swords and Ten of Cups (left to right)

Three-Card Readings: A Nod to Hegel

Three-card readings are a popular way to read the tarot. The effectiveness of a three-card spread may be rooted in the philosophy of Hegel: thesis—antithesis—synthesis. The thesis refers to an idea or a proposition, the antithesis is a reaction to or negation of the proposition (thesis), and the synthesis is a creative resolution that resolves the conflict between the two. The Hegelian theme of a creative synthesis arising from the reconciliation of antithetical forces also appears on Temperance, trump XIV, a card associated with the centaur Sagittarius.

Author James Ricklef has written an entire book about three-card spreads entitled *Tarot Tells the Tale* (Llewellyn, 2004). In it he demonstrates the power of this deceptively simple spread with a host of sample readings. Among the many variations of three-card layouts in the tarot literature, one may find:

- Past—Present—Future

- Mind—Body—Spirit

- Foundation—Problem—Advice

- Central Concern—Obstacle—Resolution

- Yes, if—No, if—Maybe if …

- Dilemma—Choice 1—Choice 2

- Situation—Action—Outcome

- Yang approach—Yin approach—Creative synthesis

- Querent—Other Person—Relationship

- Spiritual Path—Practices—Posture (from the Art of Change Tarot website)

- Pros—Cons—Outcome (If confronted with various choices, you can do a "pros—cons—outcome" spread for each option to help clarify the best course of action.)

Try inventing your own three-card spreads to suit the question. You can find many examples of this layout online. It's a powerful technique that does not overwhelm the reader, but at the same time provides useful insights. The tarot owes a debt of gratitude to Hegel.

A Personal Three-Card Reading

This reading was done on Tuesday, July 29, 2014. While doing research for this book, I came across Llewellyn's tarot-reading site, which offers free computer-generated delineations. [28] There I selected a Past—Present—Future spread. Because I was in the early stages of writing this text, I asked, "How will this book turn out in the end?" The following cards appeared:

The reversed High Priestess in the past position made sense. I was feeling stuck trying to envision what to write and how to say it. Access to my intuition felt temporarily blocked.

The upright Three of Pentacles in the present position was encouraging. This card suggested making use of my talents and working in collaboration with my editor at Llewellyn to make progress in the writing. The focus should be on quality and a job well done. I would need to keep chipping away at the block of marble to reveal the form within.

The upright Four of Wands in the future position was also a welcome sign. The Llewellyn site offered the keywords "repose after difficulty" and added "achieving a state of balance, peace, and contentment after a long ordeal." The cards suggested I keep plugging away and focusing on quality despite the long ordeal. In the end, the result should be favorable and bring contentment. I hope the cards were right.

---

28.   Llewellyn Worldwide, "Tarot Reading," http://www.llewellyn.com/tarot_reading.php

High Priestess (reversed), Three of Pentacles (upright), and Four of Wands (upright) (left to right)

Theme and Variations Spread

This spread consists of five cards arranged in a square with a central card and one in each of the four corners, representing variations on a theme. If you have a particular issue you'd like to clarify, card 5 would represent the main theme and the other four cards would signify the various features on that theme.

A Sample Theme and Variations Spread

The querent is a young engineer who finished his degree in Spain but could not find a job there because of the economic crisis. He finally found work, but it involved relocating to China, to the disappointment of his family who told him that they would miss him terribly if he moved to another country. He asked for a general reading, and these cards appeared:

- **Card 1:** Page of Swords
- **Card 2:** The Hanged Man
- **Card 3:** The Hierophant (Pope, High Priest)
- **Card 4:** Three of Cups
- **Card 5:** Main theme: The Chariot

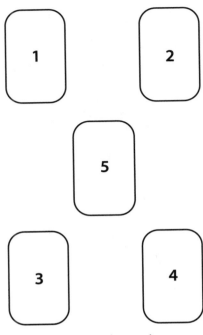

Five-Card Spread

As the central theme, the Chariot represented his journey to China to find work in his profession. As he and I discussed the variations on this theme, it became clear that the Page of Swords was linked to a recent conversation he had with his family, in which they told him that they wished that he would move back to Spain to live closer to them, get married, and start a family (themes linked to the Hierophant). To his family, the decision to live and work in China seemed a very unusual way to pursue a career (symbolized by the Hanged Man). His hope was that eventually all would be happy with his decision and celebrate his success (Three of Cups).

Interviewing a New Deck with the Theme and Variations Spread

Most tarot enthusiasts have more than one deck and use particular decks for specific purposes. For example, you might use one deck to read for yourself, another for meditation, and yet another for creative inspiration when starting a project. One way to get acquainted with a new set of cards is to "interview" the deck using a tarot spread. The theme and variations layout is useful for this purpose.

Let card 5 in the center represent your overall experience of working with the deck and assign variations on this theme to the other four cards. Decide what you want to explore and make a list of meanings for each position in the spread. For example:

- **Card 1:** What do I bring to the relationship with this deck?

- **Card 2:** What special qualities and learning experiences does this deck have to offer?

- **Card 3:** How can I most productively use these cards?

- **Card 4:** What limitations or obstacles might I face when using this deck?

- **Card 5:** What will be my overall experience of working with this deck?

Horseshoe Spread

The Horseshoe spread is helpful when you are unsure about an optimal course of action. It is so called because the cards are laid in the shape of a horseshoe, each card representing an aspect of the situation. Horseshoes are said to bring good luck, and some people hang horseshoes over the door to their home to protect it and attract good fortune. A point of contention is whether the horseshoe should be hung with its opening facing up or facing down. Placing the two ends of the horseshoe facing up (in a U shape) presumably helps to collect and store the good vibrations.

The accompanying diagram depicts the typical arrangement of a horseshoe spread. If you believe that pointing the ends of the horseshoe downward is likely to spill out all the good fortune, just flip the diagram over to hold in all your good luck!

There are many variations in the literature about ways to use this spread. The following approach is often helpful, but readers should feel free to assign their own meanings to the positions to suit the matter at hand.

1. Past influences affecting the current situation.

2. Present issues related to the problem.

3. Future developments that will need attention.

4. Advice about an optimal course of action.

5. How those around the querent (family, friends, associates, etc.) relate to the issue.

6. Obstacles and hidden influences the querent may need to take into account to resolve the problem.

7. The likely outcome of the proposed course of action.

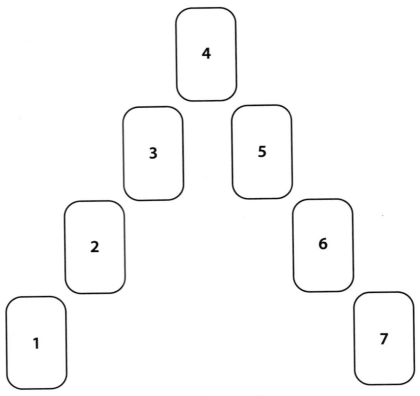

Horseshoe Spread

A Sample Horseshoe Spread

Here is an example of a horseshoe spread. The male querent was worried about his adult son who had recently been arrested for driving under the influence of alcohol. The querent and his wife had helped their son to find an attorney, and they accompanied him to court. The son's driver's license was suspended, and he was sentenced to a year's probation. In the days following the court hearing, the son became increasingly isolated and depressed. The parents got worried that their son might become suicidal. The father asked the open-ended question, "How can I best help my son in this situation?" We did a horseshoe spread.

- **Card 1,** past influences: *The King of Wands.* The querent felt that the King of Wands referred to his active role in helping his son to find a lawyer.

- **Card 2,** present issues: *The High Priest.* Most likely the High Priest, who is a spokesperson for moral behavior and traditional values, referred to the need for his son to seek counseling for his alcohol problem and meet the requirements of probation.

- **Card 3,** near future: *Three of Coins*. This card might refer to seeking a creative solution in cooperation with others.

- **Card 4,** advice: *Ten of Cups*. The advice of the Ten of Cups is to keep the focus on family love and support. Blaming and recriminations were unlikely to be helpful. The querent's wife had also drawn the Ten of Cups in her two-card spread about the same issue.

- **Card 5,** those around the querent: *Two of Coins*. Other family members were likely to have their hands full as they were juggling many responsibilities. In fact, the querent's other children were also in need of attention at this time.

- **Card 6,** obstacles and hidden issues: *The Empress*. The querent thought that the Empress probably referred to his wife, who was deeply distressed about their son's depressed mood and the risk of suicide. He felt a need to be emotionally available to both his depressed son and his wife because of her distraught state of mind.

- **Card 7,** likely outcome: *Four of Wands*. This card generally depicts peace and security. The spread appeared to advise the querent to continue supporting his son in a loving manner as a cherished member of the family. Despite the son's guilt and depression, his awareness of his parents' love and caring would help him get through this difficult time.

Clarifying Choices with the Horseshoe Spread

You can also use the seven-card horseshoe spread to clarify two options. In this case, the central card (4) represents the situation you are asking about. Branching off from the central position are cards 3, 2, and 1, which represent respectively the pros, cons, and likely outcome of the first choice; and cards 5, 6, and 7, which signify the pros, cons, and likely outcome of the second choice.

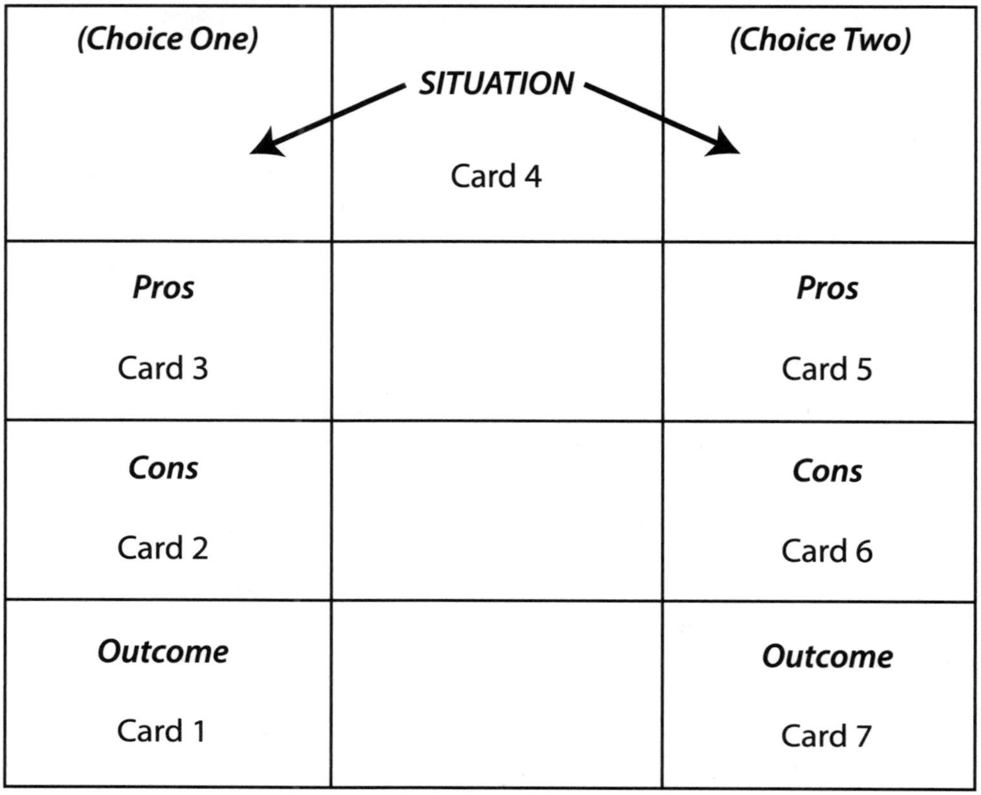

(Choice One)	SITUATION Card 4	(Choice Two)
Pros Card 3		*Pros* Card 5
Cons Card 2		*Cons* Card 6
Outcome Card 1		*Outcome* Card 7

Clarifying Choices

The Celtic Cross Layout

The Celtic Cross is my favorite tarot layout. It was popularized by A. E. Waite in his 1910 book *The Pictorial Key to the Tarot*, where he offered it as an alternative to the lengthy and complex Opening of the Key spread used by the Golden Dawn. The method I follow is close to Waite's original with some minor modifications.

Waite began by choosing a significator card to represent the querent. He then used the direction in which the figure on the card was facing to determine past and future positions in the spread. The future lay ahead of the querent's significator; and the past, behind. My own practice is to omit the significator and launch immediately into the spread.

The Celtic Cross consists of two crosses, a small two-card inner cross with a larger four-card outer cross surrounding it, plus a column of four cards to the right. I lay the cards as in the accompanying diagram.

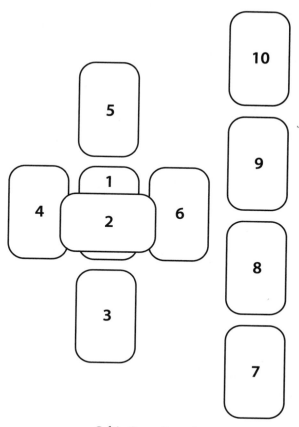

Celtic Cross Spread

- **Card 1** "covers" the significator, if you use one, and is the central card that signifies the main theme of the reading.

- **Card 2** "crosses" the central card and signifies a challenge or issue that the querent must traverse in dealing with the central issue of card 1. Taken together, these two cards form the central cross of the reading.

Cards **3**, **4**, **5**, and **6** form a second cross surrounding the central cross.

- **Card 3** is the basis or foundation of the matter.

- **Card 4** refers to an event, feeling, or idea from the recent past that has direct bearing on the central issue.

- **Card 5** shows a potential or an ideal outcome, that is, what might happen or what the querent may wish to have happen. Some readers use this card to refer to what is going on at present in the querent's life.

- **Card 6** points to something that will occur in the near future that is related to the issue at hand.

The column of four cards to the right of these two crosses gives additional information.

- **Card 7** represents the attitude and experience of the querent with regard to the central theme.

- **Card 8** shows the attitude and experience of those who surround the querent with regard to the central theme.

- **Card 9** refers to the querent's hopes and fears in this matter.

- **Card 10** suggests the likely outcome.

A Sample Celtic Cross Reading

The following example will make the process clear. The querent is a professional man in his early thirties. He lives with his girlfriend of many years. He asked for a general reading to reveal which issues might be important in his current life.

Card 1 was the Queen of Swords. This could represent an important woman in his life or a personality trait that he needs to cultivate at this time. If this card refers to a situation, it would involve a certain amount of sadness, grieving, or loss. The Queen of Swords is often called the "widow" card because she is a woman who has experienced loss or privation. Interestingly, one of the traditional meanings of this card is "sterility."

Card 2 was the Empress. The Empress is a fertile, productive woman who is often concerned about issues of marriage, pregnancy, and motherhood. Seeing the Queen of Swords crossed by the Empress, a combination of two powerful women, I asked if something involving his girlfriend was on his mind. The querent replied that his girlfriend had been to see the doctor the day before and was told that if she did not get pregnant soon, she might never be able to have children. She had always wanted to have a child and was worried about growing old without a family of her own.

Card 3 was the Queen of Wands, another significant woman, this time in the foundation position of the reading. This queen is an energetic woman who likes keeping busy and being in charge. In light of what the querent said about his girlfriend, I wondered if she felt a need to do something to ensure she could get pregnant soon and have a family. He said that his girlfriend was this type of energetic person.

Card 4, the recent past position, was the Tower, a card of sudden disruption. His girlfriend had experienced the doctor's words as a bolt from the blue. The possibility of forgoing motherhood would upset the life plan she had envisioned for herself.

Card 5, the possible outcome, was the Five of Wands, a group of young men engaged in rivalry and competition. This card suggests that he and his girlfriend were likely to be at odds about having a baby at this time. He agreed, adding that it would be very disruptive to his career to start a family just now.

Card 6, the near future, was the Nine of Swords, sometimes called the nightmare card. It depicts a woman, perhaps a cloistered nun, sitting up in bed at night in a state of worry and pre-occupation. The querent said that the possibility of not being able to have children was weighing heavily on his girlfriend's mind. In addition, her mother's health has recently concerned her.

Card 7, the querent's experience of the matter, was Judgment depicting an angel sounding a trumpet at the end of time to awaken the souls of the dead and call them to a new phase of existence. The querent felt that having a child now would be like entering a completely new phase of life. He added that the angel on the Judgment card reminded him of his girlfriend's name, which was Angela!

Card 8, the experience of those surrounding the querent, was the Nine of Cups, often called the "wish card." Most likely this card referred to his girlfriend's belief that getting pregnant would be a wish come true.

Card 9, hopes and fears, was the Page of Cups. Pages represent children, so the Page of Cups could represent his own wish for children as well as his fear of dependency.

Card 10, the final outcome, was the Wheel of Fortune. The spread seemed to be indicating that forces greater than either member of the couple were at work. The outcome could depend somehow on a twist of fate. The Wheel might also signify that the opportunity to have children was now pre-senting itself but would vanish with the passage of time, just as the doctor had counseled. The two of them had an important decision to make while the possibility of having children was still open.

A Celtic Cross Reading for a Skeptical Student

Every so often a skeptical but curious querent asks for a reading. In this case, the querent was a university student who was studying translation and linguistics. Because of his interest in foreign languages, he asked for a reading to get a sense of how the cards are read.

Card 1 was the Ace of Pentacles. This card suggests that the main theme of the reading has to do with material opportunities and resources.

Card 2 was the King of Cups. This king is often a professional person who can be of assistance to the querent, perhaps someone who could help him achieve the financial goal of card one.

Card 3 was the Devil, a major arcana card suggesting that a matter of major importance was at the foundation of the reading. The Devil card often refers to a material ambition being pursued, sometimes obsessively, to the exclusion of other matters of a more spiritual significance.

Card 4, the recent past position, was the Chariot, a major arcana card that might indicate that a significant journey or important ambition has been on his mind in the recent past.

Card 5, the possible or ideal outcome, was the *Five of Wands* depicting a group of young men engaged in rivalry and competition.

Card 6, the near future, was the Four of Pentacles, showing someone holding tightly to money and resources. Perhaps in the near future he would need to be saving his money for the purpose indicated by card 1.

Card 7, the querent's experience of the matter, was the Eight of Cups depicting a character walking away from eight cups, perhaps in search of a more satisfying situation.

Card 8, the experience of those surrounding the querent, was the *Ten of Wands* showing a man walking along with a burden of ten wands. Perhaps those around him were feeling a bit overwhelmed.

Card 9, hopes and fears, was the Four of Wands, depicting people celebrating a job well done.

Card 10, the final outcome, was the Ace of Wands. The spread seemed to be indicating that he would be given an opportunity to pursue an exciting personal or professional ambition.

Putting the cards together with the fact that he was a student of foreign languages, I suggested that the main theme of the reading might be related to seeking a scholarship (Ace of Pentacles) with the aid of a mentor or advisor (King of Cups) to pursue a goal of studying abroad (Chariot) to advance his career (Ace of Wands) because of a certain sense of dissatisfaction with what he could learn at his current university (Eight of Cups). This goal might feel like an obsession to him (the Devil) and would require careful management of resources (Four of Pentacles) and involve competition with other students (Five of Wands).

The skeptical student replied that my comments were true in a general way, but that it was probably just coincidence that these cards appeared in the reading. He confirmed that he had been hoping to spend a year abroad studying languages but that it would be costly to do so and he would need to be very careful with his finances. He remained unconvinced that the tarot had anything useful to offer him.

Houses of the Horoscope Spread

For those interested in astrology, the Houses of the Horoscope layout provides useful insight into the various aspects of life described by the twelve houses. Each astrological house represents a distinct field of experience.

To use this spread, lay one or more cards in each house of the horoscope wheel and interpret the cards in the context of the meaning of the house. Many readers lay a thirteenth card (or set of cards) in the center of the wheel to represent the general theme of the reading. The following keywords apply to the houses:

- **House 1:** One's body, vitality, physical integrity, character, personality style, basic motivation in life, the beginning of matters.

- **House 2:** Income, resources, assets, possessions, values, finances, business skills, talents, ability to make money, material wealth.

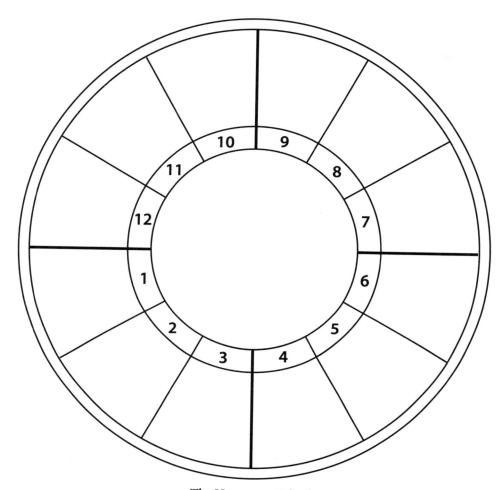

The Horoscope Wheel

- **House 3:** Local travel, short trips, motor skills, practical mind, speech, ability to use language, mental capacities, communication, news, letters, documents, messages, vehicles, siblings, kin, neighbors, local environment.

- **House 4:** Home, early childhood environment, place of residence, family, father, roots, patrimony, houses, real estate, landed property, weather, old age, ancestry, tradition, conditions at the end of life, endings.

- **House 5:** Romance, lovers, matters of the heart, what you do for fun, pleasures, sex, creativity, children, pregnancy, leisure, games, recreation, holidays, vacations, adornment, creative activities, hobbies, theater, sports, risks, gambling, speculative ventures.

- **House 6:** Daily labor, coworkers, servants, subordinates, employees, work environment, dependents, service, health concerns, diet, medical treatments, illness, worry, misfortune, diet, small animals, pets.

- **House 7:** Spouse, partner, marital relationship, significant other, one-to-one relationships, contractual or binding agreements, diplomacy, lawsuits, adversaries, open enemies.

- **House 8:** Other people's money and resources, taxes, legacies, death, mortality, goods of the dead, occult matters, profound understanding, transformation, penetration, medical and surgical procedures, personal crises, major life changes, partial loss of some aspect of one's life.

- **House 9:** Higher education, abstract thinking, long-distance journeys, publishing, broadcasting, foreign languages, dealings with foreigners, travel to unfamiliar realms, divination, religion, priestly duties, philosophy, wisdom, science, the law, the quest for truth and justice, expanding one's horizons.

- **House 10:** Career, professional matters, authority figures, honors, success, recognition, public image, reputation, dignity, ambitions, advancement, worldly status, one's boss, one's mother.

- **House 11:** Friendships, counselors, advisors, benefactors, humanitarian concerns, clubs, groups of like-minded people; our aspirations, objectives, ideals, hopes, and wishes.

- **House 12:** Undoing, confinement, limitation, sacrifice, adversity, obstacles, seclusion, introspection, spirituality, the subconscious mind, fantasy, illusion, spiritual retreat, institutions that restrict freedom (e.g., hospitals, monasteries, prisons), chronic illness, hospitalization, large animals, personal limitations, self-sabotage, scandal, secret enemies, behind-the-scenes activities.

Reading the Houses Spread with the Entire Deck

This method makes use of the entire seventy-eight-card deck divided into thirteen six-card spreads (13 x 6 = 78). Choose a significator card to represent the querent. This can be done by matching the querent's personality to one of the court cards, or in any other way you and the querent see fit. Shuffle and cut the cards, and then reassemble the deck. Beginning with house 1, proceed around the wheel placing one card in each house and one card in the center of the wheel (13 cards in all).

Continue this process until the entire pack is used up. You will now have thirteen stacks of cards, one stack in each house and one stack in the center of the wheel. Each stack will contain six cards.

Find the stack that contains the significator. If you have placed the cards face-up, it will be easy to spot the significator while you are laying out the cards. Note which house of the horoscope the significator lies in. This house indicates the matter that most concerns the querent. Lay out the six cards of the stack in the order of their appearance, and relate them thematically to tell a story about the matters governed by the house where they fall.

Now do the same with the stack of six cards in the center of the wheel. The central stack makes a general comment on the querent's life course at this time.

If other questions arise as you are discussing these two stacks, locate the house that is relevant to the question, lay out its six cards, and interpret them in the context of the querent's concerns about this aspect of life experience.

A Briefer Twelve Houses Spread

The French tarot restorer, Paul Marteau, published his highly influential book *Le Tarot de Marseilles* in 1949, in which he presented a horoscopic spread that makes use of all seventy-eight cards. A briefer version of this method involves selecting twelve cards from the major arcana and spreading them around the wheel, one major card in each house of the horoscope. The next step is to draw a card for each house from the remaining sixty-six cards (majors and minors mixed together) and lay them around the wheel, one card in each house. The first round of major arcana cards are read just as you would read the planets and zodiac signs in the houses of a horoscope. The second card, which might be either a major or minor arcana, reveals the future trends of that house. If the querent has further questions about the matters of a house, a third card can be drawn to clarify the issue.

For example, the Empress (Venus) in the ninth house of foreign affairs might suggest a pleasant trip abroad. If the next card in the ninth house happens to be the Four of Pentacles, this trip might cost more than the querent wants to spend. The Golden Dawn associated the Four of Pentacles with the sun in Capricorn, suggesting that the querent might travel to a sunny clime (the sun) and manage trip expenses with good business sense (Capricorn).

Twelve Signs of the Zodiac Layout

The Zodiac Spread is laid out in the same way as the Houses of the Horoscope spread. The difference is that instead of interpreting the cards in the context of the individual *houses*, which represent distinct *fields of life experience*, the reader interprets the cards with reference to the archetypal meanings of the *signs* of the zodiac, which represent *modes of being* or ways of behaving in the world. An additional feature of this spread is that each zodiac sign is associated with a major arcana card that should enter into the interpretation.

In Western astrology, a zodiac sign is defined as one-twelfth of the zodiac circle. Each sign measures 30 degrees and receives its name from one of the constellations of the zodiac of antiquity. By convention, we begin the zodiac with the sign Aries on the first day of spring.

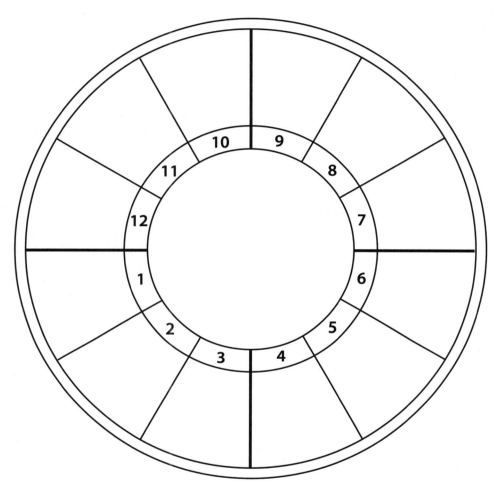

The Horoscope Wheel

Using the same diagram as you did for the Houses of the Horoscope spread, use the following concepts and sample questions to frame the interpretation of the cards. As you gain experience with the meanings of the signs and with their associated major arcana cards, feel free to substitute your own questions for the ones I have suggested.

Interpreting the Zodiacal Signs Layout

- **Sign 1: Aries and the Emperor**—How are you expressing your power, authority, and individual identity in the world?

- **Sign 2: Taurus and the Hierophant (Pope, High Priest)**—How are you seeking guidance from tradition or a higher authority to inform your sense of values and your search for meaning in life?

- **Sign 3: Gemini and the Lovers**—What do you truly love and how does it inform the major decisions you must make in life?

- **Sign 4: Cancer and the Chariot**—How are you keeping focused on an important goal or journey? Are you taking the reins so you can move forward in a self-protective manner?

- **Sign 5: Leo and Fortitude (Strength, Lust)**—How are you acting courageously to confront a situation, regulate your passions, and tame the beast within?

- **Sign 6: Virgo and the Hermit**—How are you managing to calm yourself, remain centered, and draw upon your inner wisdom?

- **Sign 7: Libra and Justice**—How are you treating yourself and others with fairness, honesty, and justice?

- **Sign 8: Scorpio and Death**—How are you embracing the need for transformation in your life? In what areas of life do you need to let go so that you can move on?

- **Sign 9: Sagittarius and Temperance**—How are you acting with balance and moderation in reconciling conflicting aspects of your life in a creative synthesis?

- **Sign 10: Capricorn and the Devil**—How are you maintaining a spiritual perspective as you pursue important material ambitions? What temptations or obsessional desires are you dealing with?

- **Sign 11: Aquarius and the Star**—How are you keeping hope alive in a manner that benefits you and those around you? What is your heart's desire?

- **Sign 12: Pisces and the Moon**—How are you remaining open to intuition and visionary ideas without falling prey to illusion and wishful thinking? In what ways are you undermining yourself?

Tree of Life Spread

Ten cards (or sets of cards) can be laid out in the pattern of the Kabbalistic Tree of Life. Each tarot card is interpreted in the context of the meaning of the Sephirah on which it falls. The Hebrew word *Sephiroth* (the plural of Sephirah) means "emanations." The ten Sephiroth of the Tree of Life can be viewed as ten emanations or attributes, by means of which the *Ein Sof* (the Infinite) reveals itself and creates the universe in all of its aspects. As mentioned elsewhere, the Tree of Life grows upside-down; its roots lie in heaven and its final fruits appear here on the Earth.

The following keywords can serve as a guide when interpreting the cards as they fall in each position. As you become more familiar with this spread, feel free to substitute your own keywords and questions for the ones suggested.

Interpreting the Tree of Life Layout

1. **Kether.** The Crown. The fiery spark of creation. Beginnings. The unmanifest. Spiritual factors. Inspiration. One's spiritual goal. What is the creative spark that is inspiring you in your current situation? What is your spiritual purpose at this time?

2. **Chokmah.** The Father. Wisdom. Masculine potency. Virility. Yang. Primordial maleness. Responsibilities. The elements in their purest form. What are you assertively and actively trying to create? How are you expressing your potency?

3. **Binah.** Understanding. The Throne. The Great Mother. Feminine wisdom. Primordial femaleness. Yin. Receptivity. The darkness inside the womb. The cycle of death and new life. Problems. Difficulties. Decisions to be made. Associated with the planet Saturn. How are you receiving creative inspiration and allowing it to grow within? What must you let die so that new life can emerge and you can create something new in the world? How are you dealing with necessary limits imposed by reality?

4. **Chesed.** Mercy. Kindness. Majesty. Benevolence. Help. Protection. Favorable factors ("pros"). Associated with the planet Jupiter. What are the "pros" favoring your potential course of action? What kind of help and support is available?

5. **Geburah.** Severity. Strength. Testing. Judging and assessing. Troubles. Opposing factors ("cons"). Associated with the planet Mars. What are the "cons" that conflict with your potential course of action? What kind of obstacles and trials do you need to confront? What battles do you need to wage to achieve your goals?

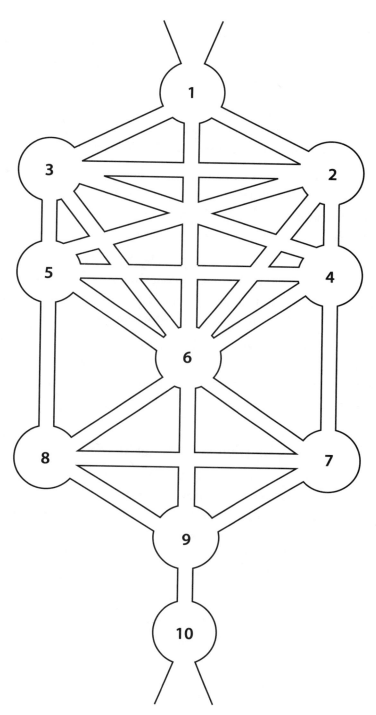

The Tree of Life Spread

6. **Tiphareth.** Harmony. Beauty. The god that dies only to be reborn. The Center. Illumination. Sacrifice for a greater good. Associated with the sun. What is the greater good that will result from your course of action? Will your choices leave you feeling more centered? What sacrifices are you willing to make?

7. **Netzach.** Victory. Success. Achievement. Relationships. Love. Desire. Art. Emotional factors. Associated with Venus-Aphrodite. How does the situation resonate with you emotionally? How will it affect your personal relationships? Will achieving your success be a work of art?

8. **Hod.** Glory. Spendor. Intellect. Career. Communication. Writing. Science. Reason. Mental factors. Associated with the planet Mercury. Are you thinking rationally and strategically about the best course of action? With whom do you need to communicate? Have you checked all the facts and gathered sufficient evidence? Are you expressing yourself clearly?

9. **Yesod.** Foundation. Unconscious factors. The collective unconscious. Mysticism. Illusion. Meditation. One's inner world. Associated with the moon. To what extent are your actions based on fantasy and wishful thinking? Are you paying sufficient attention to your inner voice? Do you need to "sleep on" a decision before taking action?

10. **Malkuth.** The Kingdom. Our Earth. Fulfillment. Completion. Form. Manifestation. Stability. Home. Family. The World. What is the final result you are seeking? Have you achieved the structure and stability you were after? How do your actions affect your home, family, and sense of rootedness?

The Inverted Cards Spread

If you decide to use reversed cards in your readings, you may find this method useful. Because inverted cards catch your attention as they stand out from the other cards in any spread, you can read the reversed cards as if they were trying to give you a special message. Simply read the inverted cards in any tarot spread in sequence while ignoring all the upright cards. Assume that the inverted cards are trying to highlight an important issue that you need to become more aware of.

For example, in my three-card spread de-scribed earlier in this chapter, the High Priestess was the only inverted card:

High Priestess (reversed)
Three of Pentacles (upright)
Four of Wands (upright)

If I assume that the reversed High Priestess has an especially important message to convey, what could it be? Perhaps she is advising that the most important ingredient in writing this book is to get in touch with my intuition.

Ten

The Major Arcana

The Trionfi Cards of the Renaissance

The fifteenth-century Renaissance artists who created the tarot added a fifth suit of trump cards (*trionfi*) to the traditional playing card deck that originally came to Europe via Mamluk, Egypt. This additional suit of trumps, now called the major arcana ("greater secrets") consists of twenty-two allegorical images inspired by Greek and Roman mythology and the Bible. Many tarot readers view the sequence of trump cards as a series of moral lessons the Fool must master on his journey to salvation. Occultists often refer to the cards as "keys" because of a 1781 speculation by Antoine Court de Gébelin that each major arcana card represents a key to the ancient magical wisdom of the Egyptian god Thoth, whose mysteries are encoded in the symbolism of the cards.

After the French conquered Milan and the Piedmont of Italy in 1499, they brought the game of tarot to the Marseille region of France as one of the spoils of war. Tarot became popular in southern France, and the playing card industry of Marseille grew into a thriving business. Perhaps for reasons of manufacturing, French card makers settled on a standardized design and a specific number and sequence of cards in their tarot decks. This pattern became known as the Tarot of Marseille and established the norm for what is considered a tarot deck today.

In card games, the sequence of the trump cards is crucial because the cards of higher rank trump those of lower rank. The images on the cards and the cards' relative importance with respect to one another no doubt reflected the cultural, political, and religious climate in which they were created.

Many books about tarot, however, minimize the role played by Christian symbolism and moral teachings in the development of the tarot.

To illustrate this point, let's trace the Fool's journey through the major arcana, as if the Fool were an initiate to Christianity who needed to learn how to achieve salvation through the teachings of the medieval church. In early tarot decks, the Fool is unnumbered. He is often shown as a madman, vagabond, or beggar; he stands completely apart from the sequence of trumps in the tarot deck. In the tarot games of northern Italy, the Fool was regarded as an "excuse card" as "playing the Fool" excused the player from following suit or playing a trump card on a particular trick. Metaphorically, the Fool functions as an outsider looking in; he gives the player an excuse for not following the established rules of the game.

The Christian Influence on the Major Arcana

Trump 1: The Juggler (Magician) is the trump of the lowest rank. Traditionally he is a street magician, trickster, or mountebank. Through sleight of hand with cups and balls he can swindle visitors out of their hard-earned money. The priests of ancient Egypt who turned their rods into serpents during Moses's confrontation with the Pharaoh are a typical embodiment of this archetypal image. The cheap tricks of the Egyptian priests were no match for the might of Yahweh, whose power could part the Red Sea and destroy the Pharaoh's army under its waters. The trickster magician is the least potent trump of the lot.

Trump 2: The Female Pope (High Priestess) is one step above the street magician but still a trickster. Modeled after the legendary Pope Joan, this brilliant woman disguised herself as a man so she could assume the papacy. In patriarchal Europe, God was unequivocally of masculine gender and *His* spokesperson on Earth could never legitimately be a lowly female. Sadly, Pope Joan came to a bitter end. After being outed as a woman, a pious Christian mob bound her feet to a horse's tail and dragged her through the streets of Rome, stoning her to death along the way. How dare a woman trick the populace by pretending to be the Holy Father!

Trump 3: The Empress. Unlike the Female Pope, the Empress was a legitimate female authority in sixteenth-century Europe. Being female, however, she ranked toward the bottom of the heap. Much of her authority was due to her status as wife of the male Emperor.

Trump 4: The Emperor is the ultimate secular authority in the tarot, but he ranks only fourth in the order of trumps. Apparently an even higher authority exists on the way to salvation.

Trump 5: The Pope (Hierophant) outranks the Emperor because the Holy Father (a man, of course) forms the bridge between humanity and the deity. He is the patriarchal God's spokesman on Earth with divine authority to appoint a secular ruler to serve as Emperor of the Holy Roman Empire.

Trump 6: The Lover(s). Even higher than the Pope's canonical authority is the power of love, the greatest of the church's three theological virtues of faith, hope, and love. According to I Corinthians 13:13, the greatest of these virtues is love. This card is also an allusion to the Pharisees testing Jesus about his knowledge of Jewish law:

"Master, which is the great commandment in the law? Jesus said unto him, Thou shalt love the Lord thy God with all thy heart, and with all thy soul, and with all thy mind. This is the first and great commandment. And the second is like unto it, Thou shalt love thy neighbor as thyself. On these two commandments hang all the law and the prophets" (Matthew 22:36–40, KJV).

Trump 7: The Chariot depicts an ancient image of a rational charioteer controlling the competing forces of two horses, one white (will) and the other black (appetite). The thirteenth-ccentury theologian Thomas Aquinas viewed this ancient image of a charioteer controling the black and white horses as a metaphor for the virtue of Prudence. Aquinas learned from Aristotle that there are four cardinal virtues upon which all others depend: Prudence, Justice, Fortitude, and Temperance, in that order. The virtues depicted on the trump cards of the Tarot of Marseille follow the same order as specified by Aquinas in his writings: the Chariot (Prudence, trump 7), Justice (trump 8), Strength (Fortitude, trump 11), and Temperance (trump 14). A virtuous life characterized by Prudence (the Charioteer) trumps even the power of love.

Trump 8: Justice is often exchanged for Strength in modern decks. Here the Tarot of Marseille follows the order of cardinal virtues set down by Thomas Aquinas in his *Summa Theologica*. The Justice card reminds us that everyone is subject to the Law.

Trump 9: The Hermit. Despite living a life characterized by Love, Prudence, and Justice, we may need to get away for a while to ponder who we are, where we are going, and how to put our lives in perspective. Prayer and meditation are powerful practices that rank ninth in the order of trump cards.

Trump 10: The Wheel of Fortune. No matter how virtuous or hardworking we are, sometimes bad things just happen and there is nothing we can do about it.

Trump 11: Strength (Fortitude, often exchanged for Justice in modern decks). Here the tarot is again following the order of cardinal virtues laid out by Thomas Aquinas. We must cultivate the virtue of Fortitude to deal successfully with the slings and arrows of outrageous fortune (trump 10, the Wheel of Fortune).

Trump 12: The Hanged Man. Despite our most valiant efforts (trump 11, Fortitude), life can throw us for a loop and leave us feeling suspended and at the mercy of fate. We may have no choice but to adopt a new perspective as we accept our fate, just as Jesus accepted his destiny of hanging on a cross to save humankind.

Trump 13: Death. One might think that death trumps all, but in the tarot Death ranks only thirteenth out of twenty-one in its ability to overpower other cards. Jesus demonstrated that he could defeat death by rising from the dead on the third day after his crucifixion.

Trump 14: Temperance. Here again the tarot follows the order of cardinal virtues laid down by Thomas Aquinas. The angel of Temperance is mixing water and wine, just as a Catholic priest does during the sacrifice of the Mass. The sacrificial wine symbolizes the divine nature of Christ; and the water, his human nature. In Christian lore, Jesus was a perfect blending of God and Man. By overcoming Death (trump 13), Christ offered humanity eternal life. These accomplishments were certain to make the Devil (trump 15) quite unhappy.

Trump 15: The Devil. The Prince of Darkness is upset by the words of the New Testament: "For God so loved the world that he gave his only begotten Son, that whosoever believeth in him should not perish, but have everlasting life" (John 3:16, KJV). Satan will do whatever he can to lure people away from the righteous path, often appealing to their pride and ambition as can be seen in the next trump, the Tower.

Trump 16: The Tower. The biblical Tower of Babel was an outgrowth of the pride and ambition of humans who wanted to build a structure that reached the heavens. By building such a tower, they hoped to claim dominion over God's creation. Clearly Satan (trump 15) must have prompted humans to display such arrogance. The Old Testament deity was not pleased with such human arrogance. As Genesis 11:9 explains, at Babel "the Lord confused the language of all the earth; and from there the Lord scattered them abroad over the face of all the earth" (King James Bible).

Trump 17: The Star. Hope of salvation is embodied in the Star of Bethlehem, the celestial body announcing the impending birth of Jesus. The tarot Star out-trumps the machinations of Satan (trump 15) and the human arrogance and swift retribution of the Old Testament deity (trump 16). The Star is the first glimmer of hope for humanity, the new religion of Christianity that will show the way to eternal life in the Spirit.

Trump 18: The Moon. The moon, whose cycles parallel the menstrual periods of the human female, is a profound maternal symbol. From a Christian perspective, the moon symbolizes the immaculate conception of the Virgin Mary and the gestation of Jesus in her womb. In many religious paintings, Mary is depicted standing on a crescent moon—a symbol of fertility, maternity and protection of the newborn infant.

Trump 19: The Sun. In the history of mythology, Jesus is one in a long line of sun gods who die only to be reborn a short time later. In the Christian version of this myth, Jesus dies on the cross on a Friday and rises from the dead three days later on Easter morning, a *sun* day.

Trump 20: The Last Judgment. At the end of time, Jesus returns to judge all souls, determining whether they are fit to enter into the Kingdom of Heaven (trump 21) or else condemned to spend eternity with the Devil (trump 15). The difference between these two cards, 21 minus 15, is 6, the number of the trump card of Love.

Trump 21: The World. This highest-ranking trump card represents the final destination: the New Jerusalem, Salvation, Paradise Regained, Life Eternal, the Pearly Gates. The Fool has finally made it to the Promised Land.

How to Use the Associations for the Seventy-Eight Cards

In this and the following chapters, each tarot card is discussed in detail in the form of a list of associations for each card. These associations are grouped under the following headings, not all of which appear for every card.

Key: The occultists who developed the modern tarot regarded each card, especially the major arcana, as "keys" to unlock doors to esoteric knowledge. Presumably these mysterious truths were encoded in the tarot symbols by none other than the Egyptian god Thoth.

Astrology: The tarot shares much symbolism with astrology. Both tarot and astrology, for example, use the four elements of antiquity (Fire, Air, Water, and Earth). The Golden Dawn associated the major arcana with the planets and the signs of the zodiac. They also paired the numbered pip cards with the thirty-six decans of the zodiac. For readers familiar with astrology, these correlations add an extra dimension to tarot reading.

Timing: Some readers use the cards to time their predictions. Temporal associations, rooted in astrology, can be helpful in judging when future events might occur.

Numerology and Number Symbolism: The numbers on each card are important symbols in their own right. Number symbolism can be traced back to the ideas of Pythagoras in ancient Greece. The Golden Dawn connected the numbers on the cards with the Sephiroth of the kabbalistic Tree of Life, and these numerical associations became the basis for many of the modern meanings of the minor arcana.

Hebrew Letter: Associating the letters of the Hebrew alphabet with the kabbalistic Tree of Life and with other occult systems dates back at least to the sixteenth century.[29] Occultists, such as Eliphas Levi and the members of the Golden Dawn, used these associations to develop interpretations for the cards. The meanings of Hebrew letters used in this text are based on the research of the Ancient Hebrew Research Center and shed further light on the associations between symbolism of the Hebrew alphabet and the corresponding major arcana cards.[30]

Myths/Archetypes: Carl Jung beleived that mythology and literature owe their power to stir the human soul to the embodiment of certain archetypal patterns and images that have universal significance. Many modern readers find the tarot cards to be manifestations of these potent archetypes.

---

29. Helen Farley, *A Cultural History of Tarot: From Entertainment to Esotericism* (London: I.B. Tauris, 2009), 114.

30. The website of this center is at www.ancient-hebrew.org/3_al.html.

Etteilla: This name is the pseudonym of Jean-Baptiste Alliette (1738–1791), the French occultist who first popularized tarot divination to a wide audience (1785). Etteilla's card meanings became the standard method for interpreting the cards throughout Europe in the eighteenth and nineteenth centuries. [31]

Mathers: Samuel Liddell MacGregor Mathers was a British occultist and founding member of the Hermetic Order of the Golden Dawn, whose tarot delineations have powerfully influenced tarot interpretation in the English-speaking world since the end of the nineteenth century. Mathers's book, *The Tarot,* was first published in London in 1888 and had a profound impact on future generations of tarot readers. The meanings listed here are quoted from Mathers's 1888 text. [32]

Waite: Arthur Edward Waite, with Pamela Colman Smith, developed the Rider-Waite-Smith tarot deck, the most popular tarot in the English-speaking world since its debut in 1909. Waite's delineations became a standard for interpreting the tarot in the twentieth century. Because of Waite's overwhelming influence on the practice of tarot in the English-speaking world, his delineations (now in the public domain) are quoted verbatim from *The Pictorial Key to the Tarot* (London, UK: W. Rider, 1911, reproduced by Citadel Press, Secaucus, NJ, with an introduction by Gertrude Moakley, 1959). [33]

Crowley and Golden Dawn: Aleister Crowley was a British occultist who broke with the Golden Dawn but continued to develop his own interpretations, which closely followed the Golden Dawn's occult teachings. With Lady Frieda Harris, Crowley published the Thoth Tarot, one of the most influential esoteric decks of the later part of the twentieth century.[34]

Keywords (+): These "positive" keywords reflect some of the fruitful and constructive uses of the energies symbolized by the card.

Keywords (-): These "negative" keywords reflect some of the challenging and potentially harmful uses of the energies symbolized by the card.

---

31.   The keywords presented here are my translation of a representative sample from Etteilla's *Dictionnaire synonymique du Livre de Thot* (Paris, 1791) and *l'Astrologie du Livre de Thot* (Paris, 1785) published by Guy Trédaniel, editor, with commentary by Jacques Halbronn (Paris, 1990).

32.   Mather's public domain text is available as a Kindle e-book from Amazon Digital Services (ASIN: B004IE9Z14) and online at sacred-texts.com: http://www.sacred-texts.com/tarot/mathers/.

33.   Waite's *The Pictorial Key to the Tarot* is in the public domain and available as a Kindle eBook from Amazon Digital Services (ASIN: B00L18UZG4).

34.   The meanings presented here are a paraphrase of a representative sample of keywords from Crowley's *The Book of Thoth* (San Francisco: Weiser Books, 2008) and Regardie's *The Golden Dawn,* 6th ed. (St. Paul, MN: Llewellyn Publications, 1989).

Upright Card: This section briefly describes a typical meaning of the upright card. It should be used only as a suggestion of possible meanings. With continued practice and experience, you will come to assign your own meanings and develop a richer personal understanding of the cards.

Reversed Card: This section describes a possible interpretation of the inverted card. Reversed card meanings should not be taken literally, as each card has a core meaning that remains valid regardless of its upright or reversed orientation. Some readers prefer to use only upright cards.

0. The Fool: The Idealistic Sorcerer's Apprentice

Key 0: The Fool (traditionally not numbered, but labeled 0 in some modern decks)

Astrology: The element Air (the planet Uranus in some modern decks)

Numerology: 4 (Emperor) ~ 1 + 3 (Death) ~ 2 + 2 (The Fool)

Hebrew letter: [35] *Aleph* (an ox head; a Hebrew word meaning strength, power, chief, leader; also, to learn, teach, guide; to team up and plow—the ox was used for plowing).

Myths/Archetypes: The Court Jester. Perceval. *Puer aeternus*. The Innocent. The Orphan. The Seeker. The Idealist. The Wanderer. The Novice. The Sorcerer's Apprentice.

Mathers (1888): *The Foolish Man.* Folly, expiation, wavering; (R) hesitation, instability, trouble arising therefrom.

Waite (1911): Folly, mania, extravagance, intoxication, delirium, frenzy, bewrayment [betrayal]; (R) negligence, absence, distribution, carelessness, apathy, nullity, vanity.

Golden Dawn: A foolish person in the material affairs of everyday life in which folly, stupidity, instability, and eccentricity occur due to the Fool's high level of idealism.

Keywords (+): Opening up to new possibilities, idealism, a leap of faith, a fresh start, opportunities for growth, childlike wonder, trust, innocence, enthusiasm, curiosity, inexperience, initiation, an unexpected opening, embarking on an exciting journey, experimentation, freedom to explore, a spiritual quest, opening your mind to new learning, taking a risk, living in the now, not following the established rules of the game.

Keywords (-): Folly, madness, stupidity, an unrealistic attitude, confusion, immaturity, eccentricity, insecurity, silliness, gullibility, foolishness, infatuation, intoxication, frenzy, needless risk, irresponsibility, uncertainty, premature action, muddleheadedness, questionable advice, recklessness, a pointless enterprise, foolish abandonment of material goods; a jester, madman, drifter, beggar; "fools rush in where angels fear to tread."

The Fool Upright

When upright, the Fool suggests a leap of faith and a desire to explore the unknown with a "beginner's mind." The Fool has a basic trust that things will turn out well in the end, but he has not yet acquired the ability to navigate his way skillfully through the practical affairs of everyday life. He is starting out on a new and exciting journey in which he will encounter marvelous adventures and seek spiritual growth. When this card appears in a reading, it is important to keep your wits about you as you take risks and explore the unknown. At the same time, this card cautions you to avoid foolish idealism and not undertake mundane projects unless you are well prepared for handling any pragmatic aspects.

---

35. The meanings of Hebrew letters are based on the research of the Ancient Hebrew Research Center at www.ancient-hebrew.org/3_al.html, accessed 10 November 2014.

....
The Fool Reversed

At some point during childhood, most kids hear their parents remonstrate: "If all your friends jumped off a bridge, would you jump too?" When reversed, the Fool cautions against unrealistic planning, naiveté, gullibility, irresponsibility, immaturity, premature action, and foolish risk-taking. The inverted Fool displays poor judgment and a lack of basic trust. Be sure to look before you leap or you may go off half-cocked on a pointless enterprise. Consider the consequences before engaging in impulsive or risky behavior. Especially avoid excessive use of drugs or alcohol.

1. THE MAGICIAN: AS ABOVE, SO BELOW

Key 1: The Magician (Juggler)

Hebrew letter: *Beyt* or *Beth* (the floor plan of a tent; a Hebrew word meaning tent, house, dwelling, household, family, sanctuary, the temple or house of the Lord; also, the prepositions "in" and "within").

Astrology: Mercury, messenger of the gods (Mercury rules Gemini and Virgo).

Element: Air

Numerology: 1 (Magician) = 1 + 0 (Wheel of Fortune) = 1 + 9 (The Sun)

Myths/Archetypes: Thoth. Hermes Trismegistus. Merlin. Faust. The Magus. The Juggler. The Con Artist.

Mathers (1888): *The Juggler.* Will, willpower, dexterity; (R) will applied to evil ends, weakness of will, cunning, knavishness.

Waite (1911): Skill, diplomacy, address, subtlety; sickness, pain, loss, disaster, snares of enemies; self-confidence, will; the querent if male; (R) physician, magus, mental disease, disgrace, disquiet.

Golden Dawn: Craft, cunning, skill, adaptability, magic, occult wisdom (these meanings are derived from the Roman god Mercury and his resemblance to the gods Thoth of Egypt and Hermes of Greece).

Keywords (+): Skill, mastery, cleverness, intelligence, cunning, expertise, initiative, impetus, self-confidence, determination, purpose, assertiveness, focused intent, dexterity, ability to juggle, strength of will, striving for power, transforming ideas into realities, control of natural forces, ability to manipulate the physical world; "as above, so below."

Keywords (-): Trickery, illusion, parlor tricks, deceit, sleight of hand, hesitancy, impotence, lack of confidence, confusion of purpose, the ill use of one's skills; a trickster, con artist, mountebank, stage magician, quack doctor, sleight of hand artist, swindler, thief.

The Magician Upright

When upright, the Magician symbolizes a person of great willpower who has mastered the knowledge, and skills needed to achieve his goals. As depicted in Llewellyn's Classic Tarot, the Magician can access the cosmos above and the earth below as he juggles the four elements to manifest his desires. Ruled by the planet Mercury, the Magician is a gifted communicator of intense mental focus who can translate ideas into effective action. Themes related to the Magician have to do with directing one's will and focusing one's consciousness to manipulate physical reality.

The Magician Reversed

When reversed, the Magician may be using his willpower, knowledge and skills for less than honorable purposes. An ill-dignified Magician may be engaged in deception, manipulation, or the misuse of power. He may be weak-willed or lacking in confidence and thus fail to use his communication skills in a productive manner. When the Magician appears reversed in a reading, it is wise to explore what is preventing you from maintaining the mental focus that will enable you to act like a magician in your life.

2. THE HIGH PRIESTESS: GUARDIAN OF SECRET WISDOM

Key II: The High Priestess (Female Pope)

Astrology: the Moon (ruler of the Water sign Cancer, the Crab)

Element: Water

Numerology: 2 (High Priestess) ~ 1 + 1 (Justice or Strength) ~ 2 + 0 (Judgment)

Hebrew letter: *Gamal* or *Gimel* (foot, or camel; a Hebrew word meaning to come together at a drinking hole, to walk to the watering place, to deal, to recompense)

Myths/Archetypes: Persephone. Cassandra. Pope Joan. The Virgin Mary. Sor Juana. Matris Spiri-tuale. The Oracle at Delphi. Gestation in the womb.

Mathers (1888): Science, wisdom, knowledge, education; (R) Conceit, ignorance, unskillfulness, superficial knowledge.

Waite (1911): Secrets, mystery, the future as yet unrevealed; the woman who interests the querent if male; the querent herself if female; silence, tenacity; mystery, wisdom, science; (R) passion, moral or physical ardor, conceit, surface knowledge.

Golden Dawn: Change, fluctuation, alteration (meanings derived from the shifting phases of the watery moon).

Keywords (+): Secrets, the future not yet known, the revelation of hidden matters, spiritual wisdom, occult knowledge, intuitive awareness, lunar consciousness, one's inner voice, sacred space, listening to one's dreams, extraordinary knowing, lifting the veil, walking to the watering hole, seeing beneath the surface, the seed of an idea, mystery, fluctuation, psychic intuition, piercing the veil of the unconscious; a woman who interests the querent.

Keywords (-): Superficial knowledge, escape into fantasy, inconstancy, daydreaming, inaccurate hunches, the spilling of secrets, suppressing one's true feelings, ignoring one's intuition, not heeding one's inner voice.

....
The High Priestess Upright

When upright, the High Priestess represents feminine intuition and empathic sensitivity. She gives you access to hidden knowledge (symbolized by the body of water on the card), and she encourages balanced judgment through intuitive awareness. Now is the time to quiet your mind and open yourself to the inner wisdom that lies within. Pay special attention to your dreams and intuitive hunches. In this way, you can gain access to something unrevealed or not yet known about your future plans. In the words of Einstein: "But there is no logical way to the discovery of these elemental laws. There is only the way of intuition, which is helped by a feeling for the order lying behind the appearance, and this *Einfühlung* is developed by experience." [36]

....
The High Priestess Reversed

When reversed, the High Priestess warns that important information may be hidden or otherwise obscured from view. Perhaps you feel somehow blocked in accessing your intuition, or you may be

---

36. Albert Einstein, "Preface" to Max Planck's *Where is Science Going?*, translated and edited by George Murphy (London: George Allen & Unwin, Ltd., 1933).

choosing to ignore important gut feelings. You can't quite find your way to the watering hole. Some aspect of the future as yet unrevealed may cause a delay or a change in plans.

3. THE EMPRESS: FERTILE GODDESS OF THE BIRTH CANAL

Key III: The Empress

Astrology: Venus, goddess of love and beauty. (Venus rules Taurus and Libra)

Element: Earth

Numerology: 3 (Em-press) ~ 1 + 2 (Hanged Man) ~ 2 + 1 (The World)

Hebrew letter: *Daleth* (a tent door, a pathway; a Hebrew word meaning to move, hang, dangle, draw water; also an entrance, doorway, or a back-and-forth movement). *Daleth* symbolizes the birth canal, that is, the doorway through which the fetus emerges as a separate entity in need of maternal care and protection.

Myths/Archetypes: Demeter. Mother Nature. The Earth Goddess. The Great Mother. The Caregiver. Gaia. Mary Magdalene. Queen of Queens. The Garden of Eden.

Mathers (1888): Action, plan, undertaking, movement in a matter, initiative.

Waite (1911): Fruitfulness, action, initiative, length of days; the unknown, clandestine; also difficulty, doubt, ignorance; (R) light, truth, the unraveling of involved matters, public rejoicings; according to another reading, vacillation.

Golden Dawn: Luxury, beauty, pleasure, happiness, success; with negative cards, indulgence, dissipation (meanings derived from Venus, goddess of love and sensual pleasures).

Keywords (+): Fertility, pregnancy, marriage, motherhood, the desire to have children, material abundance, luxury, sensuality, attraction, physical comfort, gestation, the womb, childbirth, the birth canal, nurturing, growth, feminine power, love of nature, enjoyment of sex, a fertile imagination, productivity, bearing fruit, protecting the environment, enjoyment of the outdoors.

Keywords (-): Overindulgence, temptation, sex without love, avarice, infertility, indolence, withholding affection, refusal to cultivate one's garden, miscarriage, menopause, unwanted pregnancy, delay in fulfilling a desire, deciding not to have children, failure to care for one's offspring, squandering natural resources.

The Empress Upright

When upright, the Empress symbolizes fertility, pregnancy, motherhood, sensuality and creative imagination. This card may herald an impending marriage, the desire to have children, or the birth of a child. You are entering a period of productivity and abundance, often in the form of offspring of either the body or the mind. You are capable of great productivity as you assist the passage of your creative ideas through their birth canal. Support and nurturing are available. It is important to exercise proper care of the body at this time.

The Empress Reversed

When reversed, the Empress suggests that you may be failing to care for the natural resources that have been entrusted to you. Perhaps you have been neglecting your body or squandering the abundance in your life. Alternatively, you may be going through a period of infertility, either literally or figuratively, in which it seems difficult to produce any type of offspring of either the physical or mental variety. A creative idea may be stuck in its birth canal. The Empress is connected with marriage, and the reversed card may signify difficulty with wedding plans or a delay in starting a family.

4. THE EMPEROR: ULTIMATE SECULAR AUTHORITY

Key IV: The Emperor

Astrology: Aries, the Ram (a Fire sign ruled by Mars)

Dates of Aries: 21 March–20 April (tropical); 14 April–13 May (sidereal)

Element: Fire

Numerology: 4 (Emperor) ~ 1 + 3 (Death) ~ 2 + 2 (The Fool)

Hebrew letter: *He* or *Hey* (a man with his arms erect; a Hebrew word meaning to look, reveal, to behold a great sight, "Lo and behold!" Also the article *the,* and a breath or sigh). Aleister Crowley paired the Emperor with the Hebrew letter *Tzaddi,* a letter the Golden Dawn associated with XVII, the Star.

Myths/Archetypes: The Great Father. The Ruler. The King of Kings. Zeus. Yahweh. Ouranos. Priapus. George Washington. Head of State.

Mathers (1888): Realization, effect, development; (R) Stoppage, check, immature, unripe.

Waite (1911): Stability, power, protection, realization; a great person; aid, reason, conviction; also authority and will; (R) benevolence, compassion, credit; also confusion to enemies, obstruction, immaturity.

Golden Dawn: Ambition, domination, victory, conquest, strife, war (meanings derived from the pioneering sign Aries, which is ruled by Mars, the god of war).

Keywords (+): Authority, splendor, power, awe, ambition, leadership, order, control, dominion, logic, reason, objectivity, visibility, setting limits, potency, forcefulness, courage, self-confidence, discipline, responsibility, majesty, impressiveness, maturity, protection, realization, will, decisiveness, life force, fathering, masculine power, the phallus, stability, structure, realism, firm foundations, taking charge, ability to get things done.

Keywords (-): Domination, arrogance, inflexibility, conventionality, butting heads, wimpishness, impotence, lack of confidence, immaturity, lack of reason or excessive rationality, indecision, disorder, loss, lack of structure, male infertility, abuse of power, vanity, inability to get things done, failure to take charge when you need to.

The Emperor Upright

Hail to the chief! When upright, the Emperor represents a person of authority, will, planning, organization, analysis, strategic thinking and phallic masculinity. Lo and behold! The Emperor is the Father Archetype, the Lord and Master who knows how to get things done. A powerful leader, he takes charge, puts things in order, and protects those in his domain. He rules with his mind rather than with his heart. The Emperor appears in a reading to remind you to step up to the plate, be true to your principles, and use your power to structure your life to accomplish what must be done. You need to set clear goals and establish firm limits so that you can provide stability and get the job done.

The Emperor Reversed

When reversed, the Emperor suggests that in some way you may have been remiss in fulfilling your role as a leader, organizer, or person in charge. Perhaps you have been pussyfooting around or, at the other end of the spectrum, acting in a dictatorial manner. Don't be a wimp; it's time to act your age and put your life in order. You need to analyze the situation, establish boundaries and limits, and develop a plan so that you do what needs to be done. President Harry S. Truman kept a sign on his desk that said *"The buck stops here!"* to remind him that the president has final authority to make decisions but also ultimate responsibility for their consequences.

5. The Hierophant: Bridge Connecting Humanity with the Divine

Key V: The Hierophant (Pope, High Priest)

Astrology: Taurus, the Bull (an Earth sign ruled by Venus)

Dates of Taurus: 21 April–21 May (tropical); 14 May–14 June (sidereal)

Element: Earth

Numerology: 5 (Hierophant) = 1 + 4 (Temperance)

Hebrew letter: *Vau, Vav,* or *Waw* (a tent peg; a Hebrew word meaning to hook, add, fasten or secure something to prevent it from slipping; the hook, peg, or nail that is used to secure the curtains of the tabernacle). The Hierophant often "fastens" people together in matrimony.

Myths/Archetypes: The prophet Moses. Pontifex Maximus. Hierophant. High Priest. The deity's spokesperson. The Holy of Holies (which housed the Ark of the Covenant and the Ten Commandments). Emily Post. The Wizard of Oz.

Mathers (1888): Mercy, beneficence, kindness, goodness; (R) Over-kindness, weakness, foolish exercise of generosity.

Waite (1911): Marriage, alliance, captivity, servitude; by another account, mercy and goodness; inspiration; the man to whom the querent has recourse; (R) society, good understanding, concord, over-kindness, weakness.

Golden Dawn: Divine wisdom, teaching, explanation.

Keywords (+): Traditional values, wise teaching, the ultimate religious authority, spiritual guidance, helpful advice, divine revelation, good counsel, the Ten Commandments, learning, teaching, formal education, instruction, mentoring, listening to a higher authority, kindness, sacred rites, church ceremonies, the sacrament of matrimony, established organizations, conventional social norms, conforming to orthodoxy, conservative views, mediation with the divine, seeking information, caring for the soul.

Keywords (-): Intolerance, rigidity, inflexibility, arrogance, dogmatism, conformity, oppressive religious doctrines, rigid orthodoxy, religious fundamentalism, perverse spirituality, misguided advice, following the letter rather than the spirit of the law, foolish generosity.

....
The Hierophant Upright

When upright, the High Priest is a wise, spiritually oriented guide to whom the querent has recourse. This person may be a kindly teacher, a mentor, or a spiritual adviser, not infrequently connected with a religious or academic setting. One role of the Hierophant is to perform sacred rites that pass traditional wisdom on to the next generation. The High Priest often officiates at ceremonies such as weddings, baptisms, bar mitzvahs, funerals, and the like. Because this priestly figure has authority to unite ("hook") couples in matrimony, this card can be a harbinger of marriage. In any case, when the Hierophant appears in a reading, you are likely to be dealing with the traditional values of your family, culture, or religion.

....
The Hierophant Reversed

When reversed, the High Priest warns that you may be taking a rigidly dogmatic stance dictated by traditional values. There is a tendency to follow the letter rather than the spirit of the law. Such extreme rigidity with its unthinking appeal to traditional authority is often adopted to subjugate others and deny them basic human rights. The inverted Hierophant is reminiscent of the words of Karl Marx that religion is the opium of the people. Marx went on to explain that his view of religion as an opiate "disillusions man, so that he will think, act, and fashion his reality like a man who has discarded his illusions and regained his senses, so that he will move around himself as his own true Sun." [37] Are you taking advice from the man behind the curtain of the Wizard of Oz?

6. THE LOVERS: CHOOSING HOW TO PLOW YOUR FIELDS

Key VI: The Lovers

Astrology: Gemini, the Twins (an Air sign ruled by Mercury)

Dates of Gemini: 22 May–21 June (tropical); 15 June–15 July (sidereal)

Element: Air

---

37. "Karl Marx—A Contribution to the Critique of Hegel's Philosophy of Right" in the *Deutsch-Französische Jahrbücher*, published in Paris on 7 and 10 of February, 1844. Source: www.age-of-the-sage.org/quotations/marx_opium _people.html

Numerology: 6 (Lovers) = 1 + 5 (Devil)

Hebrew letter: *Zayin* or *Zain* (a plow, mattock, hoe, or sharp weapon; a Hebrew word meaning harvest, crop, food, nourish, cut or sever as with a sword). Plowing a field to produce a harvest is a metaphor for the sexual intercourse of a couple to produce offspring.

Myths/Archetypes: Adam and Eve. Eros and Psyche. Cupid's arrow. Abelard and Heloise. Romeo and Juliet. Dante and Beatrice. The Lover. Don Juan. Casanova.

Mathers (1888): Wise dispositions, proof, trials surmounted; (R) unwise plans, failure when put to the test.

Waite (1911): Love, attraction, beauty, trials overcome; (R) failure, foolish designs; another account speaks of marriage frustrated and contrarieties of all kinds.

Golden Dawn: Inspiration passively received rather than actively pursued (as in the Hermit card), action arising from inspiration, sometimes mediumistic inspirations.

Keywords (+): An important decision or the need to choose, devotion, harmony, relatedness, friendship, reciprocity, commitment, true love, romance, enchantment, knowledge of good and evil, inseminating one's fields, judicious use of one's plow, sexual union.

Keywords (-): Indecision, bad choices, doubt, temptation, lack of commitment, seduction, infidelity, betrayal, disappointments in love, injudicious use of one's plow, failure to cultivate one's fields properly, eating the forbidden fruit, being hoist with one's own petard; "idle hands are the devil's workshop."

The Lovers Upright

When upright, the Lovers card represents an important choice that will significantly influence the course of one's life. This choice may have to do with a romantic relationship or a decision to marry and have children. The associated Hebrew letter *Zayin* conjures up the image of plowing a field and cultivating it wisely to ensure a good harvest. The decisions you make now will have long-term consequences, so it is imperative to think things through, get sound advice, and choose wisely. The association of the card with the sign Gemini suggests love between individuals that can endure for an eternity.

The Lovers Reversed

When reversed, the Lovers card suggests that you may be rushing into a decision without careful consideration. Perhaps you have been swept off your feet by a new relationship and cannot think clearly. Love is blind, and Cupid's arrows may tempt you to sow wild oats without considering the consequences. Are you behaving like a farmer who has not properly plowed his fields or adequately cultivated his crops? Without careful preparation, there cannot be a good harvest. With due deliberation, you can avoid hard times.

7. THE CHARIOT: REASON TAMES APPETITE AND WILL

Key VII: The Chariot

Astrology: Cancer, the Crab (a Water sign ruled by the Moon). In the Waite-Smith tarot, a flowing river separates the canopied chariot from the walled city behind.

Dates of Cancer: 21 June–22 July (tropical); 16 July–17 August (sidereal)

Element: Water

Numerology: 7 (Chariot) = 1 + 6 (The Tower)

Hebrew letter: *Chet, Cheth,* or *Heth* (a protective fence, a tent wall; a Hebrew word meaning a separation, boundary, dividing wall, stacked stones, outside, half, or string). The crab of the sign Cancer has a well-defined protective shell (*Chet*).

Myths/Archetypes: Hecate. Auriga virtutem. Cancer, the sign of the crab. Plato's chariot as an analogy for the three-part human soul (reason, will, appetite). The NASCAR driver.

Mathers (1888): Triumph, victory, overcoming obstacles; (R) Overthrown, conquered by obstacles at the last moment.

Waite (1911): Succor, providence; also war, triumph, presumption, vengeance, trouble; (R) riot, quarrel, dispute, litigation, defeat.

Golden Dawn: Triumph, victory, good health, success (though sometimes not enduring success).

Keywords (+): Strength of purpose, taking the reins, establishing clear boundaries, maintaining protective walls, travel, prudence, determination, controlling opposing forces, triumph over obstacles in your path, having a clear direction, setting out on a quest, staying focused on your goal, relying on inner resources, mastery, a journey, a car or other vehicle, respecting your own limits, a hard shell, the straight and narrow path.

Keywords (-): Lack of direction, loss of control, frustrating obstacles, aimless wandering, spinning one's wheels, letting go of the reins, poor boundaries, unawareness of one's limits, absence of a protective shell, inability to stay on course, being pulled in many directions.

The Chariot Upright

When upright, the Chariot urges you to master the situation in the midst of changing circumstances. You must take the reins of the chariot on which you travel through life. Inside the protective shell of your personality, you have the necessary resources to accomplish your goals. Success will depend on your ability to use reason to strike a balance between your ambitions and your appetites, which may be pulling you in different directions. It is important to set clear boundaries and to respect your own limits. Now is a time to think clearly, take control, and assume direction of your life. Often the Chariot appears when you are planning a trip or are about to embark on a significant journey, be it literal or metaphorical.

The Chariot Reversed

When reversed, the Chariot warns that you may be allowing yourself to wander aimlessly rather than assuming control of the direction of your life. You may be feeling vulnerable and at the mercy of outside forces. Your many ambitions and your desire for various pleasures may be pulling you away from your preferred path. Pay attention to establishing clear boundaries and knowing your own limits. Don't let go of the reins of your personal chariot. Now is a time to focus on what you value most and to organize your life course so that you can arrive at your most cherished destination. If the Chariot refers to a vehicle or a literal journey, your trip may be delayed or run into difficulties.

8/11. STRENGTH: COURAGE AND ANIMAL PASSION

Key VIII: Strength (Fortitude, Lust). This card is numbered XI in traditional Marseille decks.

Astrology: Leo, the Lion (a Fire sign ruled by the Sun)

Dates of Leo: 23 July–23 August; 18 August–16 September (sidereal)

Element: Fire

Numerology: 8 (Strength, or Justice) = 1 + 7 (The Star)

Hebrew letter: *Teth* or *Theth* (a clay or wicker basket; a Hebrew word meaning to surround, contain, store, catch, intertwine, coil, knot together, interweave; also mud or clay, and a snake or serpent). The coiling serpent is suggestive of the intertwining of bodies in sexual intercourse. The Hebrew letter *Teth* (basket) and this card's association with human lust bring to mind the nursery rhyme, "A-tisket a-tasket, a green and yellow basket, I wrote a letter to my love and on the way I dropped it … a little boy he picked it up and put it in his pocket."

Myths/Archetypes: The Hero. Joan of Arc. The Dragon Slayer. The Satyr. Hercules and the Nemean Lion. David and Goliath. Samson and Delilah. Kundalini.

Mathers (1888): Power, might, force, strength, fortitude; (R) the abuse of power, overbearingness, want of fortitude.

Waite (1911): Power, energy, action, courage, magnanimity; also complete success and honors; (R) despotism, abuse of power, weakness, discord, sometimes even disgrace.

Golden Dawn: Fortitude, strength, courage.

Keywords (+): Courage, bravery, passion, heroism, self-esteem, fortitude, mettle, true grit, vitality, moral fiber, strength in the face of adversity, wildness, lust, libido, burning desire, sexual instincts, powerful emotions, kundalini, taming the beast within, suppression of inordinate fear, the curbing of recklessness.

Keywords (-): Lack of courage, abuse of power, unbridled lust, perverse sexuality, satyriasis, nymphomania, addiction, repression of instinctual desires, inability to cope with powerful emotions, cowardice, self-aggrandizement.

....
Strength Upright

When upright, the Strength/Lust card suggests a need to face a situation with courage, determination, and fortitude, much as Hercules did when he confronted the Nemean Lion. Your animal passions are stirring and may conflict with your "civilized" self. You are feeling lustily powerful and thoroughly enjoy the use of your body. Health improves, and your energy increases. Issues related to sexuality come up for review. The connection of the Strength card with the sign Leo and with the Sun suggests that this may be a time of compassionate self-examination, which can lead to enlightenment. Leo is known for its warmth, generosity, and lusty enjoyment of life.

....
Strength Reversed

When reversed, Strength implies that you may need to muster the courage to confront your difficulties. Perhaps you are feeling fearful or hopeless in the face of powerful instinctual desires you imagine are beyond your control. On the other hand, you may have gone overboard in trying to win admiration for how attractive or sexually adept you are, causing others to experience you as domineering, vain, self-aggrandizing, or controlling.

9. THE HERMIT: THE SEARCH FOR MEANING

Key IX: The Hermit

Astrology: Virgo, the Virgin (an Earth sign ruled by Mercury)

Dates of Virgo: 23 August–23 September; 17 September–16 October (sidereal)

Element: Earth

Numerology: 9 (The Hermit) = 1 + 8 (The Moon)

Hebrew letter: *Yud* or *Yod* (an arm and closed hand; a Hebrew word meaning to do a deed, make, work, throw, or worship; a closed fist holding something). Notice the Hermit's arm and closed fist holding the lantern on the card.

Myths/Archetypes: The Wise Old Man. The Sage. The Philosopher. Buddha. Jedi Master Yoda (whose name contains the Hebrew letter *Yod*).

Mathers (1888): Prudence, caution, deliberation; (R) over-prudence, timorousness, fear.

Waite (1911): Prudence, circumspection; also and especially treason, dissimulation, roguery, corruption; (R) concealment, disguise, policy, fear, unreasoned caution.

Golden Dawn: Active pursuit of divine inspiration and wisdom from above.

Keywords (+): Introspection, meditation, spiritual retreat, careful attention, solitude, prudence, maturity, self-possession, the wisdom of experience, watchfulness, circumspection, discernment, perspective, patient pursuit of knowledge, quiet contemplation, spiritual illumination, philosophical insight, the search for meaning, the power of Now, replenishment of the soul.

Keywords (-): Imprudence, excessive caution, lack of wisdom, narcissism, timidity, social isolation, alienation, withdrawal, loneliness, failure to learn from experience, cutting oneself off from the support of others.

The Hermit Upright

When upright, the Hermit indicates a need to spend time far from the madding crowd. Now is a time to collect your thoughts and regroup your forces. A period of solitude and contemplation is in order. In this modern age of technology, someone quipped that meditation provides the answers you can't find on Google. You have been through a lot, and the time has come to wait and watch. An attitude of patient circumspection will allow you to put matters in perspective and learn from your experience. You might consider reading Eckhardt Tolle's book *The Power of Now.*

The Hermit Reversed

When reversed, the Hermit suggests that you are caught up in the hustle and bustle of daily life and unable to see clearly where you are headed. Consider taking some time off and allowing yourself space to meditate and get back on track. A great philosopher once commented that the unexamined life is not worth living. There is a lot of wisdom to be gleaned from your experience if only you take the time to do so. A little distance is what you need to put matters in perspective.

10. THE WHEEL OF FORTUNE: A TIME TO EVERY PURPOSE UNDER HEAVEN

Key X: The Wheel of Fortune (Dame Fortune)

Astrology: Jupiter, the greater benefic. (Jupiter rules Sagittarius and Pisces)

Numerology: 1 (Magician) = 1 + 0 (Wheel of Fortune) = 1 + 9 (The Sun)

Element: Fire

Hebrew letter: *Kaph* (the open palm of a hand; a Hebrew word meaning to open, bend, allow, tame, or to submit to another's will; also, hollow or outstretched to receive something). Palm readers claim to read our fortune in the open palm of the hand. This card suggests that we may have no choice but to stretch ourselves out and submit to the turns of the wheel of fortune.

Myths/Archetypes: Lady Luck. Dame Fortune. The three Norns. The Fates of Greek mythology. The Soothsayer. The fickle finger of fate.

Mathers (1888): Good fortune, success, unexpected luck; (R) ill-fortune, failure, unexpected ill-luck.

Waite (1911): Destiny, fortune, success, elevation, luck, felicity; (R) increase, abundance, superfluity.

Golden Dawn: Good luck, happiness, sometimes intoxication with success.

Keywords (+): Good luck, destiny, opportunities for advancement, an upward trend, seizing the moment, remaining open to opportunity, natural cycles, a turn for the better, seizing the moment, twists of fate, Lady Luck, the slings and arrows of fortune, time will tell, the acceptance of one's fate.

Keywords (-): Bad luck, a downward cycle, misfortune, a turn for the worse, fateful events, impermanence, procrastination, not seizing the moment, having no choice but to submit, feeling powerless to affect circumstances, the fickle finger of fate.

The Wheel of Fortune Upright

When upright, the Wheel of Fortune reminds us that our good fortune is often the result of twists of fate rather than our own doing. Now is a time to enjoy your good luck because it can change just as rapidly tomorrow. If things are going well now, be sure to make the best of it and put something aside for a rainy day. For the time being, destiny is smiling upon you. Seize the moment because an opportunity that presents itself today may not remain available tomorrow. Contemplate the lyrics of the Pete Seeger song "Turn, Turn, Turn," which sets the biblical words to music: "To everything there is a season, and a time to every purpose under the heaven" (Ecclesiastes 3:1, KJV).

The Wheel of Fortune Reversed

When reversed, the Wheel of Fortune cautions that your good luck can't last forever. What goes up must come down. Each season gives way to the next, and you need to be prepared for the possibility of a rainy day. Although our fate is largely what we make it, unexpected things can happen that are outside of our control. Keep in mind the words of Brutus:

There is a tide in the affairs of men,
Which, taken at the flood, leads on to fortune;
Omitted, all the voyage of their life
Is bound in shallows and in miseries.
(William Shakespeare,
Julius Caesar, Act 4, Scene 3, 1599)

11/8. JUSTICE: THE LAWFULNESS OF THE UNIVERSE

Key XI: Justice. This card is numbered VIII in the traditional Marseille deck.

Astrology: Libra, the Scales (ruled by the planet Venus)

Dates of Libra: 23 September–22 October (tropical); 17 October–15 November (sidereal)

Numerology: 2 (High Priestess) = 1 + 1 (Justice or Strength) = 2 + 0 (Judgment)

Element: Air

Hebrew letter: *Lamed* (an ox goad, or a shepherd's staff that guides the herd; a Hebrew word meaning to teach, learn, yoke, bind, control, defend, protect; to/toward; also a scholar, an authority, or a leader of the flock). The virtue of Justice is like a shepherd's staff that directs the human race toward just and lawful behavior.

Myths/Archetypes: The Scales of Justice. Karma. The Egyptian goddess Ma'at who weighed souls against a feature to determine if they were worthy of paradise. King Solomon. The Code of Hammurabi. Moses receiving the Ten Commandments.

Mathers (1888): Equilibrium, balance, justice; (R) bigotry, want of balance, abuse of justice, over-severity, inequality, bias.

Waite (1911): Equity, rightness, probity, executive; triumph of the deserving side in law; (R) law in all its departments, legal complications, bigotry, bias, excessive severity.

Golden Dawn: Justice, balance, legal proceedings, legal trials, courts of law.

Keywords (+): Justice, equality, human rights, law and order, fairness, truth, lawfulness, just behavior, balance, impartiality, tolerance, reasonable decisions, courts, legal matters, accepting responsibility, correcting imbalances, respect for the law, morality, ethics, karma, actions and consequences, the right way, just deserts of one's actions.

Keywords (-): Injustice, bias, inequality, unfair treatment, partiality, favoritism, bigotry, intolerance, hypocrisy, unreasonableness, undue influence, irresponsibility, immorality, unethical behavior, legal entanglements, an adverse ruling by a court, abuse of the legal system, refusal to accept responsibility for one's actions.

....
Justice Upright

When upright, the Justice card suggests that your current situation hinges on matters of equilibrium, balance, fair treatment, and justice. If you are involved in a legal matter, it will be judged impartially and is likely to be decided in your favor (but only if you are in the right). If you are in the wrong, the same impartiality applies and you will be held accountable. In any decision you take now, it is essential to be honest and judicious in weighing the pros and cons. In the words of the Bible: "Be not deceived; God is not mocked: for whatsoever a man soweth, that shall he also reap" (Galatians 6:7, KJV).

....
Justice Reversed

When reversed, the Justice card can mean that your situation involves injustice, unfairness, bias, or partiality. Matters may feel out of balance or tilted against you. Legal proceedings are likely to cause difficulties. Dishonesty may characterize your dealings with others. If the goddess Ma'at were to weigh your soul against a feather right now, would she find you worthy of entering into paradise?

12. The Hanged Man: Adopting a Fresh Perspective

Key XII: The Hanged Man (The Traitor)

Astrology: Water (Neptune in some modern decks)

Numerology: 3 (Empress) = 1 + 2 (Hanged Man) = 2 + 1 (The World)

Element: Water

Hebrew letter: *Mem* (waves of water; a Hebrew word meaning water, liquid, blood, the ocean, a large body of water, chaos, and fear of mighty forces such as the sea). Your image reflected in the surface of a lake appears to be upside down with respect to your upright position.

Myths/Archetypes: Jesus. Buddha. Odin. Cuauhtémoc. The Martyr. The Sacrificial Lamb. Benedict Arnold. The Traitor.

Mathers (1888): Self-sacrifice, sacrifice, devotion, bound; (R) selfishness, unbound, partial sacrifice.

Waite (1911): Wisdom, circumspection, discernment, trials, sacrifice, intuition, divination, prophecy; (R) selfishness, the crowd, the body politic.

Golden Dawn: Involuntary sacrifice, suffering, loss, punishment.

Keywords (+): Sacrifice for the greater good, a state of suspension; waiting, surrender, devotion, altruism, serenity, faith, visionary thinking, release, going with the flow, letting go, feeling like you are on hold, redemption through sacrifice, adopting a unique perspective, doing something out of the ordinary, a spiritual viewpoint, a novel way to view a situation, loving kindness, compassion, evenly suspended attention.

Keywords (-): Selfishness, egotism, betrayal, stagnation, reversal, delay, self-pity, clinging, rigid thinking, self-deception, treason, playing the victim, foolish martyrdom, helplessness, unease, disillusionment, hangups, conformity.

The Hanged Man Upright

When upright, the Hanged Man looks like an image reflected in the surface of a body of water, suggesting that what we perceive with our senses is but a reflection of a deeper reality. To understand what is really real, we may need to adopt a new perspective. If your life feels like it's on hold or in a state of suspension, it's time to adopt a spiritual perspective and pursue the greater good. We sometimes need to make sacrifices and let go of something we value to achieve a greater good. In any case, when the Hanged Man appears in a reading, you are likely to be viewing or doing something out of the ordinary in a way that sets you apart from the more accepted approach of those around you.

The Hanged Man Reversed

When reversed, the Hanged Man suggests that you may be clinging too tightly to an illusion preventing you from gaining a clearer perspective. Refusal to make a necessary sacrifice can result in further loss and suffering. Playing the martyr will not be productive. In Renaissance Italy, hanging someone upside down was a punishment reserved for traitors. After betraying Cuauhtémoc, the last Aztec emperor, the Spanish conquistador Cortés killed the Aztec warrior by hanging him upside-down in a Christ-like pose, as is vividly depicted in the mural by Diego Rivera entitled "Exploitation of Mexico by Spanish Conquistadors."

13. DEATH: A NEW CHAPTER BEGINS

Key XIII: Death

Astrology: Scorpio, the Scorpion (a Water sign ruled by Mars and Pluto)

Dates of Scorpio: 23 October–22 November (tropical); 16 November–15 December (sidereal)

Element: Water

Numerology: 4 (Emperor) = 1 + 3 (Death) = 2 + 2 (The Fool)

Hebrew letter: *Nun* (a sprouting seed; a Hebrew word meaning to propagate, bear offspring, perpetuate life, continue on to a new generation, increase; also posterity, a son or an heir). The pictograph of *Nun* resembles a human sperm. In Aramaic, the word *nun* means *fish*, a symbol important to Christianity. This card reminds us that death is part of the natural process of engendering new life.

Myths/Archetypes: Osiris. Dionysus. The Angel of Death. The Eleusinian Mysteries. The phoenix myth. Transfiguration. Easter. The Resurrection.

Mathers (1888): Death, change, transformation, alteration for the worse; (R) death just escaped, partial change, alteration for the better.

Waite (1911): The end, mortality, destruction, corruption; also, for a man, the loss of a benefactor; for a woman, many contrarieties; for a maid, failure of marriage prospects; (R) inertia, sleep, lethargy, petrifaction, somnambulism; hope destroyed.

Golden Dawn: Involuntary change (as opposed to voluntary change indicated by the Moon trump), transformation, sometimes death.

Keywords (+): Transition, transformation, a sprouting seed, major change, endings, renewal, a necessary change, propagation, a sprouting seed, new growth, the closing of a chapter, shutting a door, entering a new stage of existence, liberation, release, metamorphosis, transfiguration, moving on, the need to let go, an inevitable ending, the natural cycle of life and death, courage to face the unknown.

Keywords (-): Refusal to let go, stagnation, decay, procrastination, failing to sprout, clinging unproductively to the past, resisting necessary change, fear of the unknown.

....
Death Upright

When upright, the Death trump signals a period of significant change and transformation. A new seed is sprouting in your life. One chapter is ending and another beginning. This necessary process should not be denied or avoided. The major theme of this card is "out with the old to make way for the new." Have courage to face the unknown because new life awaits you. Keep in mind the biblical admonition: "Except a grain of wheat falls into the ground and dies, it abides alone: but if it dies, it brings forth much fruit" (John 12:24, KJV).

....
Death Reversed

When reversed, the Death card suggests that you may be avoiding necessary change and transition. Clinging to the past is not productive in the long run. Aspects of your life that are stagnant or outworn must be discarded so that new growth can take place. Are you creating conditions inimical to the sprouting of new seeds in your life? If so, now is the time to summon the courage to face the unknown.

14. TEMPERANCE: ARTFUL BLENDING AND RECONCILIATION

Key XIV: Temperance (Art)

Astrology: Sagittarius, the centaur archer (a Fire sign ruled by Jupiter)

Dates of Sagittarius: 22 November–21 December (tropical); 16 December–14 January (sidereal).

Numerology: 5 (Hierophant) = 1 + 4 (Temperance)

Element: Fire

Hebrew letter: *Samech* or *Samekh* (a sharp thorn, or a hand on a staff; a Hebrew word meaning a protective shield, a support or foundation; also to pierce, hold up, sustain, prop, lean upon, grab, hate, or protect). *Samekh* also refers to the ritual laying-on of hands in animal sacrifice and in the ordination (consecration) of priests.

Myths/Archetypes: The Centaur. The Alchemist. The Hermaphrodite. The Transsexual. The Creator. The Artist. The Healer. The Inventor. Hegel's dialectic.

Mathers (1888): Combination, conformation, uniting; (R) ill-advised combinations, disunion, clashing interests.

Waite (1911): Economy, moderation, frugality, management, accommodation; (R) things connected with churches, religions, sects, the priesthood, sometimes even the priest who will marry the querent; also disunion, unfortunate combinations, competing interests.

Golden Dawn: Combined forces, action, material realization.

Keywords (+): Temperance, moderation, consecration, self-control, right proportion, healing, ability to cope, reconciliation of competing impulses, balancing different needs, discretion, mutual respect, composure, tempering, proportionality, right mixture, proper measure, resolution, union of opposites, harmonizing conflicting viewpoints, balancing contrary forces, artful combination, the golden mean, the middle way, creative resolution, artful blending of contrarieties, ability to negotiate.

Keywords (-): Immoderation, conflict, incompatibility, excess, imbalance, impatience, going to extremes, lack of self-control, indecision, clashing interests, inconsiderate demands, inability to reconcile opposing forces, irreconcilable differences, all or nothing thinking; "it's my way or the highway."

....
Temperance Upright

When upright, the Temperance trump suggests that you are dealing with a situation involving the reconciliation of opposites within yourself. Like the alchemists of old, you are trying to convert a base metal into gold. You are called upon to act with moderation and exercise the virtue of temperance. With persistent effort you will be able to blend competing forces harmoniously to create something of greater value. The Renaissance artists who created this image were no doubt inspired by the mixing of water and wine in the Catholic Mass during which the priest prays: "Through the mystery of this water and wine, may we partake in the divine nature of Christ who humbled himself to share in our humanity."

....
Temperance Reversed

When reversed, the Temperance card implies that you are having difficulty finding a golden mean. Confronted by contradictory impulses, you feel at a loss about how to strike an artful balance. You are tempted to go to extremes rather than seek a middle ground of reconciliation. Ponder the words of the philosopher: "Moderation in all things, including moderation." As Abraham Lincoln cautioned, "A house divided against itself cannot stand."

15. THE DEVIL: A TWISTED VIEW OF THE WORLD

Key XV: The Devil (the god Pan)

Astrology: Capricorn, the Mountain or Sea Goat (an Earth sign ruled by Saturn)

Dates of Capricorn: 21 December–19 January (tropical); 14 January–12 February (sidereal)

Element: Earth

Numerology: 6 (Lovers) = 1 + 5 (Devil)

Hebrew letters: *Ayin* (an eye; a Hebrew word meaning to see, watch, experience, know; also primeval light, shade, a spring or fountain, as an eye producing purifying tears in response to pain or grief). In the Bible, Lucifer's name means "bringer of light." The letter *Ghah* is also associated with the Devil card. According to Jeff Benner, the twenty-third letter of the ancient Hebrew alphabet, *Ghah* ("a twisted rope"), was absorbed into the modern letter *Ayin*.[38] *Ghah* means "twisted," "dark," or "wicked," and refers to goats because of their twisted horns. In modern slang, "horny" has come to mean lustful or sexually preoccupied. Perhaps the combination *Ayin Ghah* associated with this card suggests adopting a twisted view of the world. Coincidentally, Capricorn—the goat of astrology—is assigned to the Devil trump.

Myths/Archetypes: Pan, the sex-crazed goat-legged god of the shepherds. Bacchanalia. Adam and Eve. Baphomet. Cernunnos. Lucifer. Faust. King Midas. Alexander the Great. Beelzebub, Lord of the Flies. The religiously obsessed suicide bomber.

Mathers (1888): Fatality for good; (R) fatality for evil.

Waite (1911): Ravage, violence, vehemence, extraordinary efforts, force, fatality; that which is predestined but is not for this reason evil; (R) evil fatality, weakness, pettiness, blindness.

Golden Dawn: Materialism, obsession, material force, material temptation (the qualities of obsession and carnal temptation are enhanced by the presence of the Lovers trump).

Keywords (+): Loosening the ties that bind, breaking free of rigid morality, enjoyable material attachments, making healthy choices, having fun, enjoying sex, confronting temptation, delighting in what gives you pleasure, adopting a spiritual perspective, confronting one's inner demons, casting off the chains of religious dogmatism, leading the life that you desire, intense devotion to a worldly ambition.

Keywords (-): Bondage, obsession, entrapment, material temptation, oppression, imbalance, dishonesty, twisted thinking, ignorance, rigid morality, enslavement to religion, confining beliefs, codependency, addiction, self-deception, excessive materialism, unhealthy attachments, lust for power, overindulgence, wild abandon, horniness, sexual perversion, wickedness, secret scheming, going to extremes, self-imposed restrictions, religious fanaticism, no way out, fear of the unknown, one's shadow self.

---

38. Jeff A. Benner, "Ghah," *Ancient Hebrew Research Center*, www.ancient-hebrew.org/3_ghah.html, accessed 17 November 2014.

....
The Devil Upright

When upright, the Devil suggests that you have an opportunity to pursue activities that provide intense pleasure and satisfaction. This card often appears when we are contemplating a project requiring an almost obsessional devotion to achieve a material ambition. The Devil cautions us to maintain balance in our lives as we eagerly pursue this goal and not to allow excessive attachment to material temptations to lead us astray.

Unfortunately, the Devil card has become linked to views of dour theologians who believe that bodily pleasure is sinful in the eyes of the deity who ironically created the human body with all its capacity for enjoyment. The Devil card teaches us that seeking pleasure in life is perfectly acceptable, so long as it is done with moderation (which is why Temperance, card XIV, precedes card XV, the Devil). When this card appears in a reading, it's time to lighten up and delight in activities that you may have avoided because of a rigid sense of obligation or morality. The Devil whispers in your ear: "If it feels good, do it." Thus, if there is a cherished worldly ambition you have held back from pursing, now is the time to go for it. The Devil simply cautions you to maintain a spiritual perspective so that you can avoid becoming ensnared by your material ambitions and adopt a twisted view of the world. Along these lines, a recent survey of a thousand parents in the UK found that despite the popular notion that money, professional success, and material possessions are essential for a happy life, 95 percent of them stated that the key to happiness lies in "spending quality family time together." [39]

....
The Devil Reversed

When reversed, the Devil card suggests that you may have gone too far in pursuing pleasures and sensual delights. Imbalance and extremes of behavior may be causing difficulties. Obsessive devotion to any type of materialistic goal or corporeal pleasure is a form of bondage and entrapment. Sometimes things that feel good aren't good for us. An important feature of the image on the Devil trump is that the chains are easily removed once you realize they are present. Otherwise you end up echoing the words of Oscar Wilde: "I can resist anything except temptation."

---

39. Deni Kirkova, "What's the Ultimate Modern Luxury?" in *Daily Mail*, 21 May 2013, www.dailymail.co.uk/femail /article-2328597/Spending-quality-time-family-beats-material-possessions-holidays-new-happiness-poll.html, accessed 10 May 2015.

16. THE TOWER: SUDDEN ENLIGHTENMENT

Key XVI: The Tower

Astrology: Mars, the god of wars, bloodshed, destruction. (Mars rules Aries and Scorpio)

Numerology: 7 (Chariot) = 1 + 6 (The Tower)

Element: Fire

Hebrew letter: *Pey* or *Pe* (an open mouth; a Hebrew word meaning mouth, word, vocalization, speech, or the edge of something; also, to speak, blow, or scatter).

Myths/Archetypes: The Tower of Babel. Thor, the Norse god of lightning. Zeus of the thunderbolt. Buddha under the Bodhi Tree. Hades abducting Persephone.

Mathers (1888): Ruin, disruption, over-throw, loss, bankruptcy; (R) these in a more or less partial degree.

Waite (1911): Misery, distress, indigence, adversity, calamity, disgrace, deception, ruin. It is a card in particular of unforeseen catastrophe; (R) according to one account, the same in a lesser degree; also oppression, imprisonment, tyranny.

Golden Dawn: Courage, ambition, fighting, war (attributes of the planet Mars); when accompanied by stressful cards, destruction, ruin, danger, defeat.

Keywords (+): A bolt from the blue, a sudden revelation, abrupt changes, unexpected news that seizes your attention, disruption, overthrow, upheaval, forced change, a call to action, unanticipated events, sudden enlightenment, liberation from limiting structures, purgation, an opportunity for new growth, purification, the need to act before it is too late.

Keywords (-): Sudden upset, breakdown, crisis, ruin, catastrophe, shock, disturbing news, overthrow, destruction, elimination, trauma, defeat, distressing change, being left speechless.

. . . .

Tower Upright

When upright, the Tower suggests that you need to critically evaluate the structures that are confining you or limiting your life. If you don't do so voluntarily, the universe will find a way to force change upon you. Longstanding routines that have been hindering your progress need to be abandoned. Unanticipated changes may at first appear traumatic but in the long run can open the door to renewal. There's an old adage that says every crisis presents an opportunity. Unexpected and sometimes drastic alterations in one's life course are often accompanied by sudden and profound insights into the nature of one's reality and belief system. Concretely, such events may include separation, divorce, job loss, school failure, financial setbacks, an upsetting medical diagnosis, and so on.

. . . .

Tower Reversed

When reversed, the Tower implies that you may be avoiding necessary change or failing to learn from a traumatic situation. We cannot avoid the fact that bad things happen to good people, but we can take advantage of the opportunity to grow in wisdom from whatever we experience in our lives. Consider the parable of the house built on sand: " ... a foolish man, which built his house upon the sand, and the rain descends, and the floods came, and the winds blew and beat upon the house and it fell: and great was the fall of it" (Matthew 7:26–27, KJV). In what ways have you built your house on sand?

17. THE STAR: A GLIMMER OF HOPE

Key XVII: The Star

Astrology: Aquarius, the Water Bearer (an Air sign ruled by Saturn and Uranus)

Dates of Aquarius: 20 January–17 February (tropical); 13 February–13 March (sidereal)

Element: Air

Hebrew letter: *Tsadhe, Tsade, Tzaddi,* or *Tsadiq* (a trail leading to a destination, or a figure lying on its side; a Hebrew word meaning a stronghold built on the side of a mountain; also a journey, desire, need; to chase, hunt, catch, or capture; just or righteous). The Star of Bethlehem provided a trail that led the Magi to the birthplace of Jesus. The Hebrew letter is also said to resemble a fishing hook. Aleister Crowley pairs the Star with the letter *He,* which the Golden Dawn, in contrast, associates with the Emperor.

Myths/Archetypes: The Star of Bethlehem. The Fairy Godmother. The Egyptian sky goddess Nuit (aka Nut, Neuth, Newet). Aquarius, the Water Bearer.

Mathers (1888): Hope, expectation, bright promises; (R) hopes not fulfilled, expectations disappointed or fulfilled in a minor degree.

Waite (1911): Loss, theft, privation, abandonment; another reading say: hope and bright prospects; (R) arrogance, haughtiness, impotence.

Golden Dawn: Faith, hope, help coming from unexpected sources; when ill-dignified, false hopes, dreaminess.

Keywords (+): Hope, support, bright prospects, a guiding light, a trail leading to a destination, faith in a better future, inspiration, clarity, peace, tranquility, the possibility of improvement, opportunity for renewal, following a righteous path, the light at the end of the tunnel.

Keywords (-): Loss of hope, pessimism, expectations not met, neglected opportunities, lack of trust in the future, refusal to accept helpful guidance.

....
The Star Upright

When upright, the Star trump offers hope and support after the disruption of the Tower card. You are beginning to see the light at the end of the tunnel. You have located a trail leading to your destination. There is a promise of peace and tranquility if you continue on your current path. Help may materialize from unexpected sources. You can proceed with faith that the future holds brighter prospects. As Marcus Tullius Cicero said some two thousand years ago, "Where there is life, there is hope."

....
The Star Reversed

When reversed, the Star card suggests that you are not feeling hopeful about a positive outcome. You may be suffering a crisis of faith or feeling beset by doubts that things will not work out in the end. Now is a time to assess your situation realistically and banish any false hopes or expectations based on illusion. Are you able to see the glass only as being half empty? Are you unable to recognize the guiding trail beneath your feet? Keep in mind the moral of Aesop's fable: the gods help those who help themselves.

18. THE MOON: THINGS THAT GO BUMP IN THE NIGHT

Key XVIII: The Moon

Astrology: Pisces, the Fishes (a Water sign ruled by Jupiter and Neptune)

Dates of Pisces: 18 February–19 March (tropical); 14 March–13 April (sidereal)

Element: Water

Numerology: 9 (The Hermit) = 1 + 8 (The Moon)

Hebrew letter: *Quph* or *Qoph* (the sun on the horizon; a Hebrew word meaning the sun, revolution, a compass, circuit, cycle, circular motion, going around, behind, the back of the head, horizon, a revolution of the sun, time, or to condense). The moon is known for its dark side (back of the head) hidden from our earthly viewpoint and for its phases that resonate with natural cycles on earth.

Myths/Archetypes: The Moon Goddess. Hecate, gatekeeper between the worlds and the Queen of the Night. Diana, goddess of the moon, birthing, and the hunt.

Mathers (1888): Twilight, deception, error; (R) fluctuation, slight deceptions, trifling mistakes.

Waite (1911): Hidden enemies, danger, calumny, darkness, terror, deception, occult forces, error; (R) instability, inconstancy, silence, lesser degrees of deception and error.

Golden Dawn: Voluntary change (as opposed to the involuntary change of the Death card), dissatisfaction; when ill-dignified the Moon may signify deception, error, falsehood.

Keywords (+): Illusion, mystery, haziness, unseen influences, intuitive knowledge, things are not what they seem; voluntary change, phases, cycles, dreams, imagination, psychic awareness, unconscious knowledge, introspection, gut instincts, the menstrual cycle, facing one's fears.

Keywords (-): Confusion, deception, error, disillusionment, lack of clarity, unreality, nebulous thinking, apprehension, fearing the worst, misunderstanding, darkness, loneliness, bad dreams, depression, insecurity, hidden enemies, ambiguity, instability, intoxication, substance abuse, the dark side, fluctuating circumstances, failure to keep promises, concerns about women's health; things that go bump in the night.

. . . .

The Moon Upright

When upright, the Moon suggests that circumstances may be elusive, unclear, confusing, fluctuating, or unsteady at this time. The Moon has a dark side, always hidden from human view. Individuals under the influence of drugs or alcohol can cause problems. Important information may have been misunderstood or may not yet be within your grasp. Unseen influences may be at work, and matters are likely to look different in the light of day. You may be in one phase of a cycle, and only with the passage of time will the next phase reveal itself. Don't jump to conclusions or act on impulse. Be sure you have accurate and verifiable information before making a major decision.

. . . .

The Moon Reversed

When reversed, the Moon can indicate that you are about to emerge from a period of confusion or uncertainty. Many readers regard the inverted Moon card as posing milder problems than the card upright. Sometimes the reversed Moon appears when a female querent is facing gynecological difficulties.

19. THE SUN: A RAY OF SUNSHINE

Key XIX: The Sun

Astrology: the Sun (ruler of the Fire sign Leo)

Element: Fire

Hebrew letter: *Resh* (a man's head; a Hebrew word meaning a person, chief, leader, head, captain, that which comes first, summit, top, or beginning). The sun comes first in our solar system; without the sun's rays we would not exist. The Hebrew letter *Resh* is associated with the sun and refers to a man's head facing you. In contrast, the Hebrew letter *Qoph* associated with the moon refers to the back of the head.

Numerology: 1 (Magician) = 1 + 0 (Wheel of Fortune) = 1 + 9 (the Sun)

Myths/Archetypes: The Egyptian god Amun-Ra. The Sun god. Apollo. Logos.

Mathers (1888): Happiness, contentment, joy; (R) these in a minor degree.

Waite (1911): Material happiness, fortunate marriage, contentment; (R) the same in a lesser sense.

Golden Dawn: Gain, riches, honor, glory, arrogance, display, vanity (the latter connotations apply only when the Sun is accompanied by negative cards).

Keywords (+): Success, attainment, optimism, illumination, joy, ovation, recognition, vitality, achievement, good health, sunshine, healing, positive energy, youthful vigor, warmth, happiness, contentment, clear vision, consciousness, daylight, the bright side, brilliance, exultation, clarity, radiance, lucidity, transparency, enlightenment, childlike delight, justice tempered with mercy; "a good deed in a weary world."

Keywords (-): A lesser degree of the above; also pride, smugness, vanity, egotism, arrogance, unrealistic ambitions, megalomania, delayed success, lack of appreciation.

....
The Sun Upright

When upright, the Sun is a positive card that typically symbolizes a period of success, achievement, recognition, warmth, happiness, popularity, and contentment. Health improves and personal relationships prosper. Work situations and new ventures go well. Because of the Sun's connection with Leo and the fifth house of the natural zodiac, modern astrologers believe that this card can also signify romance, marriage, creative self-expression, the birth of children, or other matters related to offspring. Now is a time of clarity, illumination, and enlightenment. Ponder the words of the bard: "How far that little candle throws his beams! So shines a good deed in a weary world" (William Shakespeare, *The Merchant of Venice*, 1600).

....
The Sun Reversed

When reversed, the Sun is still a positive card but presumably to a lesser degree. It may be that something is blocking you from fully experiencing the joy and clarity that is possible at this time. Perhaps your inflated ego is getting in the way; excessive pride is one of the faults of the sign Leo. You may not get the standing ovation you were hoping for.

20. Judgment: What Goes Around, Comes Around

Key XX: Judgment (Aeon)

Astrology: Fire (Pluto in some modern decks). Both the element Fire and the dwarf planet Pluto are associated with purgation, renewal, and purification.

Element: Fire

Numerology: 2 (High Priestess) = 1 + 1 (Justice or Strength) = 2 + 0 (Judgment)

Hebrew letter: *Shin* or *Sin* (the two front teeth, ivory; a Hebrew word meaning tooth, sharp; also to sharpen, press, eat, consume, destroy, to sharpen a blade, to say sharp words, to sharpen one's mind; two of something, both, second). The letter *Shin's* appearance in the *lex talionis* probably accounts for its association with the Last Judgment: "…an eye for an eye, a *tooth* for a *tooth*…"

Myths/Archetypes: The Last Judgment. The Angel of Resurrection. The Avenging Angel. The phoenix rising from its ashes. Persephone being rescued from the underworld. The Tooth Fairy.

Mathers (1888): Renewal, result, determination of a matter; (R) postponement of result, delay, a matter reopened later.

Waite (1911): Change of position, renewal, outcome; another account specifies total loss though lawsuit; (R) weakness, pusillanimity, simplicity; also deliberation, decision, sentence.

Golden Dawn: A judgment, sentence, final decision.

Keywords (+): A calling, awakening from slumber, a new era, judging and being judged, re-assessment, judgment day, reanimation, someone clamoring for your attention, stepping into a new life, a final reckoning, rebirth, resurrection, renewal, a last chance, release from the underworld, being reenergized, rising from the dead, forgiveness, entering another phase of existence, rising from one's ashes, rescue, starting anew, a clean slate.

Keywords (-): Sentencing, not heeding a call, self-recrimination, worry, regret, delay, shame, remorse, stagnation, isolation, bad karma, condemnation, vengeance, a negative judgment, clinging to old ways, remaining stuck in the past, postponing a matter until it's too late, an unsatisfactory ending, failure to rise from one's ashes; an eye for an eye, a tooth for a tooth.

Judgment Upright

When upright, the Judgment card's trumpet awakens you to a new phase of existence. Perhaps you are entering a period of rebirth and transformation that will require you to make an important decision. Having heard the call, are you ready to make the necessary changes and set out on the path of rejuvenation and renewal? Redemption requires the acceptance of responsibility for past behavior and a commitment to do things better next time.

Judgment Reversed

When reversed, the Judgment card suggests that you may not be heeding the call to wake up and change the direction of your life. If you reject this opportunity to become reanimated, you may end up stagnating and feel stuck in a rut. Perhaps your reluctance is due to fear of change, a sense of regret, or feelings of self-recrimination. Ponder the biblical verse: "Except a grain of wheat falls into the ground and dies, it abides alone: but if it dies, it brings forth much fruit" (John 12:24, King James 2000 Version).

21. The World: Paradise Regained

Key XXI: The World (the Universe)

Astrology: Saturn, the outermost visible planet. (Saturn rules Capricorn and Aquarius.) The four figures surrounding the central wreath in this card represent the four fixed signs of the zodiac: Taurus the bull, Leo the lion, Scorpio the scorpion and eagle, Aquarius the water bearer.

Element: Earth

Numerology: 3 (Empress) = 1 + 2 (Hanged Man) = 2 + 1 (the World)

Hebrew letter: *Tav, Tau,* or *Taw* (two sticks laid out in the shape of an X or the sign of a cross to mark a location; a Hebrew word meaning a cross, sign, scribble, limit, mark, signal, boundary, monument, covenant, or signature). This card marks the end of the Fool's journey: X marks the spot. The sign of the cross is also an important symbol in Christianity. A cross divides space into four quarters, symbolic of the four elements and the four fixed signs of the zodiac, which are depicted on the World card.

Myths/Archetypes: The Second Coming. The New Jerusalem. The Garden of Eden. Paradise Regained. The Sign of the Cross.

Mathers (1888): Completion, good reward; (R) evil reward, or recompense.

Waite (1911): Assured success, recompense, voyage, route, emigration, flight, change of place; (R) inertia, fixity, stagnation, permanence.

Golden Dawn: Synthesis, world, kingdom; the matter inquired about, hence what the World signifies will depend largely on the accompanying cards.

Keywords (+): Culmination, wholeness, completion, the end of the road, "X marks the spot," a successful outcome, fulfillment, reward, promotion, opportunity, a clearly defined goal, a trip, one's destiny, going for the gold, reaching one's destination, knowing your limits, paradise regained, a journey to a desired location, return to the Source.

Keywords (-): Lack of commitment, failure to pursue one's dream, aimlessness, stagnation, not establishing a goal, an unattainable ambition, weak boundaries, paradise lost.

> I, who e're while the happy Garden sung
> By one man's disobedience lost, now sing
> Recovered Paradise to all mankind,
> By one man's firm obedience fully tried
> Through all temptation, and the Tempter foiled
> In all his wiles, defeated and repulsed,
> And *Eden* raised in the vast Wilderness.
> (John Milton, *Paradise Regained*, 1671)

....

The World Upright

When upright, the World card highlights an important goal or destination in your life. You may be approaching the completion of a significant ambition or perhaps you are about to embark on a journey to achieve a cherished desire. In any case, you are dealing with a major stage in your development, and you will need all the resources at your disposal to bring matters to a successful conclusion. Just as Saturn, the last planet visible to the naked eye, marks the outermost visible boundary of the solar system, the World trump marks the end of the Fool's journey toward enlightenment. Arriving at this card is a sign of completion, enlightenment, and success. You are returning to the Garden of Eden.

....

The World Reversed

When reversed, the World card suggests that you are somehow hindered or delayed in your journey toward an important destination. Perhaps you are unaware of your own limits and have failed to set realistic goals. You need to examine and confront what is holding you back so that you can resume your forward movement. Will your current attitude or behavior result in expulsion from the Garden of Eden?

Eleven

The Numbered Pip Cards

The Suit of Wands

The Wands of the modern tarot owe their origin to the game of polo. As mentioned previously, the Egyptian Mamluk deck from which the tarot derived has four suits: cups, dinari (an ancient coin), scimitars, and polo sticks. The traditional Marseille deck retained the curved blades of the scimitars and called them swords. The Tarot of Marseille also replaced the Mamluk polo sticks with batons or wands, which were more familiar to European culture.

Polo, the exciting sport of kings, is a competitive fast-paced, high-energy activity that began as a war game some two thousand years ago. Its passionate enthusiasts refer to polo as "hockey on horseback." In a *60 Minutes* interview, polo superstar Nacho Figueras described the game as "war … you're trying to score more goals, to go faster and hit someone harder and do whatever it takes to win." [40] In the game of polo, winning isn't everything; it's the only thing. How typical of the suit of Wands!

In astrology, the suit of Wands is related to the "yang" group of active Fire signs (Aries, Leo, Sagittarius) as befits the phallic nature of the budding Wands. To get a sense of the archetypal nature of this symbol, review the following list of keywords for the Wands (Polo Sticks):

---

40. CBS News," The Sport of Kings: Polo" at www.youtube.com/watch?v = DAs2OQDuJNk, accessed 9 June 2014.

Fortitude	Enthusiasm	Boldness
The spark of life	Creativity	Bravery
Fast-paced enthusiasm	Excitement	Faith
Action	Impulse	Power
Enterprise	Animation	Growth
Ambition	Adventure	Career advancement
New business initiatives	Risk-taking	Dominion
Aspiration	Energetic activity	An overweening desire to win
Inspiration	Power and strength	Expanding one's horizons
Passion	Competitiveness	Going for the gold
Courage	Quarreling	*Per aspera ad astra* (through hardships to the stars)
Liveliness	Opposition	

A Suit of Wands Exercise

According to the Golden Dawn, several major arcana cards are associated with the element Fire and the suit of Wands. These include:

- The Sun, Trump XIX (the fiery star at the center of our solar system)

- The Emperor, Trump IV (the Fire sign Aries)

- Strength, Trump VIII or XI (the Fire sign Leo)

- Temperance, Trump XIV (the Fire sign Sagittarius)

- The Tower, Trump XVI (the fiery red planet Mars)

- Judgment, Trump XX (the element Fire)

Lay out these cards and note any qualities they have in common. Do they share any symbolism with a forest fire or a burning candle? Do they have anything in common with the game of polo? Repeat this exercise after you have studied the suit of Wands. Record your observations in your tarot notebook.

ACE OF WANDS: THE SPARK OF LIFE

Etteilla (1791): Birth, origin, source, first fruits; (R) decline, failure, bankruptcy.

Mathers (1888): Birth, commencement, beginning, origin, source; (R) persecution, pursuits, violence, vexation, cruelty, tyranny.

Waite (1911): A hand issuing from a cloud grasps a stout wand or club. *Divinatory Meanings*: Creation, invention, enterprise, the powers which result in these; principle, beginning, source; birth, family, origin, and in a sense the virility which is behind them; the starting point of enterprises;

according to another account, money, fortune, inheritance; (R) fall, decadence, ruin, perdition, to perish also a certain clouded joy.

Crowley/GD: Phallic solar energy. Strength, power, natural force, vigor, speed, energy. Natural force as distinct from the invoked force of the Ace of Swords.

Number Symbolism: 1—initial spark, will, creation, beginnings, new life.

Astrology: Root-force of Fire, the element associated with the season of spring.

Timing: Astrologically, Fire is linked to springtime.

Keywords (+): Birth, creation, inspiration, excitement, passion, initial spark, commencement, inception, new life, pregnancy, source, beginning, the seed of Fire, the sprouting of a seed, conception, self-actualization, career opportunities.

Keywords (-): Decline, weakening, false start, failure to ignite, lack of motivation, weakness, frustration, insufficient effort, barrenness, a seed that does not sprout.

In Llewellyn's Classic Tarot a hand emerging from a cloud on the left-hand side of the card holds a wooden staff upright in the light blue sky. The knuckles of the hand face the viewer. The cloud dips down and touches the surface of the water. The staff must have been carved recently from a living tree because fresh green leaves are sprouting along its length, symbols of vitality and new life. Beneath the staff is a country landscape of verdant pastures and trees in bloom. A river cuts through the scene on its way to a large body of water, perhaps a lake or the sea. A stony crag at the edge of the water supports a well-appointed castle overlooking the entire landscape.

Ace of Wands Upright

When upright, the Ace of Wands suggests new beginnings and promises success related to enterprise, ambition, identity formation, career, and self-realization. Your creative juices are flowing. You may be expanding your career, starting a new job, or initiating a business venture. This is a time characterized by enthusiasm, inventiveness, ambitious goals, and innovative projects. Wands are associated with the element Fire, the spark of life. This ace sometimes signals a pregnancy or the birth of a child. In the Prometheus myth, the fire this mythical figure steals from the gods signifies the awakening of the human mind.

Ace of Wands Reversed

When reversed, the Ace of Wands points to problems with starting something new. Perhaps you are lacking in motivation or your creative ideas seem to have dried up. Maybe you have gotten off to a bad start or you are not making the optimal kind of effort to get your project off the ground. You have planted some seeds but they are refusing to sprout. Your creative juices don't seem to be flowing, and you feel as if you are passing through a barren period. Keep in mind the words of the Sufi poet: "This too shall pass."

TWO OF WANDS: WHERE DO I GO FROM HERE?

Etteilla (1791): Dark thoughts, sorrow, distress, sadness, displeasure, melancholy; (R) fear, shock, domination, surprise, astonishment, unforeseen events, a miracle.

Mathers (1888): Riches, fortune, opulence, magnificence, grandeur; (R) surprise, astonishment, event, extraordinary occurrence.

Waite (1911): A tall man looks from a battlemented roof over sea and shore; he holds a globe in his right hand, while a staff in his left rests on the battlement; another is fixed in a ring. The Rose and Cross and Lily should be noticed on the left side. *Divinatory Meanings*: Between the alternative readings there is no marriage possible; on the one hand, riches, fortune, magnificence; on the other, physical suffering, disease, chagrin, sadness, mortification. The design gives one suggestion;

here is a lord overlooking his dominion and alternately contemplating a globe; it looks like the malady, the mortification, the sadness of Alexander amidst the grandeur of this world's wealth; (R) surprise, wonder, enchantment, emotion, trouble, fear.

Crowley/GD: Dominion, the will at its most exalted, influence over others, Fire in its highest form.

Number Symbolism: 2—duality, partnership, choice, decision, balance, gestation.

Astrology: The assertive and pioneering planet *Mars* (dignified) in the first decan of fiery *Aries* (the first ten days of spring); also the realm of the *Queen of Wands* (Water of Fire) and the *Emperor* (Aries). Mars is linked to the *Tower*. The fiery Queen of Wands gives birth to the season of spring at the beginning of Aries.

Timing: 0 Aries–10 Aries. Tropical, 20 March–30 March. Sidereal, 14 April–23 April

Keywords (+): Dominion, influence over others, the power to control things, confidence, choosing one's direction in life, planning for the future, effective use of one's will, envisioning future developments, astonishment, an important decision, trying to figure a way out of a difficult situation.

Keywords (-): Hesitation, sadness, displeasure, dark thoughts, an unexpected occurrence, risky behavior, feeling stuck.

Two of Wands Upright

When upright, the Two of Wands suggests that you are pondering a course of action or deciding on a future path your life will take. The young man on the card is contemplating a globe with a stance of self-assurance. Traditionally this card represented dark thoughts and sorrow. It reminds Waite of the sorrow of Alexander the Great amidst the grandeur of this world's wealth. Modern interpretations view the Two of Wands as a card of fortune, grandeur, dominion, and influence over others. Perhaps it encompasses both meanings simultaneously. You may feel a sense of sadness as you contemplate a potential future course of action. The number two is related to partnerships, collaboration, and making important choices, which usually involve a sense of loss in giving up something to pursue another goal that you desire.

Two of Wands Reversed

When reversed, the Two of Wands traditionally has meant surprise, a miracle, or an extraordinary occurrence. Something may take place that fills you with wonder and astonishment. On the other hand, the inversion of the Two of Wands can suggest that you may be having difficulty making an important decision about your future. Perhaps you are lacking sufficient confidence or feeling plagued by self-doubt about the best course of action. Problems with a partner may also be coming to the surface.

THREE OF WANDS: PUTTING YOUR DUCKS IN A ROW

Etteilla (1791): Enterprise, daring, audacity, start, effort; (R) repose, intermission, interruption of misfortunes, the end of worry.

Mathers (1888): Enterprise, undertaking, commerce, trade, negotiation; (R) hope, desire, attempt, wish.

Waite (1911): A calm, stately personage, with his back turned, looking from a cliff's edge at ships passing over the sea. Three staves are planted in the ground, and he leans slightly on one of them. *Divinatory Meanings*: Established strength, enterprise, effort, trade, commerce, discovery; those are his ships, bearing his merchandise, which are sailing over the sea; able cooperation in business, as if the successful merchant prince were looking from his side toward yours with a view to help you; (R) the end of troubles, suspension or cessation of adversity, toil, and disappointment.

Crowley/GD: Virtue, power, established strength, pride, arrogance.

Number Symbolism: 3—fertility, a creative environment, a triadic relationship, the first fruits of a joint venture.

Astrology: The mighty *Sun* (exalted) in the second decan of fiery *Aries*, realm of the *Queen of Wands* (Water of Fire) and the *Emperor* (Aries). The exaltation of the Sun in Aries enhances its power, virtue, pride and strength.

Timing: 10 Aries–20 Aries. Tropical, 30 March–9 April. Sidereal, 24 April–3 May

Keywords (+): Enterprise, foresight, cooperation in business, trade, commerce, launching a new venture, exploring possibilities, creating something new, awaiting results, maximizing chances of success, long-range planning, realistic goals, collaborating with others to pursue a goal, embarking on a new course of action, taking a calculated risk, the end of troubles, your ships departing or coming in.

Keywords (-): poor planning, lack of foresight, carelessness, arrogance, half-baked schemes, unrealistic goals, missed opportunities, false starts, foolish risks, lack of cooperation, unreliable partners, unsound advice, misguided effort, neglect, the need to reassess the situation.

Three of Wands Upright

When upright, the Three of Wands shows a man looking out to sea, watching his ships departing or coming in, perhaps carrying goods from a strategically planned business venture. This man and his partners, if he has any, have set realistic goals and acted with foresight. There is every expectation that this cooperative enterprise will succeed; but, to make sure, he is carefully overseeing each step of the process. When this card appears, you are given the green light to expand your horizons and plant the seeds for future success. The number 3 often refers to cooperative ventures, that is, to two or more people pooling their efforts over a period of time to create something new (for example, a married couple having a baby).

Three of Wands Reversed

When reversed, the Three of Wands suggests that something is holding you back from starting a new venture or from taking the proper steps for your future growth and development. Perhaps your goals are unrealistic, or the advice you have followed is unsound. Your efforts may have been careless or misguided. You need to reevaluate the situation and re-assess your skills and commitment as well as those of the people you have selected as associates. Have you planned optimally and created the proper structure to increase your chances for success?

FOUR OF WANDS: PERFECTING WORK THROUGH ALLIANCES

Etteilla (1791): Social success, association, community, alliance, agreement, pact, contract; (R) happiness, good fortune, increase, prosperity.

Mathers (1888): Society, union, association, concord, harmony; (R) prosperity, success, happiness, advantage.

Waite (1911): From four great staves planted in the foreground there is a great garland suspended; two female figures uplift nosegays; at their side is a bridge over a moat, leading to an old manorial house. *Divinatory Meanings*: Country life, haven of refuge, a species of domestic harvest-home, repose, concord, harmony, prosperity, peace, and the perfected work of these; (R) prosperity, increase, felicity, beauty, embellishment.

Crowley/GD: Completion, perfected work, settlement.

Number Symbolism: 4—structure, stability, building, order, foundation, manifestation.

Astrology: Lovely and affectionate *Venus* (debilitated) in the third decan of fiery *Aries*, realm of the Waite *King*/Thoth *Prince of Pentacles* (Air of Earth) and the *Emperor* (Aries). Venus is linked to the *Empress*.

Timing: 20 Aries–30 Aries. Tropical, 9 April–19 April. Sidereal, 4 May–13 May.

Keywords (+): Establishing security and structure, settling down, a harvest-home, concord, harmony, peace, happiness, joy, shelter, prosperity, successful completion, a traditional ceremony, a rite of passage, a significant step in personal development, perfected work, joint venture, working in alliance with others, a job well done, rest after labor, a haven of refuge.

Keywords (-): Delay in completing a task, unrealized goals, worry about getting the job done, more work is required, no rest for the weary.

....
Four of Wands Upright

When upright, the Four of Wands suggests that you are establishing a firm foundation as you manifest the results of your work. If you have been involved in a project, you are now at a stage of completion and able to rest and enjoy the fruits of your labors. If your question concerns a relationship or business partnership, it is on a firm footing. This card often represents rites of passage such as weddings, births, bar mitzvahs, graduations, etc. The symbolism of a harvest-home is linked to the possibility of purchasing a dwelling or moving to a new residence.

....
Four of Wands Reversed

When reversed, the Four of Wands hints at interruptions in completing a project or committing to a relationship. An offer on a house you were hoping to buy may not be accepted. An important goal may go unrealized, as you learn that more work is required to make it a reality. Rather than preoccupying yourself with worry, put your effort into getting the job done. This is generally a positive card, and any delays are likely to be short-lived.

FIVE OF WANDS: RICH KIDS PLAYING WAR GAMES

Etteilla (1791): Riches, affluence, gold, splendor, abundance, luxury, brilliance; (R) disputes, annoyances, legal proceedings, wrangles, harassment, opposition, litigation, court case.

Mathers (1888): Gold, opulence, gain, heritage, riches, fortune, money; (R) legal proceedings, judgment, law, lawyer, tribunal.

Waite (1911): A posse of youths, who are brandishing staves, as if in sport or strife. It is mimic warfare, and hereto correspond the *Divinatory Meanings*: Imitation, as, for example, sham fight, but also the strenuous competition and struggle of the search after riches and fortune. In this sense it connects with the battle of life. Hence some attributions say that it is a card of gold, gain, opulence; (R) litigation, disputes, trickery, contradiction.

Crowley/GD: Strife, quarrels, fights, the element Fire burdened and embittered by Saturn.

Number Symbolism: 5—instability, disruption, loss, crisis, tension, competition, conflict.

Astrology: The stern taskmaster *Saturn* (debilitated) in the first decan of fiery *Leo*, realm of the Waite *King*/Thoth *Prince of Wands* (Air of Fire) and *Strength* (Leo). Saturn is linked to the *World*. The Golden Dawn regarded this decan as the beginning of the zodiac.

Timing: 0 Leo–10 Leo. Tropical, 23 July–2 August. Sidereal, 18 August–26 August.

Keywords (+): Competition, assertiveness, friendly disagreement, disparate interests, conflicting ambitions, a lovers' quarrel, rivalry, mock battle, celebrating diversity, confrontation, testing your mettle, fighting for what you want, successful speculation, luxury, affluence, diversity, pursuing your desires, engaging with peers in the game of life.

Keywords (-): Quarrels, strife, disputes, disagreements, harassment, annoyances, litigation, trickery, hostile competition, unfair aggression, blocked efforts.

Five of Wands Upright

When upright, the Five of Wands is a card of competition. It suggests that you are assertively pursuing your desires, even though your personal interests may conflict with those of your colleagues. You are willing to compete fairly and enthusiastically with your rivals to achieve your goals. This card advises you to "put your pedal to the metal" as you engage in the game of life. A mock battle can prepare you for the real thing. Allowing for diversity of opinions is a sign of strength in a relationship. Traditionally this is a card of riches and opulence; perhaps only the affluent could afford the expensive outfits and leisure time to play at the mock battles depicted on this card.

Five of Wands Reversed

When reversed, the Five of Wands warns of being ambushed or unfairly attacked by your adversaries. Be sure you have the proper resources before engaging in battle. You may need to confront disputes, strife, quarrels, and unfair competition to achieve your goals. A divergence of opinions may be causing difficulty in a relationship. Sometimes this card indicates the need to settle differences in a court of law.

SIX OF WANDS: LEADER OF THE PACK

Etteilla (1791): Housework, domestic workers, servants, attendants, messengers; (R) hope, trust, confidence, expectation, foresight, apprehension.

Mathers (1888): Attempt, hope, desire, wish, expectation; (R) infidelity, treachery, disloyalty, perfidy.

Waite (1911): A laurelled horseman bears one staff adorned with a laurel crown; footmen with staves are at his side. *Divinatory Meanings*: A victor triumphing; also great news, such as might be carried in state by the king's courier; expectation crowned with its own desire, the crown of hope, and so forth; (R) apprehension, fear, as of a victorious enemy at the gate; treachery, disloyalty, as of gates being opened to the enemy; indefinite delay.

Crowley/GD: Victory, gain, triumph, success.

Number Symbolism: 6—harmony, communication, sharing, compassion.

Astrology: The expansive benefic *Jupiter* in the second decan of fiery *Leo*, realm of the Waite *King*/Thoth *Prince of Wands* (Air of Fire) and *Strength* (Leo). Jupiter is linked to the *Wheel of Fortune*.

Timing: 10 Leo–20 Leo. Tropical, 3 August–12 August. Sidereal, 27 August–5 September.

Keywords (+): Success, victory, triumph, gain, overcoming obstacles, achieving goals, great news, popularity, leadership, honors, recognition; getting housework done.

Keywords (-): Vanity, false pride, resting on one's laurels, undeserved recognition, apprehension, temporary setback, facing challenges, defeat.

Six of Wands Upright

Kudos! When upright, the Six of Wands is a card of accomplishment, recognition, honors, and victory. You are rewarded for a job well done, even if it's just cleaning the house, and can enjoy the fruits of your labors. Creative energy and the cooperation of others are available to help you to advance and accomplish your goals. Great news may be on its way. In Etteilla's day, this card implied dealings with messengers, housework, and domestic workers.

Six of Wands Reversed

When reversed, the Six of Wands can quite literally depict resting on one's laurels. You may have to struggle to enlist the cooperation and goodwill of others. Any honors or recognition you receive may be undeserved. You may be facing a temporary setback in which your creativity feels blocked. Facing this challenge can be a journey in self-discovery.

SEVEN OF WANDS: SPEAKING FROM A BULLY PULPIT

Etteilla (1791): Conversation, discourse, an interview, communications, negotiation, commerce, the use of words; (R) uncertainty, indecision, wavering, fickleness, hesitation, vacillation.

Mathers (1888): Success, gain, advantage, profit, victory; (R) indecision, doubt, hesitation, embarrassment, anxiety.

Waite (1911): A young man on a craggy eminence brandishing a staff; six other staves are raised toward him from below. *Divinatory Meanings*: Valor, for six are attacking one, who has, however, the vantage position. On the intellectual plane, it signifies discussion, wordy strife; in business—negotiations, war of trade, barter, competition. It is further a card of success, for the combatant is on the top and his enemies may be unable to reach him; (R) perplexity, embarrassments, anxiety, a caution against indecision.

Crowley/GD: Valor, bravery, courage in the face of opposition.

Astrology: Brave and warlike *Mars* in the third decan of fiery *Leo*, realm of the *Knight of Pentacles* (Fire of Earth) and *Strength* (Leo). Mars is linked to the *Tower*.

Number Symbolism: 7—assessment, reflection, reevaluation, standing at a threshold, seeking advantage.

Timing: 20 Leo–30 Leo. Tropical, 13 August–22 August. Sidereal, 6 September–16 September.

Keywords (+): A position of advantage, bravery, valor, success, courage in the face of danger, self-defense, standing one's ground, speaking out assertively, stating one's position, seeking to be at the top of the heap, a bully pulpit, decisive action, determination, striving for advantage, overcoming the odds, discussion, negotiation, oratory, interviews, the use of words.

Keywords (-): Worry, consternation, embarrassment, vacillation, hesitancy, indecision, anxiety, perplexity, doubt, threats, opposition to one's efforts, feeling attacked.

Seven of Wands Upright

When upright, the Seven of Wands suggests that you need to stand your ground and assertively articulate your position. Challenges may be coming at you from several directions, but you have the courage to defend yourself and overcome the odds. Success is possible despite the competing forces confronting. There may be profit or advantage in negotiation, barter, and discourse with your adversaries. You excel at the skillful use of the written and spoken word.

Seven of Wands Reversed

When reversed, the Seven of Wands warns of vacillation and hesitancy in standing up for what you believe in. The opposition you face may be causing an uncomfortable level of anxiety. Fierce competition may be filling you with uncertainty and self-doubt. Feeling under attack, you may be too timid or embarrassed to assert your position forcefully.

EIGHT OF WANDS: FLYING WITH HASTE OVER THE COUNTRYSIDE

Etteilla (1791): Countryside, rural life, landed property, farm, garden, tranquility, sport, festivities, merrymaking; (R) uncertainty, doubt, remorse, repentance, argument, inner agitation.

Mathers (1888): Understanding, observation, direction; (R) quarrels, domestic strife, internal disputes, discord, a troubled conscience.

Waite (1911): The card represents motion through the immovable—a flight of wands through an open country; but they draw to the term of their course. That which they signify is at hand; it may be even on the threshold. *Divinatory Meanings*: Activity in undertakings, the path of such activity, swiftness, as that of an express messenger; great haste, great hope, speed toward an end which promises assured felicity; generally, that which is on the move; also the arrows of love; (R) arrows of jealousy, internal dispute, stingings of conscience, quarrels; and domestic disputes for persons who are married.

Crowley/GD: Swiftness, speed, high velocity, rapid thought, hasty communication.

Number Symbolism: 8—movement, action, power, determination.

Astrology: Quick and clever *Mercury* (debilitated) in the first decan of fiery *Sagittarius*, realm of the *Knight of Wands* (Fire of Fire) and *Temperance* (Sagittarius). Mercury is linked to the *Magician*.

Timing: 0 Sagittarius–10 Sagittarius. Tropical, 23 November–2 December. Sidereal, 16 December–24 December.

Keywords (+): Swiftness, great haste, rapid progress, controlled acceleration, sport, enthusiasm, speeding toward a goal, the end of delay, confidence, quick thinking, rapid transfer of information, inspirational ideas, news from afar, an express messenger, contact with foreigners or people at a distance, Cupid's arrow, love letters, flight, travel by air, rapid transit, a visit to the countryside.

Keywords (-): Doubt, hesitation, travel difficulties, a disrupted flight, delayed messages, haste makes waste, precipitous action, taking unnecessary risks, feeling up in the air, uncontrolled acceleration, the stings of conscience.

Eight of Wands Upright

When upright, the Eight of Wands signifies swiftness in thought and deed. You are able to progress rapidly in a controlled and thoughtful manner. Your enthusiasm and confidence propel you forward. Your quick thinking and readiness to act decisively augur success in your endeavors. Messages and information pass quickly to and fro. This is one of the "travel" cards of the tarot, suggesting that a journey or plane flight may be in the offing. Time spent in the countryside can be pleasant and refreshing. The flying wands on this card also symbolize Cupid's arrows and may mean being smitten by love.

Eight of Wands Reversed

When reversed, the Eight of Wands warns that "haste makes waste." You may be moving too quickly in a risky or uncontrolled fashion. Alternatively you may be plagued by doubts and hesitation and thus unable to proceed at a proper pace. Be sure to consider the potential consequences of your actions before rushing ahead impulsively. Is it wise to be in such a hurry to get things done? Travel plans may be disrupted or delayed. A love affair may take an unexpected turn.

NINE OF WANDS: FIGHTING THE GOOD FIGHT

Etteilla (1791): Hindrance, suspension, deferral, slowing down, delay, separation, sending back; (R) opposition, disadvantage, adversity, obstacles, unhappiness, misfortune.

Mathers (1888): Order, discipline, good arrangement, disposition; (R) obstacles, crosses, delay, displeasure.

Waite (1911): The figure leans upon his staff and has an expectant look, as if awaiting an enemy. Behind are eight other staves—erect, in orderly disposition, like a palisade. *Divinatory Meanings*: Strength in opposition. If attacked, the person will meet an onslaught boldly; and his build shews that he may prove a formidable antagonist. With this main significance there are all its possible adjuncts—delay, suspension, adjournment; (R) obstacles, adversity, calamity.

Crowley/GD: Great strength, power, energy, health, a change in stability.

Number Symbolism: 9—the final single digit, culmination, fruition, attainment.

Astrology: The emotional and sensitive *Moon* in the second decan of fiery *Sagittarius*, realm of the *Knight of Wands* (Fire of Fire) and *Temperance* (Sagittarius). The Moon is linked to the *High Priestess*.

Timing: 10 Sagittarius–20 Sagittarius. Tropical, 3 December–12 December. Sidereal, 25 December–3 January.

Keywords (+): Strength in opposition, order, discipline, preparedness, endurance, resilience, caution, self-determination, bodily health, resourcefulness, facing challenge, taking the initiative, going it alone, Herculean effort, deciding to suspend a course of action, choosing one among many options.

Keywords (-): Obstacles, disadvantages, hindrances, opposition, isolation, adversity, inflexibility, weariness, bodily weakness, exhaustion, lack of preparedness, overwhelming odds, delay, sending back.

Nine of Wands Upright

When upright, the wounded warrior on this card must muster the courage to face another challenge and defend himself against his adversaries. His strength, fitness, and self-determination has gotten him this far, and he may need to go the rest of the way alone. Although the odds against succeeding may appear overwhelming, he is well-prepared for the oncoming attack. The warrior knows that he must make careful choices and call on all his inner resources. Such persistence, in the face of difficulties and delays, is necessary if there is to be victory. Should the outcome be defeat, the warrior will know that he fought honorably and with distinction. Sometimes an exit strategy is the wisest course of action.

Nine of Wands Reversed

When reversed, this card suggests that the querent is acting at a disadvantage. He or she may be ill-prepared and feel like giving up in the face of obstacles, perhaps feeling isolated, overwhelmed, or exhausted by circumstances. A rigid or inflexible approach to the problem is not likely to succeed. Sometimes you have to admit that a challenge is insurmountable or that you have taken on more than you can chew; in such a case, the best course of action is to accept that you are not up to the task and move on to something new.

TEN OF WANDS: WEIGHTED DOWN

Etteilla (1791): Lies, deceit, falsehood, duplicity, betrayal, treason, conspiracy; (R) hindrances, obstacles, travail, toil, objection.

Mathers (1888): Confidence, security, honor, good faith; (R) treachery, subterfuge, duplicity, bar.

Waite (1911): A man oppressed by the weight of the ten staves he is carrying. *Divinatory Meanings*: The chief meaning is oppression simply, but it is also fortune, gain, any kind of success, and then it is the oppression of these things. It is also a card of false-seeming, disguise, perfidy. The place which the figure is approaching may suffer from the rods that he carries. Success is stultified if the Nine of Swords follows, and if it is a question of a lawsuit, there will be certain loss; (R) contrarieties, difficulties, intrigues, and their analogies.

Crowley/GD: Oppression, cruelty, malice, injustice, revenge, overbearing strength.

Number Symbolism: 10—one too many, the fullness of completion, readiness to begin a new cycle.

Astrology: The stern taskmaster *Saturn* in the third decan of fiery *Sagittarius*, realm of the *Queen of Pentacles* (Water of Earth) and *Temperance* (Sagittarius). Saturn is linked to the *World*.

Timing: 20 Sagittarius–30 Sagittarius. Tropical, 13 December–23 December. Sidereal, 4 January–13 January.

Keywords (+): Willingness to take on a heavy load, carrying the weight of success, a sense of responsibility, ability to delegate, sharing the workload with others, accepting support.

Keywords (-): An oppressive burden, lies, deceit, obstacles, difficulties, feeling overwhelmed, injustice, falsehood, inability to delegate, workaholism, over-commitment, carrying the weight of the world on your shoulders, the straw that broke the camel's back.

Ten of Wands Upright

When upright, the Ten of Wands suggests that you have worked hard and have achieved a great deal, but now your success is weighing you down. Your sense of duty and your willingness to shoulder obligations have been assets along the way, but the time has come to delegate and share the load. Make sure that the burden you carry is not the result of deceit or falsehood. Your commitment to a job well done is admirable, but there are others who are now willing to share the responsibility for the future outcome. You need to lighten up; otherwise your workaholism will take a toll in other areas of your life.

Ten of Wands Reversed

When reversed, the Ten of Wands implies an inability to delegate and an undue sense of responsibility for all aspects of a project. Others may be taking advantage of your willingness to do everything yourself. It's time that they stepped up to the plate and pulled their fair load. If you don't trust your colleagues to participate fairly, perhaps you should not be working with them. Consider the proverb, "All work and no play makes Jack a dull boy and Jill a dull girl."

The Suit of Cups

You typically find cups on the scene when people gather to share a meal or have a good time. Chalices are goblets traditionally used in the Catholic Mass to celebrate the sacrifice of Christ, who gave up his life out of love for humanity. In ordinary life, people use chalices as goblets for the consumption of wine. The theme that runs through these uses of cups is celebration, socializing, and human interconnectedness. It would be difficult to "eat, drink, and be merry" if chalices were not available.

In astrology, the suit of Cups is related to the inner-directed "yin" group of Water signs (Cancer, Scorpio, Pisces) as befits the receptive nature of the chalices of the tarot. To get a sense of the archetypal nature of this tarot symbol, review the following list of keywords for the suit of Cups (Chalices):

Temperance	Sharing	Fantasy
Love	Healing	Dreams
Joy	Empathy	Looking inward
Pleasure	Grace	Intuition
Merriment	Compassion	Contentment
Romance	Concern for others	Touchy-feely issues
Feelings	Relationships	Matters of the heart
Moods	Fertility	Spiritual attunement
Emotions	Celebration	Psychic awareness
Marriage	Good times	Emotional intelligence
Caring	Human connectedness	
Nurturing	Creative imagination	

A Suit of Cups Exercise

According to the Golden Dawn, several major arcana are associated with the element Water and the watery suit of Cups. These include:

- The High Priestess, Trump II (the watery Moon)
- The Chariot, Trump IX (the Water sign Cancer)
- Death, Trump XIII (the Water sign Scorpio)
- The Moon, Trump XVIII (the Water sign Pisces)
- The Hanged Man, Trump XII (the element Water)

Lay out these cards and note any qualities they have in common. Do they share any symbolism with a body of running water? Repeat this exercise after you have studied the suit of Cups. Record your observations in your tarot notebook.

ACE OF CUPS: EAT, DRINK, AND BE MERRY AS LOVE BLOSSOMS

Etteilla (1791): A table, a meal, feast, treat, reception, hosting, an inn, abundance, fertility; (R) inconstancy, weakness, diversity, changeability.

Mathers (1888): Feasting, banquet, good cheer; (R) change, novelty, metamorphosis, inconstancy.

Waite (1911): The waters are beneath, and thereon are water-lilies; the hand issues from the cloud, holding in its palm the cup, from which four streams are pouring; a dove, bearing in its bill a cross-marked Host, descends to place the Wafer in the Cup; the dew of water is falling on all sides. It is an intimation of that which may lie behind the Lesser Arcana. *Divinatory Meanings*: House of the true heart, joy, content, abode, nourishment, abundance, fertility; Holy Table, felicity hereof; (R) house of the false heart, mutation, instability, revolution, unexpected change of position.

Crowley/GD: The receptive feminine counterpart of the phallic Ace of Wands. Union with God. The Supernal Mother: fertility, pleasure, productivity, elegance, happiness.

Number Symbolism: 1—initial spark, will, creation, beginnings, new life.

Astrology: Root-force of elemental Water, the element associated with the season of summer.

Timing: Astrologically, Water is linked to summertime.

Keywords (+): Pleasure, feasting, enjoyment, love, friendship, receptivity, fulfillment, fertility, pregnancy, nurturing, healing, creative inspiration, a new relationship, the beginning of romance, good cheer; "eat, drink, and be merry."

Keywords (-): Instability, changeability, excess, infertility, loneliness, inconstancy, dissatisfaction, inadequate nourishment.

In Llewellyn's *Classic Tarot,* a hand comes out of a cloud on the right-hand side of the card, holding a chalice upright in the light blue sky. Of the four Aces in the Classic Tarot, only the Ace of Cups is offered by a hand emerging from the right-hand side of the card. Inside this chalice sits a dove bearing an olive branch, a symbol of peace. Water overflows the brim of the chalice creating five streams pouring into the body of water below, on whose surface rest five lotus blossoms. In Christian symbolism, the dove represents the Holy Spirit sent by God the Father as a symbol of divine love after the sacrifice of Christ on the cross to save humankind. The five streams and five lotus blossoms—symbols of redemption through sacrifice—are a reference to the five wounds Christ endured during his crucifixion. The Catholic Mass still makes use of the chalice to commemorate this event. There is a noticeable absence of dry land in the image on this card, as water and clouds dominate the scene.

....

Ace of Cups Upright

When upright, the Ace of Cups suggests new beginnings in your emotional life. You are experiencing a period of joy, contentment, camaraderie, feasting, affection, and creativity. Love and fertility are in the air. It is possible to deepen a current relationship or to start a new friendship or love interest. Artists find themselves full of creative ideas. The nurturing waters of the Ace of Cups represent a fertile time, able to produce offspring of the body or the mind. Moving spiritual experiences and opportunities for compassion also accompany this card.

....
Ace of Cups Reversed

When reversed, the watery Ace of Cups hints at delays or difficulties in beginning a new love relationship or initiating a creative project. This can result in a sense of dissatisfaction, instability, and loneliness. Some type of overabundance in the boundlessness of the element Water may be interfering with your ability to focus. Water is a necessary element for life and continued growth, but the myth of Noah and the Great Flood teaches us that an excess of water can act as a destructive force.

TWO OF CUPS: SOUL MATES FALLING IN LOVE

Etteilla (1791): Love, affection, attraction, friendship; (R) lust, passion, desire, sensuality, jealousy.

Mathers (1888): Love, attachment, friendship, sincerity, affection; (R) crossed desires, obstacles, opposition, hindrance.

Waite (1911): A youth and maiden are pledging one another, and above their cups rises the caduceus of Hermes, between the great wings of which there appears a lion's head. *Divinatory Meanings:* Love, passion, friendship, affinity, union, concord, sympathy, the interrelation of the sexes, and—as a suggestion apart from all offices of divination—that desire which is not in nature, but by which nature is sanctified; (R) favorable in things of pleasure and business, as well as love, passion, wealth, and honor.

Crowley/GD: Love, marriage, joy, pleasure, harmony, warm friendship.

Number Symbolism: 2—duality, partnership, choice, decision, balance, gestation.

Astrology: Affectionate *Venus* in the first decan of watery *Cancer*, realm of the lovely *Queen of Cups* (Water of Water) and the *Chariot* (Cancer). Venus is linked to the *Empress*. The watery Queen of Cups gives birth to the season of summer at the start of Cancer.

Timing: 0 Cancer–10 Cancer. Tropical, 21 June–1 July. Sidereal, 16 July–26 July.

Keywords (+): Affection, sexual attraction, falling in love, union, intermingling, harmony, affinity, intimacy, friendliness, cooperation, reconciliation, companionship, finding one's soulmate.

Keywords (-): Disaffection, false friendship, disharmony, unrequited love, lack of commitment, the inability to reconcile differences, lack of sexual attraction.

Two of Cups Upright

When upright, the Two of Cups suggests involvement in a positive personal relationship with someone. A friendship, business partnership, or love interest may be forming. You genuinely like the other person and they, in turn, enjoy your company and want to form a closer tie. Such a relationship is likely to be mutually beneficial. If you've been having difficulties in a relationship, you will have an opportunity for reconciliation. The healing waters of Cups can bring positive changes to your life and inspire creative self-expression. The two snakes coiled around the rod of Hermes represent the mingling together of the two partners. The winged lion's head refers to the sign Leo and the fifth astrological house, which has to do with pregnancy, romance, fun, sexual pleasure, and creative activities.

Two of Cups Reversed

When reversed, the Two of Cups implies that you might be having difficulty with a friendship or romantic interest. It may be that the close bond you thought existed was really a false friendship or that the other person does not truly have your best interests at heart. There appears to be some sort of lack of commitment to the relationship. If you are unable to resolve the disharmony, it could result in estrangement or the dissolution of a relationship. In terms of romance, it may be that sexual attraction between the partners is simply lacking. There is no point continuing to pursue someone if the only response you get is disinterest or unrequited love. A relationship based on sex without love and mutual respect is doomed to failure.

THREE OF CUPS: HAPPY CELEBRATION

Etteilla (1791): Solace, relief, cure, success, healing, victory, perfection, happy outcome; (R) daily work, expedience, accomplishment, dispatch, termination.

Mathers (1888): Success, triumph, victory, favorable issue; (R) expedition of business, quickness, celerity, vigilance.

Waite (1911): Maidens in a garden-ground with cups uplifted, as if pledging one another. *Divinatory Meanings*: The conclusion of any matter in plenty, perfection, and merriment; happy issue, victory, fulfillment, solace, healing; (R) expedition, dispatch, achievement, end; excess in physical enjoyment, and the pleasures of the senses.

Crowley/GD: Abundance, plenty, merriment, abounding joy, pleasure, new clothes.

Number Symbolism: 3—fertility, creativity, a triadic relationship, the first fruits of a joint venture.

Astrology: Quick and clever *Mercury* in the second decan of watery Cancer also the realm of the *Queen of Cups* (Water of Water) and the *Chariot* (Cancer). Mercury is linked to the *Magician*.

Timing: 10 Cancer–20 Cancer. Tropical, 2 July–11 July. Sidereal, 27 July–5 August.

Keywords (+): Happy times, joyous celebration, a fortunate outcome, friendship, sensual pleasures, merriment, partying, exuberance, healing, creativity, favorable issue, fulfillment, a good harvest, showing gratitude for abundance, enjoying material goods.

Keywords (-): Excess sensuality, overindulgence, excess, overspending, selfishness, triangular love relationships, marital difficulties.

....
Three of Cups Upright

When upright, the Three of Cups depicts three friendly individuals in a happy celebration, perhaps of a good harvest. It is a time of happiness, success, favorable issue, and abundance. Why are the maidens rejoicing? Perhaps they have received good news about a project, a promotion, recovering from illness, an engagement, a wedding, or the birth of a child. Their creative juices are flowing. The harvest has been abundant and they know how to have a good time.

....
Three of Cups Reversed

When reversed, the Three of Cups suggests overindulgence in merriment. Rather than enjoying their good fortune, the individuals on the card may be selfishly exploiting the situation and getting on each other's nerves. There is a sense of excess or too much of a good thing. Perhaps they are behaving like party animals. If the querent inquired about a relationship, then difficulties with a partner or marital strife may be indicated.

FOUR OF CUPS: MISSED OPPORTUNITY, WEARINESS, AND DISCONTENT

Etteilla (1791): Ennui, boredom, discontent, worry, disquiet; (R) novelty, new instruction, prediction, prescience, premonition, setbacks.

Mathers (1888): Ennui, displeasure, discontent, dissatisfaction; (R) new acquaintance, conjecture, sign, presentiment.

Waite (1911): A young man is seated under a tree and contemplates three cups set on the grass before him; an arm issuing from a cloud offers him another cup. His expression notwithstanding is one of discontent with his environment. *Divinatory Meanings*: Weariness, disgust, aversion, imaginary vexations, as if the wine of this world had caused satiety only; another wine, as if a fairy gift, is now offered the wastrel, but he sees no consolation therein; also a card of blended pleasure; (R) novelty, presage, new instruction, new relations, presentiment.

Crowley/GD: Luxury, blended pleasure, new goals, the kindness of others, new relationships, awakening after contemplation.

Number Symbolism: 4—structure, stability, order, logic, foundation, manifestation.

Astrology: The emotional and inconstant *Moon* (dignified) in the third decan of watery *Cancer*, realm of the Waite *King*/Thoth *Prince of Wands* (Air of Earth) and the *Chariot* (Cancer). The Moon is linked to the *High Priestess*.

Timing: 20 Cancer–30 Cancer. Tropical, 12 July–21 July. Sidereal, 6 August–17 August.

Keywords (+): Ennui, reflection, blended pleasure, anticipation, presage, premonition, novelty, new instruction, fresh possibilities, new goals, the need to wait for a desired outcome to manifest.

Keywords (-): Disquiet, feeling unfulfilled, dissatisfaction, weariness, discontent, a missed opportunity, indifference, satiety, cloying of appetites, boredom, disenchantment, stagnation, apathy, lethargy, self-pity, depression, imaginary vexation, lack of motivation, feeling stuck in a rut, problems with health.

Four of Cups Upright

When upright, the Four of Cups suggests that you are going through a period of discontent, apathy, stagnation, and dissatisfaction. The pleasures of life just don't seem to perk you up. You may feel unfulfilled, as if something essential were missing from your life. Perhaps you are suffering from depression or wallowing in self-pity. You feel stuck in a rut as you focus on the glass being half empty. You need to confront your imaginary vexations and find a way to motivate yourself to move forward. Are you focusing on the cloud rather than its silver lining? Take advantage of the gifts and opportunities that surround you. This card's association with the Moon suggests that you may need to wait until the proper moment in the cyclic to achieve your goal. The phases of the Moon are a reminder that "to every thing there is a season, and a time to every purpose under the heaven" (Eccleisates 3, KJV).

Four of Cups Reversed

When reversed, the Four of Cups points to novelty and fresh possibilities entering your life. These may take the form of new acquaintances, new learning, or the setting of new goals for yourself. The inverted Four of Cups may also herald the experience of presentiments, premonitions, and accurate hunches, so keep open to gut feelings and signs from the universe thatmay signal new paths to fulfillment.

FIVE OF CUPS: EVERY CLOUD HAS A SILVER LINING

Etteilla (1791): Heritage, patrimony, transmission, tradition, bequest, gift, donation, inheritance, legacy, resolution; (R) kin, relatives, family, consanguinity, ancestry, marriage, alliance, rapport.

Mathers (1888): Union, junction, marriage, inheritance; (R) arrival, return, news, surprise, false projects.

Waite (1911): A dark cloaked figure looking sideways at three prone cups; two others stand upright behind him; a bridge is in the background, leading to a small keep or holding. *Divinatory Meanings*: A card of loss, but something remains over; three have been taken, but two are left; it is a card of inheritance, patrimony, transmission, but not corresponding to expectations; with some interpreters it is a card of marriage, but not without bitterness or frustration; (R) news, alliances, affinity, consanguinity, ancestry, return, false projects.

Crowley/GD: Disappointment, loss in pleasure, separation, worry, a breakup, loss of friendship, unkindness from friends, onset of illness.

Number Symbolism: 5—instability, disruption, loss, crisis, tension, competition, conflict.

Astrology: Assertive and warlike *Mars* (dignified) in the first decan of watery *Scorpio*, realm of the Waite *King*/Thoth *Prince of Cups* (Air of Water) and *Death* (Scorpio). Mars is linked to the *Tower*.

Timing: 0 Scorpio–10 Scorpio. Tropical, 23 October–2 November. Sidereal, 16 November–24 November.

Keywords (+): Loss with something remaining, good news mixed with bad, finding emotional fulfillment within, renewal of a relationship, ancestry, hope in the midst of apparent defeat, a gift or inheritance that does not meet expectations.

Keywords (-): Regret, sorrow, remorse, separation, dejection, feelings of emptiness, disappointment in love, loneliness, possible onset of illness.

....
Five of Cups Upright

When upright, the Five of Cups depicts a scene of emotional disappointment. You are likely to have suffered a loss and to be focusing on the three overturned cups that have spilled their contents rather than on the two full cups that remain standing. Even though you feel dejected because of a separation or breakup, some hope of fulfillment remains. Sometimes your emotional fulfillment will need to come from within rather than from another person. Are you crying over spilt milk? Traditionally this card also stands for a gift or inheritance, but one that does not live up to your hopes and expectations. Though it may sound trite, remember that every dark cloud has a silver lining.

....
Five of Cups Reversed

When reversed, the Five of Cups suggests that you need to adopt a different perspective in order to find the good in the situation. Even though you have suffered a loss, hope remains if you will only look for it. Two of the cups remain standing, having not spilled their contents. You may be able to salvage a relationship you thought was irretrievably lost, or perhaps a new relationship will enter your life to dispel these feelings of emptiness. A gift or inheritance may be better than anticipated. News of someone's return may reach you. Remember the words of Alexander Pope: "Hope springs eternal in the human breast."

SIX OF CUPS: REMEMBRANCE OF THINGS PAST

Etteilla (1791): Then! The past, formerly, in the past; age, antiquity, times gone by, decrepitude; (R) the future, in the future, yet to come, renewal, advent, reproduction, regeneration.

Mathers (1888): The past, passed by, faded, vanished, disappeared; (R) the future, that which is to come; shortly, soon.

Waite (1911): Children in an old garden, their cups filled with flowers. *Divinatory Meanings*: A card of the past and of memories, looking back, as—for example—on childhood; happiness, enjoyment, but coming rather from the past; things that have vanished. Another reading reverses this, giving new relations, new knowledge, new environment, and then the children are disporting in an unfamiliar precinct; (R) the future, renewal, that which will come to pass presently.

Crowley/GD: Pleasure, harmony, well-being, enjoyment, sexual satisfaction.

Number Symbolism: 6—harmony, communication, sharing, compassion.

Astrology: The mighty *Sun* in the second decan of watery *Scorpio*, realm of the Waite *King*/Thoth *Prince of Cups* (Air of Water) and *Death* (Scorpio).

Timing: 10 Scorpio–20 Scorpio. Tropical, 3 November–12 November. Sidereal, 26 November–5 December.

Keywords (+): In the past, happy memories, nostalgia, longing, reunion, harmony, pleasure, enjoyment, betterment, gift giving, old friends, renewal of old relationships, a blast from the past. Traditionally the Six of Cups meant "in the past" and the Six of Coins referred to "in the now"—we tend to reminisce about the good old days when we sip wine from a cup. The reversed Six of Cups traditionally meant "in the future"—perhaps because the inverted cups do not yet hold the wine we will drink at a future time. These traditional "past-present-future" meanings derive from the fortune-telling history of the tarot.

Keywords (-): In the future, yet to come; also, clinging to the past, not letting go of an old relationship, wallowing in past hurts, retreating into nostalgia.

Six of Cups Upright: In the Past

When upright, the nostalgic Six of Cups refers to pleasant memories and enjoyable relationships returning from the past. It can herald a friendly reunion or the revival of a former friendship or love interest. You may find yourself exchanging gifts or sharing sexual pleasures with someone you care about. This is a card of joy, harmony, and satisfaction. Traditionally it is a marker of things past.

Six of Cups Reversed: Yet to Come

When reversed, the Six of Cups can refer to things that will happen shortly or at some unspecified time in the future. This card can also indicate a desire to take refuge in pleasant memories of past pleasures rather than facing your current situation. Nostalgia can become a form of escapism. For some reason you may be having difficulty experiencing joy and satisfaction in your life at this time.

SEVEN OF CUPS: REFLECTIONS IN THE POOL OF CONTEMPLATION

Etteilla (1791): Ideas, thought, reflection, contemplation, deliberation, imagination, opinion, viewpoint, sentiment, mind, intelligence; (R) plans, intentions, projects, desire, will, resolution.

Mathers (1888): Idea, sentiment, reflection, project; (R) plan, design, resolution, decision.

Waite (1911): Strange chalices of vision, but the images are more especially those of the fantastic spirit. *Divinatory Meanings*: Fairy favors, images of reflection, sentiment, imagination, things seen in the glass of contemplation; some attainment in these degrees, but nothing permanent or substantial is suggested; (R) desire, will, determination, project.

Crowley/GD: Debauch, illusionary success, promises unfulfilled, errors, deceit, lies, deception, mild and brief success, external splendor but internal corruption.

Number Symbolism: 7—assessment, reevaluation, standing at a threshold, seeking advantage.

Astrology: Lovely and affectionate *Venus* (debilitated) in the third decan of watery *Scorpio*, realm of the *Knight of Wands* (Fire of Fire) and *Death* (Scorpio). Venus is linked to the *Empress*.

Timing: 20 Scorpio–30 Scorpio. Tropical, 13 November–22 November. Sidereal, 6 December–15 December.

Keywords (+): Images of reflection, imaginings, daydreams, fantasies, visualizations, possibilities, illusionary choices, a multitude of options, scrying, visions seen in the glass of contemplation.

Keywords (-): Escapism, wishful thinking, illusion, pipe dreams, unrealistic desires, confusion, uncertainty, lies, deceit, misuse of alcohol or drugs, intoxication, drunkenness, excessive sensuality.

....
Seven of Cups Upright

When upright, the Seven of Cups highlights the importance of sentiments and images that come to mind during moments of reflection and contemplation. Such imaginings may reveal our wildest desires but they may not be grounded in reality. Many possibilities seem available, making it difficult to decide which path to follow. At some point we must stop daydreaming, soberly assess our options, and make hard choices. Otherwise we risk wandering in a state of confusion or unreality, like the fictional character Walter Mitty.

....
Seven of Cups Reversed

When reversed, the Seven of Cups suggests that you are in the process of resolving the confusion of the upright card and choosing realistically from among many possibilities. The period of daydreaming is over. Now is the time to plan your course of action with determination and take into account what you genuinely want to achieve. An opportunity may arise allowing you to deal with problems related to the misuse of drugs or alcohol.

EIGHT OF CUPS: THE DECLINE OF A MATTER

Etteilla (1791): A blond girl, a sincere girl, modesty, timidity, sweetness, attractiveness, honor, moderation; (R) joy, pleasure, happiness, satisfaction, festivity, diversion, pomp.

Mathers (1888): A fair girl, friendship, attachment, tenderness; (R) gaiety, feasting, joy, pleasure.

Waite (1911): A man of dejected aspect is deserting the cups of his felicity, enterprise, undertaking, or previous concern. *Divinatory Meanings*: Some say joy, mildness, timidity, honor, modesty, but in practice, the card usually shews the decline of a matter, or that a matter which has been thought to be important is really of slight consequence—either for good or evil; (R) great joy, happiness, feasting.

Crowley/GD: Indolence, abandoned success, decline of interest, sloth, laziness, ennui, the soul poisoned.

Number Symbolism: 8—movement, action, power, determination.

Astrology: The stern taskmaster *Saturn* in the first decan of watery *Pisces*, realm of the *Knight of Cups* (Fire of Water) and the inconstant *Moon* (Pisces). Saturn is linked to the *World*.

Timing: 0 Pisces–10 Pisces. Tropical, 19 February–28 February. Sidereal, 14 March–23 March.

Keywords (+): Renewed interest, walking away from a relationship or situation that is no longer satisfying, a new perspective, travel, a journey, seeking greater meaning in life, searching for something that is missing, renewal of intimacy, lifestyle changes, feasting, joy, finding happiness; the grass looks greener on the other side; a blonde girl loses interest.

Keywords (-): The decline of a matter, disillusionment, abandoned success, instability, unsteady emotions, dissatisfaction, resignation, giving up, recklessly walking away, aimless travel, chasing an illusion, emotional withdrawal, fear of intimacy, dejection, loss of interest, feeling stuck, indolence, sluggishness, laziness; do blonds really have more fun?

....
Eight of Cups Upright

When upright, the Eight of Cups indicates that you have surveyed your current situation and it no longer feels emotionally satisfying. Because of this dissatisfaction with circumstances, you have decided to move on in search of greener pastures. Perhaps a project or a relationship has not lived up to expectations. You may be feeling "stuck in the mud" and wanting to look for fulfillment elsewhere. The bottom line is that you are seeking greater joy and happiness because it does not appear to be available in your present circumstances. It is important to determine whether your discontent is based on a valid assessment of your situation or whether you are acting on some illusory notion, for instance, that blonds have more fun.

....
Eight of Cups Reversed

When reversed, the Eight of Cups cautions you to be thoughtful about a temptation to abandon your current life circumstances in search of greener pastures. You may be feeling dissatisfied with some aspect of your life, but now may not be the optimal time to walk away from difficulties; it may be wiser to try to resolve problems in your current situation. If you run away from troubles, you may take them with you because they are of your own making. The grass may not be greener on the other side. Ponder the words of Eric Samuel Timm: "We are often unaware of the gradual decline and the erosion in our lives but not unaware of the gnawing feeling it brings." [41]

---

41.   Eric Samuel Timm, *Static Jedi: The Art of Hearing God through the Noise.* (Lake Mary: FL, Charisma House, 2013), 4.

NINE OF CUPS: CONTENT IN POMPOUS CIRCUMSTANCES

Etteilla (1791): Success, triumph, achievement, advantage, pomp, gain, pageantry, attire; (R) sincerity, candor, loyalty, ease, lack of affectation, success in business.

Mathers (1888): Victory, advantage, success, triumph, difficulties surmounted; (R) faults, errors, mistakes, imperfections.

Waite (1911): A goodly personage has feasted to his heart's content, and abundant refreshment of wine is on the arched counter behind him, seeming to indicate that the future is also assured. The picture offers the material side only, but there are other aspects. *Divinatory Meanings*: Concord, contentment, physical *bien-être*; also victory, success, advantage; satisfaction for the querent; (R) truth, loyalty, liberty; but the readings vary and include mistakes, imperfections, etc.

Crowley/GD: Material happiness, wishes fulfilled, pleasure, success.

Number Symbolism: 9—the final single digit, culmination, fruition, attainment.

Astrology: The expansive benefic *Jupiter* (dignified) in the second decan of watery *Pisces*, realm of the *Knight of Cups* (Fire of Water) and the dreamy *Moon* (Pisces). Jupiter is linked to the *Wheel of Fortune.*

Timing: 10 Pisces–20 Pisces. Tropical, 1 March–10 March. Sidereal, 24 March–2 April.

Keywords (+): Satisfaction, happiness, contentment, enjoyment, success, advantage, pleasure, creativity, celebration, material delights, blessings, dreams come true, fulfillment of desires, cause for celebration, the "wish card."

Keywords (-): Vanity, conceit, egotism, pomp, pageantry, complacency, unfulfilled desires, superficiality, materialism, overindulgence, reckless generosity, smugness, self-satisfaction, spoiled by success.

....
Nine of Cups Upright

When upright, the Nine of Cups indicates a period of pleasure, creativity, and enjoyment. Wishes are fulfilled and dreams come true. This is a time of material happiness and success in mundane matters. You feel particularly creative and sociable at this time. Your many blessings are cause for celebration and sharing your happiness with others.

....
Nine of Cups Reversed

When reversed, the Nine of Cups suggests an excessive focus on material pleasures and conspicuous consumerism. Such superficial behavior makes you come across as smug and complacent. Success can be a two-edged sword: it can grant all your wishes, but it can also turn you into a grown-up version of an egocentric spoiled child.

TEN OF CUPS: REPOSE OF THE HEART

Etteilla (1791): Home, place of residence, domicile, dwelling, homeland, city, village, town; (R) anger, rage, wrath, strife, indignation, violence.

Mathers (1888): The town wherein one resides, honor, consideration, esteem, virtue, glory, reputation; (R) combat, strife, opposition, differences, dispute.

Waite (1911): Appearance of Cups in a rainbow; it is contemplated in wonder and ecstasy by a man and woman below, evidently husband and wife. His right arm is about her; his left is raised upward; she raises her right arm. The two children dancing near them have not observed the prodigy but are happy after their own manner. There is a home-scene beyond. *Divinatory Meanings*: Contentment, repose of the entire heart; the perfection of that state; also perfection of human love and friendship; if with several picture-cards, a person who is taking charge of the querent's interests; also the town, village, or country inhabited by the querent; (R) repose of the false heart, indignation, violence.

Crowley/GD: Satiety, good fortune, perfected success, matters settled as one wishes; the element Water has been fully expressed and disturbance is due.

Number Symbolism: 10—one too many, the fullness of completion, readiness to begin a new cycle.

Astrology: Assertive and warlike *Mars* in the third decan of watery *Pisces*, the last ten days of winter and also the realm of the *Queen of Wands* (Water of Fire) and the dreamy *Moon* (Pisces). Mars is linked to the *Tower*. The heat of the red planet Mars in this last decan of Pisces brings winter to a close and ushers in the first day of spring.

Timing: 20 Pisces–30 Pisces. Tropical, 11 March–20 March. Sidereal, 3 April–13 April.

Keywords (+): Family happiness, amiable social life, close ties, friendship, contentment, fulfillment, gratitude, family celebration, getting what you always wanted, reaching a long-term goal, home, going home, one's place of residence, hometown, the end of the rainbow, repose of the heart.

Keywords (-): Satiety, lack of fulfillment, indignation, strife, discontent in one's family or social life, quarrels, disturbance, ingratitude, disrupted ties, a fly in the ointment, dissatisfaction with what you thought you wanted after you finally get it.

....
Ten of Cups Upright

When upright, the Ten of Cups finds you surrounded by loving relationships, whether they be good friends or supportive family members. This is a time of fulfillment and achieving your heart's desires. Home is where the heart is, and you have arrived where you want to be. Since one of the meanings of Cups is the power to heal, this Ten may represent a final stage of healing and the release from suffering. As pleasant as the scene on this card may appear, it is important to remember that all good things must eventually come to an end. Enjoy your blessings but don't forget to reflect on the impermanence of life.

....
Ten of Cups Reversed

When reversed, the Ten of Cups highlights family problems, domestic disruptions, and a sense of sadness in the home. There can also be a certain amount of strife and tension in other personal relationships. You may be experiencing a lack of a sense of fulfillment or a failure to achieve your heart's desires; or else you have gotten what you want but you find it lacking. There is no pot of gold at the end of the rainbow. Crowley says of this card that having got everything you wanted, you realize that you did not want it after all, and now you must pay the piper.

The Suit of Swords

The tarot Swords were originally the scimitars of the Egyptian Mamluk playing card deck. With their curved blades, the relatively light-weight scimitars were the preferred weapon for battles on horseback. The Mamluk soldiers found that the curved blade of the scimitar was the ideal shape for slashing their enemies from atop moving horses. Straight blades, in contrast, tended to get stuck in the enemy's body, causing a delay while the warrior had to pause to pull the embedded straight sword from the wounded opponent's chest. It is no surprise, then, that phallic Swords (scimitars) became symbols of conflict, strife, and devastation.

In astrology, the suit of Swords is related to the "yang" group of active Air signs (Gemini, Libra, Aquarius) as befits the thrusting phallic nature of incisive Swords. To get a sense of the archetypal nature of this tarot symbol, consider the following list of keywords for Swords (Scimitars):

Justice	Quarrels	Legal matters
Thought	Action	Verbal ability
Ideas	Confrontation	Words as weapons
Communication	Clearing the air	Beliefs and attitudes
Logic	Detachment	Matters of the mind
Truth	Emotional coolness	Sickness
Intellect	Analysis	Surgery
Sharpness	Decision-making	Blood-letting
Incisiveness	Strategy	Clearing dead wood
Cutting	Strife	Intensive medical interventions
Pain	Loss	Jumping into the fray
Suffering	Scandal	Piercing to the quick

Separation	Worry	Clearing the air
Conflict	Sadness	Devastation
Troubles	Preoccupation	Death
Struggle	Grief	"Double-edged" words
Debate		

A Suit of Swords Exercise

According to the Golden Dawn, several major arcana cards are associated with the element Air and the airy suit of Swords. These include:

- The Magician, Trump I (the airy communicative planet Mercury)
- The Lovers, Trump VI (the Air sign Gemini)
- Justice, Trump VIII or XI (the Air sign Libra)
- The Star, Trump XVII (the Air sign Aquarius)
- The Fool, Trump 0 (the element Air)

Lay out these cards and note any qualities they have in common. Do they share any symbolism with the wind blowing through the sky or a tornado devastating the earth below? Repeat this exercise after you have studied the suit of Swords. Record your observations in your tarot notebook.

ACE OF SWORDS: INVOKING INTENSE FORCE FOR DECISIVE ACTION

Etteilla (1791): Amplification, intensification, enlargement, excess, anger, fury, quarrel, limits, boundaries; extreme, big, excessive, inordinate, utmost (R) conception, impregnation, seed, sperm, birth, increase, multiplicity.

Mathers (1888): Triumph, fecundity, fertility, prosperity; (R) embarrassment, foolish and hopeless love, obstacle, hindrance.

Waite (1911): A hand issues from a cloud, grasping a sword, the point of which is encircled by a crown. *Divinatory Meanings*: Triumph, the excessive degree in everything, conquest, triumph of force. It is a card of great force, in love as well as in hatred. The crown may carry a much higher significance than comes usually within the sphere of fortune-telling. (R) The same, but the results are disastrous; another account says—conception, childbirth, augmentation, multiplicity.

Crowley/GD: Great power invoked for good, or for evil if reversed. Strength in adversity. The Sword of Discrimination and Justice.

Number Symbolism: 1—initial spark, will, creation, beginnings, new life.

Astrology: Primordial energy of Air, the element associated with the season of autumn.

Timing: Astrologically, Air is linked to the autumn months.

Keywords (+): Decisive action, invocation of great force, intensification, enlargement, establishing one's identity, clarity of thought, seeing the truth, triumph, recognition, keen insight, a breakthrough, impregnation, birth or seed of an idea, incisive use of words, the power of the mind, the focused use of energy.

Keywords (-): Misapplication of force, hurtful use of words, anger, quarrels, troublesome excess, rupture in a relationship, indecision, the harmful use of energy.

In Llewellyn's Classic Tarot, a hand emerges from a cloud on the left-hand side of the card; the hand holds a sword upright against the light blue sky. The palm of the hand faces the viewer. Peaked mountains in the background symbolize important goals and ideas that need to be honored. The blade of the sword thrusts upright through a four-pointed golden crown, from which dangle olive and laurel branches. Each point of the golden crown is inlaid with a distinct gem representing one of the four elements: Earth, Water, Air and Fire. The olive branch is a symbol of peace; the laurel, a symbol of triumph and recognition.

....

Ace of Swords Upright

When upright, the Ace of Swords suggests new beginnings related to principled thinking and effective communication. You are able to focus your mind, see things clearly, cut through confusion, invoke intense force, and put matters in perspective. With the courage of your convictions, you cut through the crap and don't suffer fools gladly. Swords are weapons of battle, and the upright Ace indicates the courage to face obstacles and fight for what you believe. You are likely to emerge victorious from your struggles, with a greater sense of personal identity. In the myth of Perseus and Medusa, the hero uses his strategic intelligence to outwit the snake-headed monster and chop off her head with his mighty sword. Sigmund Freud pointed out that the sword has long been a symbol of a powerful phallus.

....

Ace of Swords Reversed

When reversed, the Ace of Swords warns of the misapplication of force, perhaps in the form of quarrels or other forms of strife that can lead to separations in relationships. Be careful what you say because words, like swords, can cause painful wounds. The reversed Ace of Swords can also indicate that you are expending your energy in a way that is inappropriate or not to your advantage.

Two of Swords: Rapport and Masterful Self-Regulation

Etteilla (1791): Friendship, rapport, affection, tenderness, attraction, affinity, intimacy; (R) falsity, deceit, lying, imposture, trickery, superficiality.

Mathers (1888): Friendship, valor, firmness, courage; (R) false friends, treachery, lies.

Waite (1911): A hoodwinked female figure balances two swords upon her shoulders. *Divinatory Meanings*: Conformity and the equipoise which it suggests, courage, friendship, concord in a state of arms; another reading gives tenderness, affection, intimacy. The suggestion of harmony and other favorable readings must be considered in a qualified manner, as Swords generally are not symbolical of beneficent forces in human affairs. (R) Imposture, falsehood, duplicity, disloyalty.

Crowley/GD: Peace, a quarrel settled and resolved, peace restored but some tension remaining. Crowley objects to the Golden Dawn's "peace restored" because he says there has been no disturbance, and he likens this card to the negative form of a positive idea and the masterful chastity of an honorable knight.

Number Symbolism: 2—duality, partnership, choice, decision, balance, gestation.

Astrology: The emotional and inconstant *Moon* in the first decan of airy *Libra*, realm of the *Queen of Swords* (Water of Air) and *Justice* (Libra). The Moon is linked to the *High Priestess*. The airy Queen of Swords gives birth to the season of autumn at the start of Libra.

Timing: 0 Libra–10 Libra. Tropical, 23 September–2 October. Sidereal, 17 October–26 October.

Keywords (+): Peace, true friendship, rapport, composure, intimacy, tranquility, concord, tenderness, masterful self-possession, burying the hatchet, resolving differences, balancing viewpoints, making a difficult decision, looking for answers within, perfectly balanced forces, self-regulation in the expression of impulses and desires.

Keywords (-): Disturbance of the peace, inner struggle, lack of composure, impasse, stalemate, indecision, no action possible, on the horns of a dilemma, trickery, lies, deceit, treachery, superficiality, poor self-restraint, unregulated emotions, false friendship.

Two of Swords Upright

When upright, the Two of Swords suggests that your inner state is calm and finely balanced. You are able to review your options and take reasoned decisions against a backdrop of changing circumstances and varying emotions. If you've had differences with others, you can see the value in resolving differences and burying the hatchet. This state of peace and self-possession characterizes the rapport you feel with your closest friends. True friendship is based on the tender and honest balancing of the needs, wishes, and feelings of both parties.

Two of Swords Reversed

When reversed, the Two of Swords indicates that some type of imbalance has disturbed your sense of self-possession. You may be at an impasse, unable to judge or decide on a correct course of action. Alternatively, you may have an urge to act on impulse without properly considering the consequences. Such superficial behavior will likely have negative consequences. There may be a disturbance in one or more of your friendships. Perhaps someone you considered a friend is involved in deceit or treachery, or you may be feeling tempted to lie to someone who trusts you.

THREE OF SWORDS: SEPARATION AND HEARTACHE

Etteilla (1791): Separation, estrangement, rupture, absence, departure, severance, detachment, aversion; (R) bewilderment, confusion, distraction, mental alienation, insanity, error, loss, miscalculation, detour.

Mathers (1888): Separation, removal, rupture, quarrel.

Waite (1911): Three swords piercing a heart; cloud and rain behind. *Divinatory Meanings*: Removal, absence, delay, division, rupture, dispersion, and all that the design signifies naturally, being too simple and obvious to call for specific enumeration; (R) mental alienation, error, loss, distraction, disorder, confusion.

Crowley/GD: Sorrow, unhappiness, breakups, tears, secrecy, perversion.

Number Symbolism: 3—fertility, creativity, a triadic relationship, the first fruits of a joint venture.

Astrology: The stern taskmaster *Saturn* (exalted) in the second decan of airy *Libra,* also the realm of the *Queen of Swords* (Water of Air) and *Justice* (Libra). Saturn is linked to the *World.*

Timing: 10 Libra–20 Libra. Tropical, 3 October–12 October. Sidereal, 27 October–5 November.

Keywords (+): Necessary separation, beneficial severance, detachment, surgery, absence, grieving in order to heal, the joy of release from sorrow, insightful but stormy weather for the emotions, attainment of wisdom through suffering.

Keywords (-): Stormy weather for the emotions, heartache, breakup, anguish, tears, sadness, loss, grief, sorrow, alienation, lost friendship, miscarriage, death of a loved one, painful separation, rupture, loss of love, divorce, unhappiness, betrayal, a broken heart, distress, affliction, feeling under the weather, illness, quarrels, disruption, interrupted plans, disappointment, wounds, a broken heart, misfortune, suffering.

Three of Swords Upright

When upright, the Three of Swords suggests that you are confronting some type of separation, loss, severing of ties, or suffering that will lead to important realizations about your emotional life and aid you to grow in wisdom. This card depicts "stormy weather for the emotions." You may need to deal with feeling alienated, cut off, disappointed, grief-stricken, or alone. Because Swords are a mental and conflict-laden suit, you may be involved in disputes with friends or loved ones. A hoped-for meeting with someone you care about may not materialize. Sometimes this card points to a need for surgery, either for yourself or for someone close to you. When all is said and done, the suffering and unhappiness implied by this card offer an opportunity for a fresh start.

Three of Swords Reversed

When reversed, the Three of Swords implies that you are not allowing yourself to grow as a result of your suffering. Rather than hanging on to hard feelings and keeping a dispute going, it may be time to bury the hatchet and clear the air. Clinging too long to rancor and sadness will only result in prolonged heartache. Consider the five stages of grief outlined by Elisabeth Kübler-Ross (1969): (1) denial and isolation, (2) anger, (3) bargaining, (4) depression, and finally (5) acceptance. The Three of Swords is about the process of grieving and ultimately accepting and letting go in order to restore balance in your life (Saturn in Libra).

FOUR OF SWORDS: SOLITUDE AND RETREAT

Etteilla (1791)**:** Retreat, solitude, desert, hermitage, loneliness, exile, banishment, ostracism, sepulcher, coffin, tomb; (R) prudence, proper conduct, harmony, good management, discretion, moderation, economy, thrift.

Mathers (1888)**:** Solitude, retreat, abandonment, solitary, hermit; (R) economy, precaution, regulation of expenditure.

Waite (1911)**:** The effigy of a knight in the attitude of prayer, at full length upon his tomb. *Divinatory Meanings*: Vigilance, retreat, solitude, hermit's repose, exile, tomb and coffin; (R) wise administration, circumspection, economy, avarice, precaution, testament.

Crowley/GD: Truce, rest from strife, convalescence, recovery from illness, refuge from mental chaos, a turn for the better, a time of peace away from struggle.

Number Symbolism: 4—structure, stability, order, logic, foundation, manifestation.

Astrology: The expansive benefic *Jupiter* in the third decan of airy *Libra*, realm of the Waite *King/Thoth Prince of Cups* (Air of Water) and *Justice* (Libra). Jupiter is linked to the *Wheel of Fortune*.

Timing: 20 Libra–30 Libra. Tropical, 13 October–22 October. Sidereal, 6 November–15 November.

Keywords (+): Rest from strife, time out, solitude, retreat, solace, peace, repose, a break, truce, temporary cessation of hostilities, respite, withdrawal, meditation, recuperation, R&R, convalescence, taking the time to recover from loss or illness, hermitage, oasis, tomb or final resting place, a period of tranquility away from struggle, mental attraction, going off the grid for a while, seeking spiritual guidance.

Keywords (-): Exile, ostracism, rejection, banishment, isolation, exclusion, abandonment, loneliness, being stuck in a stressful situation.

Four of Swords Upright

When upright, the Four of Swords indicates a time of repose, healing, solitude and recuperation. Note the word *PAX* (Latin for "peace") in the angel's halo on the stained glass window. Perhaps you are recovering from illness or need a break from stressful circumstances. In modern technological parlance, you may want to go off the grid for a while and recharge your batteries. After a period of rest and relaxation, you will be able to begin anew. Traditionally this card represents retreating to a meditative environment, such as a remote hermitage in the desert.

Four of Swords Reversed

When reversed, the Four of Swords warns of possible rejection or ostracism, which can leave you feeling lonely and abandoned. Sometimes feeling cut off in this way is self-imposed by your choice to withdraw from involvement with others. The meditative isolation so much sought after by hermits may not be the oasis you were expecting.

FIVE OF SWORDS: MOURNING A LOSS

Etteilla (1791): Loss, waste, decline, deprivation, affront, meanness, humiliation, degradation, setback, avarice, thief; (R) grief, mourning, despondency, distress, chagrin, bereavement, funeral rites, interment.

Mathers (1888): Mourning, sadness, affliction; (R) losses, trouble (same signification, whether reversed or not).

Waite (1911): A disdainful man looks after two retreating and dejected figures. Their swords lie upon the ground. He carries two others on his left shoulder, and a third sword is in his right hand, point to earth. He is the master in possession of the field. *Divinatory Meanings*: Degradation, destruction, revocation, infamy, dishonor, loss, with the variants and analogues of these; (R) the same; burial and obsequies, sorrow and mourning.

Crowley/GD: Defeat, loss, unfavorable outcome, malice, treachery, slander, evil-speaking, intellect defeated by sentiment.

Number Symbolism: 5—instability, disruption, loss, crisis, tension, competition, conflict.

Astrology: Lovely and affectionate *Venus* in the first decan of airy *Aquarius*, realm of the Waite *King*/Thoth *Prince of Swords* (Air of Air) and the *Star* (Aquarius). Venus is linked to the *Empress*.

Timing: 0 Aquarius–10 Aquarius. Tropical, 20 January–29 January. Sidereal, 13 February–22 February.

Keywords (+): Winning in a dispute, the ability to do what you want without regard for the feelings of others, learning a spiritual lesson from losses and defeats, a parting of ways, burying the dead; to the victor belong the spoils.

Keywords (-): Affront, rejection, hurtful humiliation, a painful parting of ways, hard feelings, wounded pride, meanness, slander, betrayal, loss, abandonment, dejection, defeat, anxiety, blame, feelings of inadequacy, Pyrrhic victory, gloating, poor sportsmanship, sorrow, mourning, licking your wounds, feeling slighted or abandoned, leaving without saying goodbye; all's fair in love and war.

....
Five of Swords Upright

When upright, the Five of Swords indicates that you are dealing with some type of loss, defeat or abandonment. There is an important spiritual lesson to be learned from this mournful experience. Sometimes this card indicates that you are the victor who is gloating over his triumph without regard for the feelings of those whom you have humiliated. Alternatively, you may be the loser who is feeling affronted, rejected, abandoned, or treated unfairly. Social science has demonstrated that experiences of humiliation can lead to feelings of anger and sometimes violence.

....
Five of Swords Reversed

When reversed, the Five of Swords suggests that you have been licking your wounds for too long. The time has come to confront your sense of defeat and humiliation and see if there is a way to effect reconciliation. Wallowing in self-pity only prolongs your hurt feelings and sense of inadequacy.

SIX OF SWORDS: LIKE A BRIDGE OVER TROUBLED WATERS

Etteilla (1791): Journey, voyage, road, path, lane, walk, passage, messenger, envoy, moving forward, thoughtfulness, kind attention; (R) proclamation, publicity, statement, knowledge, discovery, declaration, explanation, waiting, expectation.

Mathers (1888): Envoy, messenger, voyage, travel; (R) declaration, love proposed, revelation, surprise.

Waite (1911): A ferryman carrying passengers in his punt to the further shore. The course is smooth, and seeing that the freight is light, it may be noted that the work is not beyond his strength. *Divinatory Meanings*: A journey by water, route, way, envoy, commissionairy [a messenger or attendant charged with the protection of people, property or information], expedient, a pleasant voyage; (R) declaration, confession, publicity; one account says that it is a proposal of love.

Crowley/GD: Science, earned success, winning intelligence, labor, work done with words, journey over water, a balance of mental and moral faculties.

Number Symbolism: 6—harmony, communication, sharing, compassion.

Astrology: Quick and clever *Mercury*, messenger of the gods, in the second decan of airy *Aquarius*, realm of the Waite *King*/Thoth *Prince of Swords* (Air of Air) and the *Star* (Aquarius). Mercury is linked to the *Magician*.

Timing: 10 Aquarius–20 Aquarius. Tropical, 30 January–8 February. Sidereal, 23 February–3 March.

Keywords (+): Moving away from troubles, the removal of obstacles, a journey, change of scene, travel over water, safe passage, kind attention, patience, a helpful attendant, a guardian angel, moving toward less turbulent times, carrying a message afar, difficulties surmounted, resolution of legal difficulties, better times ahead; a declaration, revelation, proposal, publicity, surprise, winning intelligence, a verbal accomplishment.

Keywords (-): Difficulty leaving a troubling situation behind, feeling overwhelmed by circumstances, refusal to deal with problems, short-lived relief, travel difficulties, legal complications, unintelligent attempts to resolve a difficulty, an unhelpful attendant, poor service.

....
Six of Swords Upright

When upright, the Six of Swords indicates that you are moving away from troubling waters toward less turbulent circumstances with the aid of a strong and skillful oarsman. You are not there yet, and some residual difficulties remain on your journey. Conversely, you may be playing the role of the protective oarsman, helping someone to leave a problematic situation behind, in search of a better life. Crowley named this card "Science" because of its connection with the mental planet Mercury in the objective sign Aquarius. The clever use of words may play an important role in your current situation.

....
Six of Swords Reversed

When reversed, the Six of Swords suggests that you are having difficulty leaving your troubles behind. Something or someone is blocking your effort to make it to more tranquil seas. Difficulties or delays with travel are also possible. Perhaps because of the association of this card with the planet Mercury (communication) in Aquarius, traditional meanings of the Six of Swords reversed included proclamations, declarations, proposals, revelations, and surprises.

SEVEN OF SWORDS: UNSTABLE EFFORT

Etteilla (1791): Intention, scheme, wish, hope, expectancy, promise, longing, fantasy, expectations, overvaluing oneself; (R) thought, reflection, lesson, instruction, helpful admonition, good counsel, consultation, sage advice.

Mathers (1888): Hope, confidence, desire, attempt, wish; (R) wise advice, good counsel, wisdom, prudence, circumspection.

Waite (1911): A man in the act of carrying away five swords rapidly; the two others of the card remain stuck in the ground. A camp is close at hand. *Divinatory Meanings*: Design, attempt, wish, hope, confidence; also quarreling, a plan that may fail, annoyance. The design is uncertain in its import, because the significations are widely at variance with each other; (R) good advice, counsel, instruction, slander, babbling.

Crowley/GD: Futility, unstable effort, imaginings beyond possibility, vacillation, untrustworthiness, a policy of appeasement, a journey by land.

Number Symbolism: 7—assessment, reevaluation, standing at a threshold, seeking advantage.

Astrology: The inconstant *Moon* in the third decan of airy *Aquarius*, realm of the dreamy *Knight of Cups* (Fire of Water) and the *Star* (Aquarius). The Moon is linked to the *High Priestess*.

Timing: 20 Aquarius–30 Aquarius. Tropical, 9 February–18 February. Sidereal, 4 March–13 March.

Keywords (+): Stealth, strategic goal-setting, careful planning, wise precautions, thinking before you act, clever stratagems, tact, diplomacy, sidestepping direct confrontation, finding back-door solutions, thoughtfully directed behavior, consultation, heeding sound advice.

Keywords (-): Half-baked plans, underhanded scheming, theft, dishonesty, deception, misdirection, futility, instability, vain effort, ineffectiveness, timidity, indecisiveness, muddled intentions, chasing rainbows, ignoring good advice, being incapable of sustained effort, feeling taken advantage of, biting off more than you can chew, a sneak attack, a mole, a snake in the grass.

....
Seven of Swords Upright

When upright, the Seven of Swords urges careful planning and a strategic approach to resolving a delicate situation. Do your homework and set your goals carefully. It is best to avoid direct confrontation; instead, try to find alternative solutions to any kind of conflict or disagreement. Stealth can give you an advantage. You may wish to discuss matters with an expert consultant who can provide you with prudent counsel. Tact and diplomacy are definite assets in your current situation. Keep in mind the words of the poet:

> The best-laid schemes of Mice and Men
> Oft go awry,
> And leave us nothing but grief and pain,
> For promised Joy!
> (Robert Burns, "To a Mouse," 1785)

....
Seven of Swords Reversed

When reversed, the Seven of Swords advises you to take reasonable precautions against theft, deception, and other types of underhanded behavior. Someone you thought you could trust may turn out to be a snake in the grass. Your timidity and indecisiveness may be contributing to muddled thinking and unstable efforts. You may wish to seek wise counsel to avoid chasing after rainbows or biting off more than you can chew.

EIGHT OF SWORDS: THE PARALYSIS OF ANALYSIS

Etteilla (1791): Censure, blame, criticism, contempt, a delicate situation, a critical moment, an unfortunate circumstance, crisis; (R) delay, misfortune, hindrance, opposition, resistance, quibbling, problems, accidents.

Mathers (1888): Sickness, calumny, criticism, blame; (R) treachery in the past, event, accident, remarkable incident.

Waite (1911): A woman, bound and hoodwinked, with the swords of the card about her. Yet it is rather a card of temporary durance [confinement] than of irretrievable bondage. *Divinatory Meanings*: Bad news, violent chagrin, crisis, censure, power in trammels, conflict, calumny; also sickness; (R) disquiet, difficulty, opposition, accident, treachery; what is unforeseen; fatality.

Crowley/GD: Unexpected interference, unforeseen bad luck, shortened force, restriction, narrow-mindedness, pettiness, the will thwarted by accidental interference, prison.

Number Symbolism: 8—movement, action, power, determination.

Astrology: Expansive *Jupiter* (debilitated) in the first decan of airy *Gemini*, the realm of the *Knight of Swords* (Fire of Air) and of the *Lovers* (Gemini). Jupiter is linked to the *Wheel of Fortune*. Jupiter's debilitated state in Gemini brings about increase without accompanying good fortune.

Timing: 0 Gemini–10 Gemini. Tropical, 21 May–31 May. Sidereal, 15 June–24 June.

Keywords (+): Confronting self-imposed limitations, freeing yourself of restrictive beliefs and oppressive self-criticism, overcoming interference, clearing obstacles that hem you in, liberating yourself from a situation in which you feel censured or trapped.

Keywords (-): Feeling restricted, trapped, blocked, hemmed in, or confined; self-imposed limitations, imprisonment, problematic thoughts, unexpected interference, unforeseen bad luck, petty gossip, censure, blame, criticism, disquiet, confusion, over-thinking a situation, the paralysis of analysis, being a prisoner of your own mind, allowing others to inhibit your freedom.

Eight of Swords Upright

When upright, the Eight of Swords suggests that you are feeling trapped or hemmed in by circumstances. Some of these restrictions may be of your own making and others may be due to the interference of unforeseen events. You tend to over-think situations and to inhibit yourself though limiting beliefs, excessive self-blame, or surrendering your power to others. You may be suffering from the paralysis of analysis. Now is the time to take off your blindfold and take a good look around you. Freedom is within your grasp. Consider the words of poet Richard Lovelace (1642): "Stone walls do not a prison make nor iron bars a cage."

Eight of Swords Reversed

When reversed, the Eight of Swords has a similar meaning to the upright card but also implies that you are able to clear the obstacles in your path. The potential for liberation lies in confronting your limiting beliefs and replacing restrictive ideas with more realistic attitudes. If you have surrendered your power to others, it's time to take it back and resume control of your life.

NINE OF SWORDS: A CLOISTERED NUN SUFFERS INSOMNIA

Etteilla (1791): A cleric, priest, nun, virgin, cloistered person, ecclesiastic, recluse, unmarried person; devotion, celibacy, piety, a cult, a convent, monastery, hermitage; (R) reasonable suspicion, warranted mistrust, legitimate fear, a troubled conscience, timidity, shame, disgrace.

Mathers (1888): An ecclesiastic, a priest, conscience, probity, good faith, integrity; (R) wise distrust, suspicion, fear, doubt, shady character.

Waite (1911): One seated on her couch in lamentation, with the swords over her. She is as one who knows no sorrow which is like unto hers. It is a card of utter desolation. *Divinatory Meanings*: Death, failure, miscarriage, delay, deception, disappointment, despair; an ecclesiastic; (R) imprisonment, suspicion, doubt, reasonable fear, shame.

Crowley/GD: Cruelty, despair, suffering, despondency, illness, pain, malice, psychopathy, fanaticism, primitive instincts.

Number Symbolism: 9—the final single digit, culmination, fruition, attainment.

Astrology: Assertive and warlike *Mars* in the second decan of airy *Gemini*, the realm of the *Knight of Swords* (Fire of Air) and the *Lovers* (Gemini). Mars is linked to the *Tower*.

Timing: 10 Gemini–20 Gemini. Tropical, 1 June–10 June. Sidereal, 25 June–5 July.

Keywords (+): The need for acceptance, self-realization, legitimate fear, self-exploration, confronting self-doubt and negative thinking, moving toward resolution, accepting loss, looking at matters realistically, piety, faith, devotion, virginity, integrity, celibacy.

Keywords (-): Nightmares, insomnia, desolation, despair, worry, mental anguish, anxiety, sorrow, self-doubt, a guilty conscience, preoccupation, shame, bad dreams, cruelty, depression, ill health, miscarriage, gloomy thoughts, resigning oneself to negative thinking; "I can't get no satisfaction."

Nine of Swords Upright

When upright, this card represents anguish of mind. Sometimes you feel so bad that you'd like to run off to a sheltered refuge and cloister yourself like a monk or a nun. Worrisome thoughts may be keeping you up at night or having a negative effect on your health. Perhaps you have felt the sting of harsh words from a loved one (warlike Mars in mental Gemini), or you fear an impending split or separation in a relationship. Whatever is troubling you, just remember that matters look bleaker in anticipation and in the darkness of night than when they actually manifest in tangible reality. According to author Amber Jayanti, this card reflects "how painful it can be to let go of what you want and accept what is." [42]

Nine of Swords Reversed

When reversed, this card can indicate that you are either avoiding or refusing to face up to your deepest fears. A well-known refrain from the self-help movement goes, "What you resist persists." Acknowledge that you are worried and try to look at matters more clearly in the light of day. In the words of the serenity prayer: "God grant me the serenity to accept the things I cannot change, the courage to change the things I can, and the wisdom to know the difference."

---

42.   Amber Jayanti, *Tarot for Dummies* (Stamford, CT: U.S. Games Systems, 2001), 149.

Ten of Swords: Pain and Sorrow Gives Way to the Morrow

Etteilla (1791): Tears, sadness, crying, affliction, grief, lamentation, distress, sorrow, desolation; (R) profit, advantage, gain, winnings, favor, benefit, power, authority, kind deeds.

Mathers (1888): Tears, affliction, grief, sorrow; (R) passing success, momentary advantage.

Waite (1911): A prostrate figure, pierced by all the swords belonging to the card. *Divinatory Meanings*: Whatsoever is intimated by the design; also pain, affliction, tears, sadness, desolation. It is *not* especially a card of violent death; (R) advantage, profit, success, favor, but none of these are permanent; also power and authority.

Crowley/GD: Ruin, reason divorced from reality, the airy energy of Swords used disruptively, the logic of insanity.

Number Symbolism: 10—one too many, the fullness of completion, readiness to begin a new cycle.

Astrology: The hot dry *Sun* in the third decan of airy *Gemini*, realm of the *Queen of Cups* (Water of Water) and the *Lovers* (Gemini).

Timing: 20 Gemini–30 Gemini. Tropical, 10 June–20 June. Sidereal, 6 July–15 July.

Keywords (+): a final ending, fresh hope, new horizons, release, liberation, the darkness before the dawn, the end of a bad situation, things can't get any worse, the end of a cycle, success but at a great price, being forced to confront a problem that has been brewing for some time, starting over, a new day is dawning.

Keywords (-): hitting bottom, disruption, ruin, destruction, desolation, bad advice, loss, pain, sorrow, tears, wounding, betrayal, affliction, feeling stabbed in the back, failure, unmet goals, thwarted plans, defeat, downfall, disinformation, upset, madness, anguish, panic, anxiety, depression, surgery, legal problems, run-ins with the law, feeling pinned down, fearing there is no way out, catastrophic thinking.

....
Ten of Swords Upright

When upright, the Ten of Swords indicates that you have reached the end of a period of anguish and suffering and are ready to move on. You have hit bottom and things cannot get any worse. It's one of those times in your life when you come to understand that you were never promised a rose garden. Circumstances are forcing you to confront a problem that has been brewing for some time, and the only way forward is up. The rising sun in the background implies that there is hope of a solution; you are at the dawn of a new day. Release and liberation from suffering are at hand. Since Swords represent ideas and communications, problems created by misinformation can be resolved at this time.

....
Ten of Swords Reversed

When reversed, the Ten of Swords suggests that something is preventing you from letting go of negative thoughts. You may be following bad advice or engaging in catastrophic thinking. Perhaps you are clinging to a difficult relationship or a bad situation that has only brought trouble into your life. You feel pinned down, but your worst imaginings do not match the reality of your circumstances. If you have been hurt or betrayed, you can either swim in the cesspool of anger and resentment, or let go of rancor and embrace forgiveness so you can move forward. Sometimes hitting bottom is a blessing in disguise, as it can force you finally to deal with your problems.

The Suit of Pentacles (Coins)

The tarot Pentacles derive from the suit of gold coins (dinars) of the Mamluk deck. Dinars were the currency the Mamluk Sultanate used for business transactions and the material affairs of daily life. The suit of diamonds of ordinary playing cards corresponds to tarot Coins or Pentacles. When trying to remember keywords for Pentacles, it may help to recall the song, "Diamonds are a Girl's Best Friend."

In astrology, the suit of Pentacles is related to the receptive "yin" group of Earth signs (Taurus, Virgo, Capricorn) as befits the inner-directed nature of the earthy Coins of the tarot. To get a sense of the archetypal nature of this tarot symbol, look over the following list of keywords for the Pentacles (Coins, Disks, Dinars):

Prudence	Practical attainment	Income
Business	Health matters	Opportunities for work
Money	Heredity	Work-related projects
Finances	Good medicine	Earth
Goods	The care of one's body	Skepticism
Possessions	The five senses	Common sense
Work	Stewardship of natural resources	Learning by doing
Labor	Survival	Persistent effort
Purely material affairs	Manifestation	Slow but steady progress
Investments	Laying down roots	Values
Wealth	Tangible reality	Diligence
Security	Business acumen	Sensation
Material well-being	The material world	

A Suit of Coins/Pentacles Exercise

According to the Golden Dawn, several cards of the major arcana are associated with the element Earth and the earthy suit of Coins or Pentacles. These include:

- The High Priest, Trump V (the Earth sign Taurus)

- The Hermit, Trump IX (the Earth sign Virgo)

- The Devil, Trump XV (the Earth sign Capricorn)

- The World, Trump XXI (the planet Saturn, symbolic of structure, boundaries, and tangible reality).

- No major arcana card is assigned specifically to the element Earth.

Lay out these cards and note any qualities they have in common. Do they share any symbolism with the solid earth beneath your feet? Repeat this exercise after you have studied the suit of Pentacles. Record your observations in your tarot notebook.

ACE OF PENTACLES: OPPORTUNITY FOR MATERIAL IMPROVEMENT

Etteilla (1791): Contentment, great joy, happiness, rapture, ecstasy, pleasure, accomplishment, the perfect medicine, the color red; (R) riches, capital, wealth, opulence, treasure, precious things.

Mathers (1888): Perfect contentment, felicity, prosperity, triumph; (R) purse of gold, money, gain, help, profit, riches.

Waite (1911): A hand—issuing, as usual, from a cloud—holds up a pentacle. *Divinatory Meanings*: Perfect contentment, felicity, ecstasy; also speedy intelligence; gold; (R) the evil side of wealth, bad intelligence; also great riches. In any case it shews prosperity, comfortable material conditions, but whether these are of advantage to the possessor will depend on whether the card is reversed or not.

Crowley/GD: The phallus viewed head-on. Material gain, labor, power, wealth.

Number Symbolism: 1—initial spark, will, creation, beginnings, new life.

Astrology: Primordial energy of Earth, the element associated with the season of winter.

Timing: Astrologically, Earth is linked to wintertime.

Keywords (+): Fertility, great joy, health, finances, wealth, material happiness, riches, prosperity, physical well-being, financial opportunity, the perfect medicine, abundance, physical prowess, material accomplishment.

Keywords (-): Materialism, greed, discontent, poverty, wastefulness, bad medicine, excessive attachment, missed opportunities.

In Llewellyn's Classic Tarot, a hand emerges from a cloud on the left-hand side of the card, holding a golden coin upright in the light blue sky. The hand encircles the upper part of the chalice with its thumb facing the viewer. On its surface the golden coin features a pentacle, often used as a talisman in ritual magic. The five points of the pentacle are associated with the five points of the human body (the head and four limbs) and with the classical five senses (touch, sight, taste, smell, and hearing). People characterized by the suit of Coins or Pentacles tend to be grounded in material reality but may have difficulty making contact with their sixth sense of intuition.

Ace of Pentacles Upright

When upright, the Ace of Pentacles suggests new beginnings related to health, monetary matters, and material well-being. In the earliest tarot decks, Pentacles were gold coins, suggesting that this Ace is linked to financial security, sound business practices, and achievements in the material world. The Ace of Coins often accompanies the receipt of money, scholarship aid, a job offer, or an opportunity for increased income. Traditionally it is a card of great joy. Now is a time of reward and recognition for your persistent effort and hard work. The proper care of your body or perhaps some athletic achievement may also be part of the picture.

Ace of Pentacles Reversed

When reversed, the Ace of Pentacles (golden coins) suggests that something may have gone awry in your quest for material well-being. Perhaps you are missing a significant opportunity to improve financial security, or maybe your attitude toward wealth and prosperity needs adjusting. In the myth of King Midas, his unbridled greed for the acquisition of material goods leaves him devoid of human contact. Now may be a good time to ponder Buddha's teachings about nonattachment. Interestingly, the lilies on this card in the Llewellyn Classic Tarot resemble the lotus, a Buddhist symbol of nonattachment; the lotus has the ability to rise above the mire of the swamp and produce an object of beauty.

TWO OF PENTACLES: DESPITE THE SNAGS, KEEP ON DANCING

Etteilla (1791): Snags, upsets, unexpected obstacles, trouble, difficulty, confusion, disquiet, embarrassment, anxiety, agitation; (R) a written document, note, letter, book, literature, bill of exchange.

Mathers (1888): Embarrassment, worry, difficulties; (R) a letter, missive, epistle, message.

Waite (1911): A young man, in the act of dancing, has a pentacle in either hand, and they are joined by that endless cord which is like the number 8 reversed. *Divinatory Meanings*: A card of gaiety, recreation, and its connexions, which is the subject of the design; but it is read also as news and messages in writing, as obstacles, agitation, trouble, embroilment. (R) Enforced gaiety, simulated enjoyment, literal sense, handwriting, composition, letters of exchange.

Crowley/GD: Change, pleasant or harmonious changes, visits with friends.

Number Symbolism: 2—duality, partnership, choice, decision, balance, gestation.

Astrology: Generous and expansive *Jupiter* (debilitated) in the first decan of earthy *Capricorn*, realm of the *Queen of Pentacles* (Water of Earth) and the *Devil* (Capricorn). Jupiter is linked to the *Wheel of Fortune*. The earthy Queen of Pentacles gives birth to the season of winter at the start of Capricorn.

Timing: 0 Capricorn–10 Capricorn. Tropical, 22 December–31 December. Sidereal, 14 January–23 January.

Keywords (+): Change, juggling responsibilities, a balancing act, exchanges, ups and downs, adapting to circumstances, weighing options, multitasking, budgeting time, doing two things at once, riding the waves, fluctuating fortunes, increased stability resulting from a change, a written document, business-related travel, dealings abroad, gaiety, recreation, engaging in the dance of life.

Keywords (-): Complications, troubles, agitation, unexpected obstacles, snags, turbulence, upsets, anxiety, erratic conditions, lack of focus, sink or swim, foolish management of time or resources, too many irons in the fire.

....

Two of Pentacles Upright

When upright, the Two of Pentacles suggests that you are engaged in a balancing act. There may be a conflict, for instance, between the demands of work and those of family. Your life is full of responsibilities you must juggle efficiently to get everything done. Despite any snags, keep on trekking. At this time you are undergoing many changes that will ultimately lead to a sense of increased stability. You may feel as if you are sailing through turbulent waters in hope of calmer seas ahead. It is important to remain flexible and to adapt to circumstances. The ships on this card can imply travel or dealings abroad. A written message or document may also be indicated by this card.

....

Two of Pentacles Reversed

When reversed, the Two of Pentacles implies that you are being pulled in many directions by various commitments and having a hard time adapting and establishing balance in your life. You may feel as if you will either sink or swim. Perhaps you have taken on more than you can handle or others are placing an overwhelming number of demands on your time and energy. Unexpected obstacles and erratic conditions are creating a sense of turbulence. To decrease your anxiety and sense of agitation, you need to focus and bring more balance into your life, even if it means getting outside help or removing some irons from the fire.

THREE OF PENTACLES: TOGETHER WE CAN BUILD A BETTER MOUSETRAP

Etteilla (1791): Fame, renown, celebrity, nobility of conduct, greatness of soul; illustrious, lofty, important; (R) mediocrity, frivolity, childishness, puerility, baseness, cowardice, trifling, lowly.

Mathers (1888): Nobility, elevation, dignity, rank, power; (R) children, sons, daughters, youths, commencement.

Waite (1911): A sculptor at his work in a monastery. Compare the design which illustrates the Eight of Pentacles. The apprentice or amateur therein [in the Eight of Pentacles] has received his reward and is now at work in earnest. *Divinatory Meanings: Métier*, trade, skilled labor; usually, however, regarded as a card of nobility, aristocracy, renown, glory; (R) mediocrity in work and otherwise, puerility, pettiness, weakness.

Crowley/GD: Work, material works, paid employment, engineering, construction, gain in business transactions.

Number Symbolism: 3—fertility, creativity, a triadic relationship, the first fruits of a joint venture.

Astrology: Assertive and pioneering *Mars* (exalted) in the second decan of earthy *Capricorn*, realm of the *Queen of Pentacles* (Water of Earth) and the *Devil* (Capricorn). Mars is linked to the *Tower*.

Timing: 10 Capricorn–20 Capricorn. Tropical, 31 December–9 January. Sidereal, 24 January–2 February.

Keywords (+): Artisanship, skilled labor, the master craftsman, construction, work, high quality, artistry, masterful work, honors, dignity, renown, recognition for one's work, gain in business transactions, maturity, nobility of conduct, collaborating with others to create something new, mentoring, teamwork, a job well done.

Keywords (-): Mediocrity, pettiness, childish behavior, immaturity, laziness, lack of scruples, poor execution, low quality, cutting corners, criticism of one's work.

....
Three of Pentacles Upright

When upright, the Three of Pentacles points to the skillful use of your talents to construct something of quality, often in cooperation with others. It suggests that people will recognize your maturity and truly appreciate your training and experience. There is nothing like a job well done to enhance your reputation and sense of self-esteem.

....
Three of Pentacles Reversed

When reversed, the Three of Pentacles warns of childish, lazy, or immature behavior. You may be cutting corners or not carrying your full load at work. It will become obvious if you are not producing a quality product and failing to live up to your potential. Perhaps you need more training or experience to become better qualified for the job. Don't be content with mediocrity.

FOUR OF PENTACLES: HOLDING TIGHT TO THE GIFT OF SURETY

Etteilla (1791): A gift, favor, benefit, offering, present, donation, assistance, generosity; (R) an enclosure, obstruction, blockage, obstacle, hindrance, delay, boundary, wall, a cloister, monastery, convent.

Mathers (1888): Pleasure, gaiety, enjoyment, satisfaction; (R) obstacles, hindrances.

Waite (1911): A crowned figure, having a pentacle over his crown, clasps another with hands and arms; two pentacles are under his feet. He holds to that which he has. *Divinatory Meanings*: The surety of possessions, cleaving to that which one has, a gift, legacy, inheritance; (R) suspense, delay, opposition.

Crowley/GD: Earthly power, gain of money, gain of influence, a gift.

Number Symbolism: 4—structure, stability, order, logic, foundation, manifestation.

Astrology: The proud and powerful *Sun* in the third decan of earthy *Capricorn*, realm of the Waite *King*/Thoth *Prince of Swords* (Air of Air) and the *Devil* (Capricorn).

Timing: 20 Capricorn–30 Capricorn. Tropical, 10 January–19 January. Sidereal, 3 February–12 February.

Keywords (+): A gift, love of money and possessions, financial benefits, security, gain, surety, earthly power, sound money management, saving for a rainy day, holding on tight, an enclosed space, a cloister, an inheritance, the ability to achieve something in the material world.

Keywords (-): Avarice, greed, miserliness, fear of loss, hoarding, materialism, obstacles, blockages, setbacks, delays; King Midas.

....

Four of Pentacles Upright

When upright, the Four of Pentacles suggests that your focus now is on maintaining wealth and improving material security. To hold on to what you possess, sound financial planning and money management are called for. If you have a long-term goal that requires monetary backing, a careful plan of savings will help you achieve your dream. This card may also mark a period of gain in power, money, or influence. Business dealings go well, and a financial gift or inheritance is possible. Although tempted to cling tightly to what you have, you are also able to enjoy your material well-being and act with generosity.

....

Four of Pentacles Reversed

When reversed, the Four of Pentacles warns of miserliness. You may be clinging too tightly to material goods and earthly power to appreciate the value of human relationships. Your fear of loss may prompt excessive materialism and a cloistered existence hindering you from making important changes that are overdue. Some of your plans to increase your wealth may run into obstacles, opposition, or delays. The myth of King Midas illustrates the types of setbacks excessive greed can entail.

FIVE OF PENTACLES: MONEY CAN'T BUY YOU LOVE

Etteilla (1791): A lover, spouse, paramour, mistress, friend, person in love; concord, suitability, decorum; to love and to cherish; (R) misconduct, trouble, disorganization, disorder, wasting, dissipation, consumption.

Mathers (1888): Lover or mistress, love, sweetness, affection, pure and chaste love; (R) disgraceful love, imprudence, license, profligacy.

Waite (1911): Two mendicants in a snow-storm pass a lighted casement. *Divinatory Meanings*: The card foretells material trouble above all, whether in the form illustrated—that is, destitution—or otherwise. For some cartomancists, it is a card of love and lovers—wife, husband, friend, mistress; also concordance, affinities. These alternatives cannot be harmonized. (R) disorder, chaos, ruin, discord, profligacy.

Crowley/GD: Worry, disquiet, material trouble, unemployment, loss of money, strain, inaction, financial worries.

Number Symbolism: 5—instability, disruption, crisis, loss, tension, conflict.

Astrology: Nimble and clever *Mercury* in the first decan of earthy *Taurus*, realm of the Waite *King*/Thoth *Prince of Pentacles* (Air of Earth) and the *Hierophant* (Taurus). Mercury is linked to the *Magician*. [The church window is a reference to the Pope and the sacrament of marriage. Fickle *Mercury* brings instability to the earthy solidity reflected in *Taurus* and the *King of Pentacles*, thus exposing the marriage to fluctuations in its material security.]

Timing: 0 Taurus–10 Taurus. Tropical, 21 April–30 April. Sidereal, 14 May–24 May.

Keywords (+): Spiritual solace, seeking financial assistance, mutual support, devotion, pure love, affection, commitment, lovemaking, affinity, concord, reconciliation, married life for better or for worse; "no matter what happens, we're in this together."

Keywords (-): Marital difficulties, financial setbacks, job loss, dissipation, dissolution of a loving relationship, infidelity, misconduct, illicit love affairs, lack of commitment, absence of support, abandonment to the slings and arrows of fortune, fair-weather friendship, unfulfilling relationships, material trouble, financial loss, unexpected expenses, hardship, begging, unemployment, worry, disquiet, stress, strain, feeling pressured, troubling thoughts, neediness, fear of poverty, destitution, squandering resources, profligacy.

....

Five of Pentacles Upright

When upright, the Five of Pentacles traditionally refers to two people who remain very much in love despite any material troubles they must confront. They take seriously their marriage vows: "for better, for worse, for richer, for poorer, in sickness and in health, until death do us part." The lovers walking in a snowstorm pass the church where they got married. Despite declining finances and ill health, they remain devoted to each other in a committed relationship. This card indicates the importance of love and mutual support in weathering life's storms. It shows a willingness to face hardships with a partner in a mutually supportive way.

....

Five of Pentacles Reversed

When reversed, the Five of Pentacles suggests a reluctance to fulfill a commitment when the going gets tough. The idealism of young love comes into conflict with harsh reality, making it difficult to stay together when confronted with financial loss, ill health, or other trying circumstances. Rather than attempt to reconcile differences and make your emotional ties more satisfying, you are inclined to give up and seek satisfaction elsewhere. In essence, you may be deciding to leave your partner out in the cold, or you may find yourself undergoing such an experience.

SIX OF PENTACLES: SHARING MATERIAL SUCCESS NOW!

Etteilla (1791): Now! At this moment, currently, at the present time; surroundings, assistant, witness, vigilant, careful, attentive; (R) ambition, longing, ardor, passion, desire, cupidity, jealousy.

Mathers (1888): Presents, gifts, gratification; (R) ambition, desire, passion, aim, longing.

Waite (1911): A person in the guise of a merchant weighs money in a pair of scales and distributes it to the needy and distressed. It is a testimony to his own success in life, as well as to his goodness of heart. *Divinatory Meanings*: Presents, gifts, gratification another account says attention, vigilance, now is the accepted time, present prosperity (R) desire, cupidity, envy, jealousy, illusion.

Crowley/GD: Material success, prosperity in business, transient success, the influence of a child.

Number Symbolism: 6—harmony, communication, sharing, compassion.

Astrology: The emotional and sensitive *Moon* (exalted) in the second decan of earthy *Taurus*, realm of the Waite *King*/Thoth *Prince of Pentacles* (Air of Earth) and the *Hierophant* (Taurus). The Moon is linked to the *High Priestess.*

Timing: 10 Taurus–20 Taurus. Tropical, 1 May–10 May. Sidereal, 4 June–14 June.

Keywords (+): Generosity, kindness, material success, goodness of heart, sharing resources, receiving assistance, support, being supported, financial aid, benevolence, mentoring, patronage, charity, giving and receiving, philanthropy, accomplishment, prosperity, social responsibility, equitable distribution of wealth, taking care of present needs; now, at present, currently, at this time. (Note that traditionally the Six of Pentacles refers to now and the Six of Cups refers to the past.)

Keywords (-): Indulgence, envy, dissipation, wastefulness, financial irresponsibility, extravagance, jealousy, loss, favoritism, ingratitude, unfair distribution of wealth, trickle-down economics; the check is in the mail.

....

Six of Pentacles Upright

When upright, the Six of Pentacles implies that money and resources are being apportioned in a fair and socially responsible manner. If your financial situation is secure, you may be called upon to assist those who are less fortunate. If you are experiencing a present need, essential resources and financial aid are likely to become available. An essential meaning of this card is that something of value is being passed from one person to another in a spirit of true generosity. In the words of President John F. Kennedy's 1961 inaugural address, "Ask not what your country can do for you; ask what you can do for your country." If your question was about the best time to act, this card suggests that *now* is the opportune moment. Now! The idea that the present is the accepted time may be related to this card's association with the Moon as it goes through phases, but astrologically it is at its best when it transits the sign Taurus.

....

Six of Pentacles Reversed

When reversed, the Six of Pentacles suggests an unfair or inequitable distribution of wealth and resources. Perhaps your situation involves some sort of nepotism, favoritism, ingratitude for help received, or envy of another's good fortune. You may be squandering your fortune or using your wealth for purely selfish ends without regard for the welfare of the planet or that of your fellow human beings. Be responsible with your money. No one likes to hear that the check is in the mail. Maybe "now" is not the time.

SEVEN OF PENTACLES: WHERE YOUR TREASURE IS, THERE ALSO YOUR HEART WILL BE

Etteilla (1791): Money, riches, wealth, silverware, purification, whiteness, purity, naïveté, candor, innocence, the Moon; (R) anxiety, disquiet, impatience, worry, apprehension, fear, affliction, concern, care, attention, diligence, chagrin, mistrust, suspicion.

Mathers (1888): Money, finance, treasure, gain, profit; (R) disturbance, worry, anxiety, melancholy.

Waite (1911): A young man, leaning on his staff, looks intently at seven pentacles attached to a clump of greenery on his right; one would say that these were his treasures and that his heart was there. *Divinatory Meanings*: A card of money, business, barter; but one reading gives altercation, quarrels—and another, innocence, ingenuity, purgation; (R) cause for anxiety regarding money which it may be proposed to lend.

Crowley/GD: Failure, blight, success unfulfilled, labor without pay, work for little gain, unprofitable speculation.

Number Symbolism: 7—assessment, reevaluation, standing at a threshold, seeking advantage.

Astrology: The stern taskmaster *Saturn* in the third decan of earthy *Taurus*, realm of the *Knight of Swords* and the *Hierophant* (Taurus). Saturn is linked to the *World*.

Timing: 20 Taurus–30 Taurus. Tropical, 11 May–20 May. Sidereal, 4 June–14 June.

Keywords (+): Perseverance, long-term planning, realistic assessment, reevaluation, quality control, taking stock, investing wisely for the future, slow but steady progress, the just rewards of hard work, waiting for the proper time to harvest, an office romance, unrequited labor, getting what you deserve, planning for financial security in retirement.

Keywords (-): Worries about money, impatience, apprehension, excessive caution, feelings of insecurity, fear of failure, loss, limited success, lack of recompense, much work for little return, wasted resources, missed opportunities, a bad investment, unprofitable speculation, not focusing on the task at hand, poor planning for retirement.

....
Seven of Pentacles Upright

When upright, the Seven of Pentacles shows a farmer who has paused in the midst of his labors to assess his progress and plan his next moves. He has worked hard to get to this point and is well aware that his efforts will eventually pay off. Perhaps he is wondering what else he needs to be doing at this time. When we plant seeds, we know that no amount of impatience on our part will speed their growth. Instead, diligent care, responsible cultivation, and respect for natural cycles will produce an abundant harvest. The planet Saturn associated with this card is a strict taskmaster who, in the end, gives us what we deserve. As we read in the Bible, "Whatsoever a man soweth, that shall he also reap" (Galatians 6:7, KJV).

....
Seven of Pentacles Reversed

When reversed, the Seven of Pentacles suggests that you are feeling apprehension about financial security. Perhaps you are worried that there will not be a sufficient return on your investment of time, resources, or money. The problem is that investments typically take time to mature and cannot be rushed. Impatience can result in wasted resources, failed projects, or missed opportunities. You need to assess your situation realistically and follow principles of sound fiscal management if you wish to succeed. If you're not sure about what to do, get advice from an expert consultant. Daydreaming or focusing on irrelevant matters will not help you to reassess the situation that is causing anxiety. The planet Saturn associated with this card implies that you need to keep your nose to the grindstone. You will get as much from your project as you put into it; no pain, no gain.

EIGHT OF PENTACLES: SKILL IN THE MATERIAL WORLD

Etteilla (1791): A dark girl, a pleasant girl, gracious, amiable, passive; (R) avarice, greed, usury, miserliness, lack of ambition.

Mathers (1888): A dark girl, beauty, candor, chastity, innocence, modesty; (R) flattery, usury, hypocrisy, shiftiness.

Waite (1911): An artist in stone at his work, which he exhibits in the form of trophies. *Divinatory Meanings*: Work, employment, commission, craftsmanship, skill in craft and business, perhaps in the preparatory stage; (R) voided ambition, vanity, cupidity, exaction, usury. It may also signify the possession of skill, in the sense of the ingenious mind turned to cunning and intrigue.

Crowley/GD: Prudence, skill, artfulness, cunning, carefulness in one's work, putting something away for a rainy day.

Number Symbolism: 8—movement, action, power, determination.

Astrology: The proud and powerful *Sun* in the first decan of earthy *Virgo*, realm of the *Knight of Pentacles* (Fire of Earth) and the *Hermit* (Virgo). The Sun in Virgo is known for its perfectionism, service-orientation, and meticulous attention to detail.

Timing: 0 Virgo–10 Virgo. Tropical, 23 August–1 September. Sidereal, 17 September–26 September.

Keywords (+): Work, employment, training, apprenticeship, careful preparation, putting in the effort to do a task well, competence, dedication, patience, job satisfaction, skill in material affairs, honing one's talents, technical expertise, doing your homework, dexterity, prudence, discretion, diligent labor, perfectionism, determination to do a good job, making good use of available resources, getting paid for what you love to do.

Keywords (-): Voided ambition, inadequate training, impatience, failure to apply proper effort, ignoring obligations, rashness, intrigue, cunning, shiftiness, misuse of talents, opportunities wasted, penny wise and pound foolish.

....

Eight of Pentacles Upright

When upright, the Eight of Pentacles shows a craftsman perfecting his skills and working diligently to do an excellent job. This is a card of training and apprenticeship with the goal of honing one's abilities to produce a quality product. There is much satisfaction in attending to details and doing things well, even if it takes several attempts to get it right. The artisan on the card is willing to put in the necessary time and effort. He understands the need to be patient and allow things to mature properly rather than try to rush the process. Traditionally this card refers to an amiable and modest peasant girl who approaches her chores diligently without complaint or pretension, as symbolized by the sign of Virgo associated with the card.

....

Eight of Pentacles Reversed

When reversed, the Eight of Pentacles suggests that you may not be putting in the needed time and effort to do a job well. Maybe you don't care about producing a quality product, or maybe you are cutting corners just to get the job done. Remember that Rome wasn't built in a day. Although there may be a short-term gain in your current approach, in the long run you are likely to feel a sense of dissatisfaction. When the storm arrives, it's comforting to know you have put something away for a rainy day.

NINE OF PENTACLES: SOLITARY ATTAINMENT IN MATERIAL AFFAIRS

Etteilla (1791): Attainment, realization, achievement, accomplishment, success, fulfillment; (R) deception, fraud, cheating, dupery, broken promises, aborted projects.

Mathers (1888): Discretion, circumspection, prudence, discernment; (R) deceit, bad faith, artifices, deception.

Waite (1911): A woman, with a bird upon her wrist, stands amidst a great abundance of grapevines in the garden of a manorial house. It is a wide domain, suggesting plenty in all things. Possibly it is her own possession and testifies to material well-being. *Divinatory Meanings*: Prudence, safety, success, accomplishment, certitude, discernment; (R) roguery, deception, voided project, bad faith.

Crowley/GD: Gain, luck in material affairs, improved finances, inheritance, favor, popularity, material increase, the state of being pregnant.

Number Symbolism: 9—the final single digit, culmination, fruition, attainment.

Astrology: Lovely and affectionate *Venus* (debilitated) in the second decan of earthy *Virgo*, realm of the *Knight of Pentacles* (Fire of Earth) and the *Hermit* (Virgo). Venus is linked to the *Empress*.

Timing: 10 Virgo–20 Virgo. Tropical, 2 September–11 September. Sidereal, 27 September–6 October.

Keywords (+): Gain, accomplishment, fulfillment, discernment, fruition, discretion, refinement, favor, elegance, meticulous care, material security, financial reward, self-sufficiency, solitary satisfaction, valuable time alone, self-reliance, pregnant with ideas or with child, fondness for small animals, enjoying the bounty of the harvest.

Keywords (-): Deception, bad faith, loss, wastefulness, social isolation, solitariness, loneliness, aborted projects, blocked progress, slow maturation of plans, fraud, broken promises, vile behavior, a sense of entitlement, compromised security.

Nine of Pentacles Upright

When upright, the Nine of Pentacles depicts the discerning virgin of the sign Virgo, a self-contained maiden modeled after Astraea/Dike, the goddess of purity and justice who held a grain of wheat in her left hand. Under Astraea's rule, the human race enjoyed peace, prosperity, perfect weather, and eternal youth. Unfortunately, the increasing vileness of human behavior caused the discerning goddess to flee to the heavens where she became the constellation Virgo, isolated from the wickedness of humankind. The Nine of Pentacles is a card of accomplishment, refinement, material fortune, and enjoyment of the fruits of the harvest. It indicates being rewarded for discretion, hard work, meticulous care, and prudent planning.

Nine of Pentacles Reversed

When reversed, the Nine of Pentacles suggests a situation in which someone acts in bad faith or blocks your progress. As a result of deception or broken promises, a project may fail to materialize or need to be aborted. Perhaps you were counting on someone to keep their word, only to discover that they have left you in the lurch. You may end up feeling isolated or sensing that security has been compromised. Having carefully planned and cultivated your garden, you discover that the time has not yet come to enjoy the harvest.

TEN OF PENTACLES: A PROSPEROUS HOUSEHOLD

Etteilla (1791): Household, dwelling, household economy, savings, family, posterity; (R) lot, fate, destiny, gamble, unforeseen happenings.

Mathers (1888): House, dwelling, habitation, family; (R) gambling, dissipation, robbery, loss.

Waite (1911): A man and woman beneath an archway which gives entrance to a house and domain. They are accompanied by a child, who looks curiously at two dogs accosting an ancient personage seated in the foreground. The child's hand is on one of them. *Divinatory Meanings*: Gain, riches; family matters, archives, extraction, the abode of a family; (R) chance, fatality, loss, robbery, games of hazard; sometimes gift, dowry, pension.

Crowley/GD: Wealth, riches.

Number Symbolism: 10—one too many, the fullness of completion, readiness to begin a new cycle.

Astrology: Nimble and clever *Mercury* (dignified) in the third decan of earthy *Virgo*, realm of the *Queen of Swords* (Water of Air) and the *Hermit* (Virgo). Mercury is linked to the *Magician*.

Timing: 20 Virgo–30 Virgo. Tropical, 12 September–22 September. Sidereal, 7 October–16 October.

Keywords (+): Wealth, family prosperity, savings, abundance, financial security, social status, the wise use of money, family matters, generational bonds, posterity, an inheritance, legacy, gift, dowry, pension, using one's accumulated resources to benefit others or one's heirs, caring for one's pets; a dog is a man's best friend.

Keywords (-): Financial insecurity, loss, robbery, dissipation, family feuds, gambling debts, failed speculation, unwise use of money, reckless spending, hoarding one's wealth rather than using it to benefit others.

....
Ten of Pentacles Upright

When upright, the Ten of Pentacles depicts a secure family environment populated by several generations, including the family dogs. The patriarch of the family apparently has provided well for his children and grandchildren and will no doubt leave them an inheritance. There is little point in accumulating wealth only to hoard it. The family on this card is enjoying the benefits of sound financial planning and wise investments. Even the family's pets are well cared for.

....
Ten of Pentacles Reversed

When reversed, the Ten of Pentacles hints at a family feud related to financial insecurity or a matter of legacy or inheritance. The person in charge of planning for the needs of his or her dependents has instead been guilty of unwise speculation or poor financial planning. In some cases, this card may highlight problems related to gambling. Alternatively, the person who should be providing for the family has opted to hoard his or her wealth rather than use it for the benefit of others.

Twelve

The Court Cards

What the Court Cards Can Tell You

Traditionally the court cards represent members of the royal court: the King, Queen, Knight, and Page. The accompanying "mind map" presents one way to picture the four court cards of the tarot.

Carl Jung and the Court Cards

Over the years, many ways of conceptualizing the court cards have appeared in the literature. Several tarot readers, myself included, have been influenced by the writings of Swiss psychoanalyst Carl Jung. Not only did Jung elaborate the concept of archetypes that relate directly to the images on the cards, but he also developed a theory of personality types that is useful in understanding the court cards.

Based on his own observations and those of clients, Jung discovered that human beings experience the world in four distinct but overlapping ways. The practice of dividing phenomena into four component parts is a time-honored tradition in Western philosophy as well as in the tarot, which relies heavily on the idea of the four elements of Greek philosophy: Fire, Water, Air, and Earth.

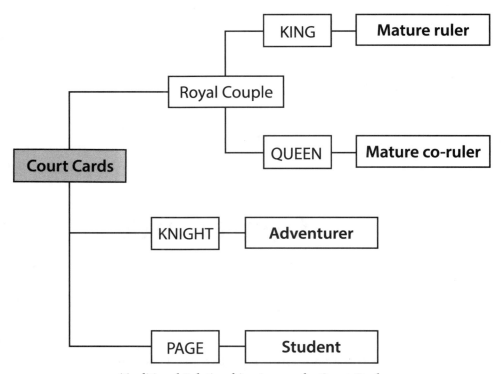

Traditional Relationships Among the Court Cards

A simple example will make Jung's ideas clear: Suppose you are walking down a street in San Francisco, California. Suddenly you hear a loud rumbling sound and you feel a strong vibration beneath your feet. You look up and notice that the buildings are swaying back and forth. A fire hydrant bursts open and water begins to gush forth. Through the information you receive from your senses, you realize that something unusual and vibratory is going on. Jung called the act of sensing that something is occurring or that something exists in your environment, the function of sensation. In the tarot, sensory perception and the awareness of tangible reality are related to the element Earth and the suit of gold coins or Pentacles.

Using the perceptions of vibration provided by your senses, your rational mind goes to work. You seek to understand what is happening. From the sensory evidence, you deduce that the city is undergoing an earthquake. Now you have a word or a concept that provides an abstract name for what is happening. Jung called the act of concept formation or rational understanding the function of thinking. In the tarot, logical thought belongs to the element Air and is characteristic of the incisive suit of Swords.

At this point you have exercised your function of sensation to become aware of a strange vibration through sensory perception. You have also thought about the unusual sensations and deduced logically that you are in the midst of an earthquake. Next your emotions kick in, and you seek to evaluate the importance of what is happening emotionally. Your feelings prompt you to form an emotional value judgment, that is, to determine the emotional significance of what is happening. You are likely to judge that something frightening is happening and to feel a need to find a safe haven from the threat of falling concrete. Jung called the act of forming value judgments based on your emotional evaluation of a situation the function of feeling. In the tarot, feeling is related to the element Water and is characteristic of the emotional suit of Cups.

Next you have a hunch, a gut feeling that you should cross the street. You don't know where the idea came from, but you follow your gut instinct and move to the other side of the road. A few minutes later, bricks fall from a building across the street onto the sidewalk where you were previously standing. Your hunch has paid off and saved your life. Jung called the act of unconscious perception, the intuitive awareness of future possibilities and the quick flashes of insight that come "out of the blue," the function of intuition. In the tarot, intuition is related to the element Fire and is characteristic of Wands, the suit of life and animation.

In understanding the court cards, Jung's ideas about the four functions are especially helpful. Each suit excels at one of these four functions, as does each type of court card. Kings are airy thinking types, Queens are watery feeling types, Knights are fiery intuitive types, and Pages are earthy sensation types.

Note that some authors prefer to associate Kings with Fire and intuition, and they assign Knights to Air and the thinking function. If you prefer this alternative method of assignment, by all means use it and adjust the comments in this text accordingly. My own preference is to view the court cards as follows:

Pages and Sensation

Pages and the earthy suit of Pentacles excel at sensation. They are especially good at observing and gathering sense impressions that establish facts about what is happening. The process of collecting tangible evidence can be slow and painstaking. Pages want to be sure their evidence is solidly based before applying their thinking function to understand the facts, or their feeling function to form value judgments based on their emotional evaluation of the sensory evidence.

Kings and Thinking

Kings and the airy suit of Swords excel at thinking. They are especially good at mental planning, logical inference, strategizing, theorizing, and concept formation. Kings seek to understand the meaning of things on the basis of the facts they have to deal with. They like to connect the dots. Sensation provides the facts; thinking provides the understanding of those facts. Kings tend to think more with their heads than with their hearts.

Queens and Feeling

Queens and the watery suit of Cups excel at feeling. They use their emotional reactions to facts to judge the value, or the lack thereof, of a situation. In other words, Queens use their emotional intelligence to evaluate whether something is agreeable or disagreeable, valuable or worthless, desirable or odious, pleasurable or painful, safe or dangerous, and so on. They might, for instance, emotionally conclude that something feels like the right thing to do. Unlike the Kings, the Queens are more likely to think with their hearts than with their heads.

Knights and Intuition

Knights and the fiery suit of Wands excel at intuition. They rely heavily on intuitive hunches and quick flashes of insight about future possibilities. Their ideas often come unbidden or out of the blue; they typically can't explain the source of these unconscious perceptions. Unlike Pages who take their time observing and gathering sense impressions, Knights act quickly, impulsively, and ambitiously in response to sudden bursts of inspiration.

Table of Jung's Typology for the Court Cards

It is important to keep in mind that none of these functions exists in isolation. Our understanding of the world is always based on a combination of sensing, thinking, feeling, and intuition. Some people and some court cards, however, excel at one or more of these functions in preference to others. For example, the Page (Earth) of Swords (Air) is a keen observer of his environment (an Earth or sensation function) and quickly connects the dots and elaborates theories about what is going on (an Air or thinking function). The remaining court cards can be analyzed in a similar way. The accompanying table illustrates Jung's typology as applied to the court cards of the tarot.

	Fire—Intuition— *Knights*	Water—Feeling— *Queens*	Air—Thinking— *Kings (Princes)*	Earth—Sensation— *Pages*
Fire **Intuition** *Wands*	Knight of Wands	Queen of Wands	King of Wands	Page of Wands
Water **Feeling** *Cups*	Knight of Cups	Queen of Cups	King of Cups	Page of Cups
Air **Thinking** *Swords*	Knight of Swords	Queen of Swords	King of Swords	Page of Swords
Earth **Sensation** *Pentacles*	Knight of Pentacles	Queen of Pentacles	King of Pentacles	Page of Pentacles

Will the Real King Please Stand Up?

The Golden Dawn introduced confusion into the notion of tarot Knights and Kings. The founders of the Golden Dawn referred to traditional tarot Knights as Kings, and to the traditional tarot Kings as Princes.

Arthur Edward Waite, a member of the Golden Dawn, used the traditional names and images of the Tarot of Marseille for his court cards. Nonetheless, Waite explicitly states, in accord with the Golden Dawn, that Knights are men over forty and Kings are younger than the Knights. Thus, Waite viewed Kings as equivalent to the Golden Dawn's Princes! In modern practice, however, the majority of tarot readers regard Knights as being younger than Kings, and Kings as men over forty—the opposite of what Waite intended.

Aleister Crowley, another former member of the Golden Dawn, also referred to Knights as youthful and acknowledged the impossibility of reconciling the various court card traditions the Golden Dawn was trying to synthesize:

"... no sooner has the Princess made her appearance than the Prince wins her in marriage, and she is set upon the throne of her Mother. She thus awakens the Eld of the original old King; who thereupon becomes a young Knight, and so renews the cycle [...] It is impossible to harmonize the multitudinous fables or parables, because each was invented to emphasize some formula that was regarded as imperative to serve some local or temporal purpose." [43]

The Golden Dawn bases its system on the correspondences between the court cards and the Tetragrammaton *Yahveh*—Yod, Heh, Vav, Heh—the four Hebrew letters in the name of the deity. The accompanying table illustrates these associations.

Tetragrammaton	Element— Jungian Function	Golden Dawn	Waite-Smith
Yod	Fire—Intuition	King (on horseback)	Knight (on horseback)
Heh (initial)	Water—Feeling	Queen	Queen
Vav	Air—Thinking	Prince (in chariot)	King (on throne)
Heh (final)	Earth—Sensation	Princess	Page, Knave

Because of the confusion introduced by the Golden Dawn, some authors associate the Golden Dawn Princes (sometimes called Kings by the Golden Dawn) with the traditional Marseille Knights, and the Golden Dawn Kings (variously called Knights, Lords, or Kings by the Golden Dawn, shown

---

43. Aleister Crowley, *The Book of Thoth*, 151.

as men riding stallions) with the traditional Kings of the Marseille deck. For a detailed discussion of the correspondences see www.lelandra.com/tarotbook/courtcorres.htm.

An Astrological Explanation

The Golden Dawn assigned the beginning of the zodiac circle to the first decan of Leo, the Lion King of the Zodiac. In the middle of the first decan of Leo (in the sidereal zodiac as the Golden Dawn used) lies the royal star Regulus, the heart of the lion ancient astrologers regarded as the ruler of the heavens. According to Israel Regardie, "The beginning of the decanates is from the Royal King Star of the Heart of the Lion, the great star Cor Leonis, and therefore is the first decanate that of Saturn in Leo." [44] Saturn comes first in the order of visible planets known to the ancient Chaldeans and thus is the proper starting place for the entire zodiac.

The Golden Dawn assigned the first decan of Leo to the Prince of the Chariot of Fire, that is, the Marseille King of Wands. The confusion arises because the Golden Dawn views Princes as traditional Kings, symbolized by the regal sign Leo and the royal star Regulus, but at the same time it views the Knights as the most senior members of the court cards. As Crowley stated, there is no easy way, based in logic, to resolve this dilemma, so choices have to be made.

My attempt to deal with this confusion about the court cards is to take a generic approach. In contrast to equating Golden Dawn Kings on horseback with traditional Knights, my preference is to follow the widely accepted practice of viewing youthful men on horseback as Knights and, like the Golden Dawn, to regard its Princes as the traditional Kings. Thus in this book and in the remainder of this chapter the convention will be as follows:

Knights (Youthful Adventurers)

Knights, the virile action-oriented young men riding powerful horses, rule the last decan of the fixed signs and the first two decans of the mutable signs. They represent the dynamic element Fire (*Yod*) and bring about the closing of one season and the transition to the next. Much as the Knights regulate the change of seasons, they also symbolize movement, action, change, progress, and relocation in the querent's life. Fiery Knights exemplify the Jungian function of *intuition*.

Queens (Mature Maternal Figures)

Queens, seated on thrones, rule the last decan of the mutable signs and the first two decans of the cardinal signs. They represent the emotional element Water (initial *Heh*). As mother figures, Queens give birth to the four seasons of the year. They symbolize women who are important in the querent's life, often in a nurturing or supportive capacity. Watery Queens exemplify the Jungian function of *feeling*.

---

44.   Israel Regardie, *The Golden Dawn* (St. Paul, MN: Llewellyn, 1989), 550.

Kings (Mature Paternal Figures)

Kings, seated on thrones, are the equivalent of the Golden Dawn's Princes riding in chariots. Kings/ Princes rule the last decan of the cardinal signs and the first two decans of the fixed signs. They represent the rational element Air (*Vav*) and govern the blossoming, maturation, and fullness of the four seasons. Kings symbolize mature persons of power and authority who are significant in the querent's life. The airy Kings exemplify the Jungian function of *thinking*.

Pages (Young Learners)

Pages, portrayed as standing rather than sitting on thrones or in vehicles or riding horses, have no zodiacal attribution. They represent the element Earth (final *Heh*). Pages are novices, youthful and inexperienced students. According to the Golden Dawn, the Pages (Princesses) rule the four quarters of the heavens around the North Pole, above the respective Kerubic signs of the zodiac, and they form the Thrones of the Powers of the four Aces. [45] The earthy Pages exemplify the Jungian function of *sensation*.

When using specific decks, however, such as the Crowley Thoth or the Liber T Tarot of Stars Eternal deck, it is best to follow the instructions of deck's author in the Little White Book (LWB) that accompanies the deck. For example, the Golden Dawn Tarot deck by Robert Wang avoids the name "Knight" entirely and uses the following designations for the court cards: Princess, Prince (in a chariot), Queen, and King (on horseback).

---

45. Ibid., 544.

The Suit of Wands

PAGE OF WANDS: A SURPRISING STRANGER

Etteilla (1791): A stranger, a foreigner, novelty, marvel, surprise, originality, extraordinary things; (R) news, advice, notice, stories, announcement, warning, admonition, education, instruction.

Mathers (1888): A Good Stranger, good news, pleasure, satisfaction; (R) ill news, displeasure, chagrin, worry.

Waite (1911): In a scene similar to the former [that of the Knight of Wands], a young man stands in the act of proclamation. He is unknown but faithful, and his tidings are strange. *Divinatory Meanings*: Dark young man, faithful, a lover, an envoy, a postman. Beside a man, he will bear favorable testimony concerning him. A dangerous rival, if followed by the Page of Cups. Has the chief qualities of his suit. He may signify family intelligence; (R) anecdotes, announcements, evil news. Also indecision and the instability which accompanies it.

Crowley/GD: Princess of the Shining Flame. Rose of the Palace of Fire. Daring, energetic, aspiring, confident, ambitious, brilliant, dramatic, superficial, sudden, shallow, cruel, violent, domineering. The traits displayed depend on the dignity of the card.

Astrology: Earth of Fire. According to Crowley in *The Book of Thoth*, the Pages (Princesses) have no zodiacal attribution but represent four types of "elemental" people.

Jungian Functions: Sensation (Earth) and intuition (Fire).

Decans/Timing: Astrology associates the element Fire with springtime.

Keywords (+): A stranger, a foreigner, a bearer of good news; passionate, energetic, ardent, enthusiastic, adventurous, surprising, future-oriented; inspiration, ambition, confidence, creativity, new life, budding sexual interests, learning, curiosity, education, an exciting opportunity, fresh possibilities, foreign travel, study abroad, new career interests, the start of an exciting relationship, something to marvel at, a surprise.

Keywords (-): Reckless, impulsive, irresponsible, domineering; bad news, warnings, indecision, worry, lack of initiative, an unwanted pregnancy.

Page of Wands Upright

Pages represent children, young people, new situations, and the beginning stages of a project or journey. They can also signify messengers or messages coming to the querent. When upright, the Page of Wands is a youthful person, full of surprises, who is ambitious to expand his or her horizons through travel, education, or involvement in an exciting adventure. A stranger or foreigner can open your mind to new vistas. Life is an adventure, and this Page wants to live it to the fullest.

Page of Wands Reversed

When reversed, the Page of Wands may bring bad news or indicate the delay of a message the querent was expecting. New projects may run into snags or have trouble getting off the ground. The querent may need to guard against reckless, impulsive, or overly ambitious behavior. A stranger or foreigner may be a source of difficulties.

KNIGHT OF WANDS: DEPARTING FOR ADVENTURE

Etteilla (1791): Change, departure, flight, alienation, displacement, emigration, moving, relocation, abandonment; (R) separation, parting, breach, discord, disruption, discontinuity, interruption. (Note that the Knight of receptive Cups *arrives* whereas the Knight of outgoing Wands *departs*. Cups, being watery, are emotionally oriented and inner-directed. Wands, being fiery, are energetically active and outer-directed.)

Mathers (1888): Departure, separation, disunion; (R) rupture, discord, quarrel.

Waite (1911): He is shewn as if upon a journey, armed with a short wand, and although mailed is not on a warlike errand. He is passing mounds or pyramids. The motion of the horse is a key to the character of its rider, and suggests the precipitate mood, or things connected therewith. *Divinatory Meanings*: Departure, absence, flight, emigration. A dark young man, friendly. Change of residence; (R) rupture, division, interruption, discord.

Crowley/GD: Lord of the Flame and Lightning. King of the Spirits of Fire. Active, swift, impetuous, daring, adventurous, revolutionary, unpredictable, proud, generous, confident, fierce, competitive, bigoted, brutal, cruel. The traits displayed depend on the dignity of the card.

Astrology: Fire of Fire.

Jungian Functions: Intuition (Fire) in double measure.

Decans/Timing: 20 Scorpio–20 Sagittarius. Tropical, 12 November–12 December; Sidereal, 06 December–04 January

Associated Trumps: Death and Temperance.

Associated Pips: Seven of Cups, Eight and Nine of Wands.

Keywords (+): Adventurous, outgoing, dynamic, brave, active, proud, generous, confident, popular, sexy, passionate, charismatic, unpredictable, charming, eloquent, fond of challenge, full of surprises; departure, long-distance travel, flight, movement, action, sexual excitement, inspiration, love of adventure, going on vacation, adding spice to your life, exploration, separation, relocation, emigration, transition, a change of job or residence, blasting off.

Keywords (-): volatile, indecisive, unreliable, cruel, intolerant, recklessly unpredictable, irresponsible, stuck in a rut; discord, alienation, disruption, abandonment, unnecessary risk, avoidance of commitment, a break-up in a relationship.

Knight of Wands Upright

Knights correspond to the element Fire, which suggests action, enterprise, movement, novelty, and excitement coming into your life. When upright, the Knight of Wands advises you to get ready for an exciting ride as he adds spice to your life. Change is in the air. This knight loves to travel. He readily picks up roots to move to a new location, so a change of job or residence is possible. The Wand Knight is full of surprises, and you can expect the unexpected. Hollywood actor James Dean might be considered a prototype for this very fiery knight.

Knight of Wands Reversed

When reversed, the Knight of Wands warns of travel difficulties and disharmony in relationships. His unpredictability can catch you off guard. He may suddenly change his mind and take off without warning on some half-baked adventure. Remaining responsibly committed to a relationship is not his strong suit. This Knight may light fires that he can't put out.

QUEEN OF WANDS: THE CHARISMATIC CAT LADY

Etteilla (1791): A rural lady, mistress of a country estate, chastity, virtue, honor, gentleness, household economy; (R) service, devotion, duty, kindness, a good wife.

Mathers (1888): Woman living in the country, lady of the manor, love of money, avarice, usury; (R) a good and virtuous woman, but strict and economical; obstacles, resistance, opposition.

Waite (1911): The Wands throughout this suit are always in leaf, as it is a suit of life and animation. Emotionally and otherwise, the Queen's personality corresponds to that of the King, but is more magnetic. *Divinatory Meanings*: A dark woman, countrywoman, friendly, chaste, loving, honorable. If the card beside her signifies a man, she is well disposed toward him; if a woman, she is interested in the querent. Also, love of money, or a certain success in business; (R) good, economical, obliging, serviceable. Signifies also—but in certain positions and in the neighborhood of other cards tending in such directions—opposition, jealousy, even deceit and infidelity.

Crowley/GD: Queen of the Thrones of Flame. Calm, commanding, steady, kind, generous, friendly, adaptable, energetic, enthusiastic, confident, attractive, proud, domineering, snobbish, obstinate, willful, brooding, vengeful, tyrannical. The traits displayed depend on the dignity of the card.

Astrology: Water of Fire. The Queen of Wands gives birth to springtime at the vernal equinox in the Northern Hemisphere.

Jungian Functions: Feeling (Water) and Intuition (Fire).

Decans/Timing: 20 Pisces–20 Aries. Tropical, 11 March–09 April. Sidereal, 03 April–04 May.

Associated Trumps: The Moon and the Emperor.

Associated Pips: Ten of Cups, Two and Three of Wands.

Keywords (+): Energetic, confident, independent, capable, strong-willed, career-oriented, gregarious, vital, sexy, passionate, sociable, extroverted, cheerful, inspiring, buoyant, proud, ambitious, dignified, protective, in command, brimming with ideas, full of vim and vigor, busy as a bee; a leader, a female authority figure, a woman in charge of her household, the life of the party.

Keywords (-): Bossy, pushy, willful, egotistical, selfish, jealous, deceitful, meddlesome, unfaithful, self-centered, over-enthusiastic; a busybody.

....

Queen of Wands Upright

Queens are mature nurturing individuals (mother figures) who are responsive to the emotional climate surrounding the querent. They represent mother figures, important women related to the current situation, and significant personality traits needed by the querent to navigate the matter at hand. When upright, the Queen of Wands is a gregarious, energetic woman who is strong-willed and gets things done. Despite her independent streak, she remains devoted to home and family. She loves being in the midst of activity, or preferably being at the center of it, and often has many irons in the fire.

....

Queen of Wands Reversed

When reversed, the Queen of Wands tends to be bossy and overbearing. She likes things done her way and doesn't tolerate much opposition to her will. Her excessive pride can result in cruelty and proneness to bearing a grudge. She tends to want what she wants when she wants it and, as a result, she may not respect the boundaries or responsibilities of a committed relationship.

KING OF WANDS: VIRILE MASTER OF THE REALM

Etteilla (1791): A rural gentleman, master of a country estate, a farmer, an honest man, integrity, decency; (R) a good man, a stern man, lenient, tolerant.

Mathers (1888): Man living in the country, country gentleman, knowledge, education; (R) a naturally good but severe man, counsel, advice, deliberation.

Waite (1911): The physical and emotional nature to which this card is attributed is dark, ardent, lithe, animated, impassioned, noble. The King uplifts a flowering wand, and wears, like his three correspondences in the remaining suits, what is called a cap of maintenance beneath his crown. He connects with the symbol of the lion, which is emblazoned on the back of his throne. *Divinatory Meanings*: Dark man, friendly, countryman, generally married, honest and conscientious. The card always signifies honesty, and may mean news concerning an unexpected heritage to fall in before very long; (R) good, but severe; austere, yet tolerant.

Crowley/GD: Prince of the Chariot of Fire. Proud, courageous, swift, strong, confident, noble, just, ambitious, hard-working, generous, romantic, impulsive, humorous, a practical joker, a boaster, intolerant, prejudiced, callous, cruel, violent, indecisive. (Aleister Crowley identified personally with the Prince of Wands.) The traits displayed depend on the dignity of the card.

Astrology: Air of Fire. (Note the airy backdrop of blue sky, clouds, and mountain peaks in the distance. In the foreground, the hot dry dessert becomes a setting for the throne capped with the head of a lion. The salamander at the King's feet is associated in mythology with Fire; the Central European "fire salamander" has fiery golden-yellow markings on its back.)

Jungian Functions: Thinking (Air) and intuition (Fire).

Decans/Timing: 20 Cancer–20 Leo. Tropical, 12 July–12 August; sidereal, 06 September–07 October.

Associated Trumps: The Chariot and the Sun.

Associated Pips: Four of Cups, Five and Six of Wands.

Keywords (+): Charismatic, adventurous, virile, enterprising, creative, assertive, strong-willed, dominant, forceful, energetic, proud, dignified, passionate, inspiring, sexy, confident, self-directed, responsible, inspiring, fond of challenge, ambitious, in charge; leadership, executive ability, king of the jungle, the boss.

Keywords (-): Impetuous, fanatical, bossy, authoritarian, orthodox, patriarchal, egotistical, arrogant, stern, intolerant, impatient, unyielding, cruel, aggressive, overpowering, domineering.

King of Wands Upright

Kings are mature accomplished individuals who are in charge of the matters related to their suit and element. They represent father figures, important men in the querent's life and significant personality traits needed by the querent to navigate the situation. When upright, the King of Wands usually represents a person of authority who is in a leadership role and has excellent managerial skills. He is likely to be a mover and shaker with entrepreneurial interests and an abundance of enthusiasm. With his thoughtful leadership and fiery personality, he is good at directing other people to get things done.

King of Wands Reversed

When reversed, the King of Wands may come across as rather domineering and egotistical. His excessive pride and arrogance often turn people off. His stern and intolerant opinions can cause difficulties for those who are in relationship with him. Religious versions of the reversed Wand King relish the words of Ephesians 5:22: "Wives, submit yourselves unto your own husbands, as unto the Lord" (KJV).

The Suit of Cups

PAGE OF CUPS: A SENSITIVE HELPER

Etteilla (1791): A blond youth, a studious child, study, application, work, employment; (R) friendship, affection, longing, desire, seduction.

Mathers (1888): A fair youth, confidence, probity, discretion, integrity; (R) a flatterer, deception, artifice.

Waite (1911): A fair, pleasing, somewhat effeminate page, of studious and intent aspect, contemplates a fish rising from a cup to look at him. It is the pictures of the mind taking form. *Divinatory Meanings*: Fair young man, one impelled to render service and with whom the querent will be connected; a studious youth; news, message; application, reflection, meditation; also these things directed to business; (R) taste, inclination, attachment, seduction, deception, artifice.

Crowley/GD: Princess of the Waters. Lotus of the Palace of the Floods. Gentle, sweet, kind, gracious, helpful, imaginative, dreamy, voluptuous, indolent, selfish, dependent. The traits displayed depend on the dignity of the card.

Astrology: Earth of Water. The Pages (Princesses) have no zodiacal attribution but represent four types of elemental people.

Jungian Functions: Sensation (Earth) and feeling (Water).

Decans/Timing: Astrology associates the element Water with summertime.

Keywords (+): Kind, affectionate, gentle, caring, studious, considerate, nurturing, helpful, introspective, sensitive, imaginative, fanciful, creative, artistic, psychic, fond of animals; a new birth, emotional renewal, meditation, reflection, study, application, work, a helper, news about a pregnancy, a message about love, a dreamlike situation, the beginning of a romantic relationship, an opportunity to care for others.

Keywords (-): Unrealistic, immature, needy, childish, living in a fantasy world, spoiled, unhappy, lazy, idle, escapist, clingy, overly dependent, fearful of dependency, deceptive, seductive, tricky, cunning, avoidant of adult responsibilities, putting your own needs ahead of the needs of others.

Page of Cups Upright

Pages represent children or young people, new learning experiences, the early stages of situations, and messages coming to the querent. When upright, the Page of Cups often indicates the receipt of happy news or of a message related to love and romance. Sometimes it heralds a pregnancy or the birth of a child, which will give you the opportunity to care for another person. This Page can also mark the start of a period of creative imagination and artistic productivity. The Page of Cups tends to be helpful and considerate.

Page of Cups Reversed

When reversed, the Page of Cups tends to spend his time in unproductive fantasy, as if living in a dream. Squandering his talents, he may come across as immature, lazy, or idle. He tends to be overly dependent on others to take care of him, and he can't be relied upon to honor his commitments. Sometimes this reversed Page highlights a fear of your own dependency needs and a reluctance to assume adult responsibilities involving care for others. Escapist tendencies, perhaps through drugs or alcohol, can become a problem. It's easy, however, to be seduced by this Page's charm.

KNIGHT OF CUPS: AN ENCHANTING ARRIVAL

Etteilla (1791): Arrival, approach, entrance, reception, reconciliation; (R) trickery, deceit, cheating, cleverness, lawlessness. (Note that the Knight of receptive Cups *approaches* whereas the Knight of outgoing Wands *departs*.)

Mathers (1888): Arrival, approach, advance; (R) duplicity, abuse of confidence, fraud, cunning.

Waite (1911): Graceful, but not warlike; riding quietly, wearing a winged helmet, referring to those higher graces of the imagination which sometimes characterize this card. He too is a dreamer, but the images of the side of sense haunt him in his vision. *Divinatory Meanings*: Arrival, approach—sometimes that of a messenger; advances, proposition, demeanor, invitation, incitement; (R) trickery, artifice, subtlety, swindling, duplicity, fraud.

Crowley/GD: Lord of the Waves and the Waters. King of the Hosts of the Sea. Amiable, graceful, quick to respond, sensitive, innocent, passive, idle, unreliable, untruthful, of little endurance. The traits displayed depend on the dignity of the card.

Astrology: Fire of Water.

Jungian Functions: Intuition (Fire) and Feeling (Water).

Decans/Timing: 20 Aquarius–20 Pisces. Tropical, 09 February–10 March; sidereal, 04 March–03 April

Associated Trumps: The Star and the Moon.

Associated Pips: Seven of Swords, Eight and Nine of Cups.

Keywords (+): Calm, graceful, attractive, romantic, imaginative, fanciful, amiable, charming, seductive, emotionally available, touchy-feely; idealism, sensitivity, the arts, creativity, idealism, falling in love, a proposal, an invitation, love affair, an approach, an arrival; a lover, artist, visionary, heart throb, musician, poet, dreamer.

Keywords (-): Escapism, illusion, deception, passivity, hedonism, impracticality, fraud, trickery, artifice, seduction, superficiality, boredom, dishonesty, unreliability, breach of confidentiality, mind-expanding drugs; a con artist, a Don Juan; "wham, bam, thank you, ma'am."

Knight of Cups Upright

Knights correspond to the element Fire, which suggests action, enterprise, movement, novelty, and excitement coming into your life. When upright, the Knight of Cups approaches with the promise of love, romance, and emotional fulfillment. He is the Prince Charming of fairy tales, who comes to help you explore your feelings. This visionary Knight can show you how to follow your bliss and make your dreams a reality. He can also provide the inspiration to get your creative juices flowing.

Knight of Cups Reversed

When reversed, the seductive Knight of Cups casts his spell so convincingly that you don't realize you are walking about in an illusion. You may think he really cares about you, but in reality he is using his charm for his own ends regardless of how it affects you in the long run. The reversed Knight of Cups is the archetypal Don Juan of classical literature. He will mislead or seduce you into providing him with momentary pleasure. Don't expect a committed relationship. Forewarned is forearmed.

QUEEN OF CUPS: EMOTIONAL INTELLIGENCE

Etteilla (1791): A blond woman, honesty, virtue, wisdom, a woman above reproach; (R) a highly placed lady, scandal, corruption, dishonesty, a dissolute woman.

Mathers (1888): A fair woman, success, happiness, advantage, pleasure; (R) a woman in good position, but intermeddling, and to be distrusted; success, but with some attendant trouble.

Waite (1911): Beautiful, fair, dreamy—as one who sees visions in a cup. This is, however, only one of her aspects; she sees, but she also acts, and her activity feeds her dream. *Divinatory Meanings*: Good, fair woman; honest, devoted woman, who will do service to the querent; loving intelligence, and hence the gift of vision; success, happiness, pleasure; also wisdom, virtue; a perfect spouse and a good mother; (R) good woman; otherwise, distinguished woman but one not to be trusted; perverse woman, a woman of equivocal character; vice, dishonor, depravity.

Crowley/GD: Queen of the Thrones of the Waters. Dreamy, receptive, tranquil, reflective, imaginative, kind, poetic, unruffled, coquettish, prone to fantasy. The traits displayed depend on the dignity of the card.

Astrology: Water of Water. The Queen of Cups gives birth to summer at the June solstice in the Northern Hemisphere.

Jungian Functions: Feeling (Water) in double measure.

Decans/Timing: 20 Gemini–20 Cancer. Tropical, 11 June–12 July; sidereal, 06 July–06 August

Associated Trumps: The Lovers and the Chariot.

Associated Pips: Ten of Swords, Two and Three of Cups.

Keywords (+): Dreamy, compassionate, sensitive, patient, empathic, intuitive, imaginative, psychic, creative, receptive, maternal, nurturing, devoted, honest, virtuous, wise, affectionate, enchanting, loving, romantic, emotionally intelligent, mystical, otherworldly, spiritually attuned; a woman above reproach.

Keywords (-): Unhappy, insecure, unstable, fickle, overly emotional, needy, brooding, passive, dependent, meddlesome, sentimental, coquettish, vain, seductive, unfaithful, dishonest, untrustworthy, dissolute, unrealistic, lacking personal boundaries, unreliable, prone to fantasy; a borderline personality.

....
Queen of Cups Upright

Queens are mature nurturing individuals (mother figures) who are responsive to the emotional climate surrounding the querent. They represent important women related to the current situation or significant personality traits needed by the querent to navigate the matter at hand. When upright, the Queen of Cups is a sensitive and nurturing woman who plays an important role in the querent's life. She is able to tune into the feeling state of those around her and to use her emotional intelligence to reconcile differences.

....
Queen of Cups Reversed

When reversed, the Queen of Cups tends to be overly sensitive and emotionally insecure. She often has poor personal boundaries and gets caught up in negative emotions. Because of her emotional instability, she is not entirely trustworthy or reliable. Sometimes she resorts to drugs or alcohol to calm her emotional storms.

KING OF CUPS: A FAIR AND AMIABLE PROFESSIONAL

Etteilla (1791): A blond man, fairness, probity, art, science; (R) a highly placed gentleman, corruption, dishonesty, extortion, scandal, a thief.

Mathers (1888): A fair man, goodness, kindness, liberality, generosity; (R) a man of good position, but shifty in his dealings, distrust, doubt, suspicion.

Waite (1911): He holds a short scepter in his left hand and a great cup in his right; his throne is set upon the sea; on one side a ship is riding and on the other a dolphin is leaping. The implicit is that the sign of the Cup naturally refers to water, which appears in all the court cards. *Divinatory Meanings*: Fair man, man of business, law, or divinity; responsible, disposed to oblige the querent; also equity, art, and science, including those who profess science, law, and art; creative intelligence; (R) dishonest, double-dealing man; roguery, exaction, injustice, vice, scandal, pillage, considerable loss.

Crowley/GD: Prince of the Chariot of the Waters. Subtle, artistic, crafty, scheming, secretive, calm, imperturbable, intensely passionate, ambitious, powerful, fierce, violent, ruthless, merciless, without conscience. The traits displayed depend on the dignity of the card.

Astrology: Air of Water. (Note the leaping fish, the watery setting, and the presence of ocean waves and a seashell on his throne.)

Jungian Functions: Thinking (Air) and Feeling (Water).

Decans/Timing: 20 Libra to 20 Scorpio. Tropical, 13 October–12 November. Sidereal, 06 November–06 December.

Associated Trumps: Justice and Death.

Associated Pips: Four of Swords, Five and Six of Cups.

Keywords (+): Kind, upright, calm, liberal, caring, amiable, loyal, generous, tolerant, fair, educated, responsible, sincere, respected, cultured, professional, self-reflective, imaginative, artistic, spiritual, nurturing, family-oriented, concerned about the welfare of others; a highly placed gentleman, a healer, a good adviser.

Keywords (-): Shifty, distrustful, scheming, manipulative, unreliable, confused, deceptive, threatening, intolerant, unprincipled, emotionally conflicted, uncommitted, dishonest, unjust, ruthless, underhanded, untrustworthy, cowardly, overly sensitive, escapist, substance-abusing, involved in scandal; gives bad advice; a thief.

....
King of Cups Upright

Kings are mature accomplished individuals (father figures) who are in charge of the matters related to their suit and element. They represent important men in the querent's life or significant personality traits needed by the querent to navigate the situation. When upright, the King of Cups is a sensitive, emotionally attuned man of accomplishment who gives good advice that can be of great assistance. He is often quite cultured and may appear in the form of a helpful physician, therapist, counselor, cleric, or other professional who ministers to the needs of the querent. Some authors feel that the King of Cups (Air of Water) comes across as cool and emotionally detached as he tries to give preference to his intellect while he keeps his own feelings under wraps.

....
King of Cups Reversed

When reversed, the King of Cups has difficulty maintaining his emotional equilibrium. He can be prone to daydreaming, escapism, or the abuse of drugs or alcohol. His personal relationships are characterized by manipulation, dishonesty, exploitation, and lack of genuine commitment. His advice cannot be trusted.

The Suit of Swords

PAGE OF SWORDS: KEEN OBSERVER, CLEVER SPY

Etteilla (1791): A spy, keen observer, curiosity seeker, artist; a remark, deduction, speculation, observation; (R) something sudden, unforeseen, astonishing or unanticipated; a lack of prudence.

Mathers (1888): A spy, overlooking, authority; (R) that which is unforeseen, vigilance, support.

Waite (1911): A lithe, active figure holds a sword upright in both hands, while in the act of swift walking. He is passing over rugged land, and about his way the clouds are collocated wildly. He is alert and lithe, looking this way and that, as if an expected enemy might appear at any moment. *Divinatory Meanings*: Authority, overseeing, secret service, vigilance, spying, examination, and the qualities thereto belonging; (R) the more evil side of these qualities; what is unforeseen, unprepared state; sickness is also intimated.

Crowley/GD: Princess of the Rushing Winds. Lotus of the Palace of Air. Dexterous, clever, strong, aggressive, firm, subtle, cunning, frivolous, vengeful, destructive. The traits displayed depend on the dignity of the card.

Astrology: Earth of Air. The Pages (Princesses) have no zodiacal attribution but represent four types of "elemental" people.

Jungian Functions: Sensation (Earth) and thinking (Air).

Decans/Timing: Astrology associates the element Air with autumn.

Keywords (+): intelligent, alert, lithe, curious, perceptive, vigilant, secretive, subtle, clever with words, discreet, observant, independent, good at keeping secrets, analytical, strategic, quick thinking, resolute, easily connects the dots; unexpected or astonishing news, a remark or opinion, a spy, a keen observer, analysis, clarity, secret service, mental planning.

Keywords (-): devious, sneaky, cunning, frivolous, secretive, suspicious, detached, unpredictable, destructive, paranoid, vengeful; spying, unforeseen difficulties, unpreparedness, cutting, illness, conflict, spite, sharp words, a hurtful communication, unwelcome news, behind-the-scenes shenanigans.

....

Page of Swords Upright

Pages represent children or young people, new learning experiences, the beginning stages of things, and messages coming to the querent. When upright, the Page of Swords is a perceptive young person who quickly connects the dots to construct theories about what is happening. His ability to plan mentally and to cut to the chase makes this Page especially adept at any type of work requiring secrecy, discernment and keen mental planning. He would be a formidable opponent in a game of chess. This page values his ability to think independently, but sometimes his sharp words or abrupt manner of communication are experienced as hurtful by those around him. Sometimes this card appears when one is dealing with unwanted news or upsetting messages.

....

Page of Swords Reversed

When reversed, the Page of Swords uses his sharp mind in an underhanded way. He can be sneaky and cunning, and sometimes paranoid and vengeful in his behavior. Typically, he is engaged in some type of behind-the-scenes dealings that may be to the detriment of the querent. Since Swords are a suit of cutting and strife, this overturned card can be a warning of surgery or illness.

KNIGHT OF SWORDS: A SOLDIER SCATTERING HIS ENEMIES

Etteilla (1791): A military man, soldier, warrior, combatant, enemy, anger, dispute, ruin; (R) stupidity, ignorance, incompetence, swindler, industriousness.

Mathers (1888): A soldier, a man whose profession is arms, skillfulness, capacity, address, promptitude.

Waite (1911): He is riding in full course, as if scattering his enemies. In the design he is really a prototypical hero of romantic chivalry. He might almost be Galahad, whose sword is swift and sure because he is clean of heart. *Divinatory Meanings*: A hero of romantic chivalry scattering his enemies, skill, bravery, capacity, defense, address, enmity, wrath, war, destruction, opposition, resistance, ruin. There is therefore a sense in which the card signifies death, but it carries this meaning only in its proximity to other cards of fatality; (R) imprudence, incapacity, extravagance.

Crowley/GD: Lord of the Wind and the Breezes. King of the Spirits of Air. Quick to act, skillful, clever, subtle, crafty, fierce, courageous, domineering, tyrannical, deceitful, indecisive. The traits displayed depend on the dignity of the card.

Astrology: Fire of Air.

Jungian Functions: Intuition (Fire) and thinking (Air).

Decans/Timing: 20 Taurus to 20 Gemini. Tropical, 11 May–10 June. Sidereal, 04 June–06 July.

Associated Trumps: The High Priest and the Lovers.

Associated Pips: Seven of Pentacles, Eight and Nine of Swords.

Keywords (+): Assertive, brave, swift, virile, forceful, eager, courageous, decisive, righteous, formidable, industrious, alert, strategic, clever with words, analytical, discerning, skillful; quick action, debate, strategy, clarity of mind, a sharp intellect, a rush to get things done, making drastic changes, defending one's rights, charging into battle, cutting away what no longer serves a purpose, adopting a new perspective.

Keywords (-): Pushy, hasty, impatient, macho, combative, inciting, headstrong, tactless, impulsive, provocative, domineering, warlike, violent, wrathful, destructive, argumentative, legalistic, oppositional, imprudent, sleazy, insensitive, self-interested; conflict, strife, combat, dispute, impatience, provocation, incitement, foolish haste, not considering consequences, harsh words, sarcasm, illness, surgery, the arrival of misfortune; death (with other cards of fatality).

....

Knight of Swords Upright

Knights correspond to the element Fire, which suggests action, enterprise, movement, novelty, and challenge coming into your life. When upright, the Knight of Swords prompts you to take decisive action to defend your rights and protect whatever you hold dear. This clever and assertive knight makes a good ally and a formidable opponent. Like the protagonist of Shakespeare's *Henry V* (1598), the Knight of Swords rallies you with the words: "Once more unto the breach, dear friends, once more." He readily connects the dots and is able to cut to the chase in any situation. His arrival is sometimes accompanied by the passing of misfortune. In many ways the Knight of Swords resembles Sir Galahad of Alfred Lord Tennyson's 1834 poem of the same name:

> My good blade carves the casques of men,
> My tough lance thrusteth sure,
> My strength is as the strength of ten,
> Because my heart is pure.

....
Knight of Swords Reversed

When reversed, the Knight of Swords tends to be impatient, insensitive, and overly assertive. He is in a rush to get things done and may be considering only his own needs to the detriment of those around him. The reversed Knight of Swords is a card of conflict and strife. His arrival sometimes heralds a period of misfortune. This knight often appears when there is concern about an illness, surgery, or possibly the death of someone to whom the querent is connected.

QUEEN OF SWORDS: A WOMAN WHO HAS KNOWN SORROW

Etteilla (1791): Widowhood, sterility, privation, poverty; (R) a cruel woman, malice, bigotry, artifice, hypocrisy.

Mathers (1888): Widowhood, loss, privation, absence, separation; (R) a bad woman, ill-tempered and bigoted, riches and discord, abundance together with worry, joy with grief.

Waite (1911): Her right hand raises the weapon vertically and the hilt rests on an arm of her royal chair; the left hand is extended, the arm raised, her countenance is severe but chastened; it suggests familiarity with sorrow. It does not represent mercy, and, her sword notwithstanding, she is scarcely a symbol of power. *Divinatory Meanings*: A woman familiar with sorrow, widowhood, female sadness, and embarrassment, absence, sterility, mourning, privation, separation; (R) malice, bigotry, artifice, prudery, bale, deceit.

Crowley/GD: Queen of the Thrones of Air. Perceptive, observant, subtle, confident, sly, graceful, deceitful, cruel, unreliable. The traits displayed depend on the dignity of the card.

Astrology: Water of Air. The Queen of Swords gives birth to autumn at the fall equinox in the Northern Hemisphere.

Jungian Functions: Feeling (Water) and thinking (Air).

Decans/Timing: 20 Virgo to 20 Libra. Tropical, 12 September–12 October. Sidereal, 07 October–06 November.

Associated Trumps: The Hermit and Justice.

Associated Pips: Ten of Pentacles, Two and Three of Swords.

Keywords (+): perceptive, thoughtful, mature, familiar with sorrow, introspective, self-reliant, independent, observant, subtle, clever, analytical, intelligent, just, critical, rational, dutiful, stoic, in control of emotions; weighing a decision, worried about an outcome, considering options, dealing with loss or abandonment, coping with grief; a strong woman who has known loss and privation.

Keywords (-): sad, embittered, worried, preoccupied, grief-stricken, isolated, abandoned, detached, ill-tempered, vindictive, cruel, icy, judgmental, hypocritical, cut off from emotions, unable to have children; loss, sorrow, worry, mourning, absence, separation, divorce, privation, emotional coolness, infertility, sterility, miscarriage, widowhood, a death in the family, malice, bigotry, intolerance, deceit, unreliability.

....
Queen of Swords Upright

Queens are mature nurturing individuals (mother figures) who are responsive to the emotional climate surrounding the querent. They represent important women related to the current situation or significant personality traits needed by the querent to navigate the matter at hand. When upright, the Queen of Swords indicates a need to keep your wits about you as you go through a period of anticipated loss, deprivation, or actual grief. This queen has known sorrow but has matured and become more self-reliant as a result of her privations.

....

Queen of Swords Reversed

When reversed, the Queen of Swords suggests that you may not be coping well with a loss of something important in your life. Perhaps you are feeling grief-stricken or bitter about what you have suffered. It is important to avoid becoming ill-tempered or vindictive in response to your loss or privations.

KING OF SWORDS: AN AUTHORITY FIGURE SITS IN JUDGMENT

Etteilla (1791): A man of law, a judge, attorney, advocate, physician, businessman; (R) a wicked man, inhumane, cruel, perverse.

Mathers (1888): A lawyer, a man of law, power, command, superiority, authority; (R) a wicked man, chagrin, worry, grief, fear, disturbance.

Waite (1911): He sits in judgment, holding the unsheathed sign of his suit. He recalls, of course, the conventional symbol of justice in the Trumps Major, and he may represent this virtue, but he is rather the power of life and death, in virtue of his office. *Divinatory Meanings*: A man who sits in judgment with power over life and death; whatsoever arises out of the idea of judgment and all its connexions—power, command, authority, militant intelligence, law, offices of the crown, and so forth; (R) cruelty, perversity, barbarity, perfidy, evil intention.

Crowley/GD: Prince of the Chariot of the Winds. Clever, intellectual, rational, full of ideas, plotting, unreliable, harsh, obstinate, overly cautious. The traits displayed depend on the dignity of the card.

Astrology: Air of Air. (Notice the clouds, high peaks, blue sky, and the presence of airy butterflies on his throne.)

Jungian Functions: Thinking (Air) in double measure.

Decans/Timing: 20 Capricorn to 20 Aquarius. Tropical, 10 January–09 February. Sidereal, 03 February–04 March.

Associated Trumps: The Devil and the Star.

Associated Pips: Four of Pentacles, Five and Six of Swords.

Keywords (+): Assertive, powerful, commanding, decisive, straightforward, authoritative, just, clever, rational, discriminating, confident, uncompromising, no-nonsense, factual, clear-thinking, pierces to the quick of a matter; clarity of communication, head over heart, confrontation, a professional, a man of law, someone who sits in judgment.

Keywords (-): Aggressive, hurtful, pushy, harsh, cold, judgmental, intimidating, obstinate, domineering, cruel, heartless, wicked, devilish, manipulative, exploitative, barbaric, evil, perverse.

....

King of Swords Upright

Kings are mature accomplished individuals (father figures) who are in charge of the matters related to their suit and element. They represent important men in the querent's life or significant personality traits needed by the querent to navigate the situation. When upright, the King of Swords represents a decisive person who uses his or her sharp intellect to achieve success. This King, for example, could be a physician, surgeon, lawyer, judge, or an astute negotiator. He can be quite confrontational in his search for the truth, and he does not suffer fools gladly.

....

King of Swords Reversed

When reversed, the King of Swords uses his sharp intellect and skill with words heartlessly to inflict harm on others. He may even delight in causing pain in a cruel and exploitative manner. Aggressive and domineering, he enjoys forcefully confronting others in an effort to make them squirm. His measure of justice is "an eye for an eye, a tooth for a tooth."

The Suit of Pentacles (Coins)

PAGE OF PENTACLES: A DILIGENT STUDENT

Etteilla (1791): A studious youth, study, application, work, apprenticeship; (R) luxury, abundance, benefit, prodigality, liberality.

Mathers (1888): A dark youth, economy, order, rule, management; (R) prodigality, profusion, waste, dissipation.

Waite (1911): A youthful figure, looking intently at the pentacle which hovers over his raised hands. He moves slowly, insensible of that which is about him. *Divinatory Meanings*: Application, study, scholarship, reflection; another reading says news, messages, and the bringer thereof; also rule, management; (R) prodigality, dissipation, liberality, luxury; unfavorable news.

Crowley/GD: Princess of the Echoing Hills. Rose of the Palace of Earth. Careful, diligent, persevering, generous, kind, benevolent. The traits displayed depend on the dignity of the card.

Astrology: Earth of Earth. The Pages (Princesses) have no zodiacal attribution but represent four types of "elemental" people.

Jungian Functions: Sensation (Earth) in double measure.

Decans/Timing: Astrology associates the element Earth with winter.

Keywords (+): studious, careful, diligent, conscientious, scholarly, persevering, meticulous, practical, dependable, hardworking, orderly, frugal, economical, detail-oriented; application of effort, hard work, study, scholarship, good management, apprenticeship, love of learning, an improvement in finances, maintenance of one's body, physical fitness, good health, steady progress, athletic prowess, survival issues, financial aid, caring for the environment, a new course of study, success on an exam.

Keywords (-): wasteful, prodigal, careless, petty, spoiled, idle, lazy, dull, slow, sickly, boring, small-minded, out of shape; loss, dissipation, wastefulness, overindulgence, pollution, prodigality, poor management, bad news, academic failure, lack of exercise, ill health; all work and no play.

....
Page of Pentacles Upright

Pages represent children or young people, new learning experiences, the beginning stages of things, and messages coming to the querent. When upright, the Page of Coins indicates the proper care of one's body and respect for the natural environment. He is a good student who works hard and systematically to perfect his abilities and achieve his goals. This scholarly and diligent Page is often the bearer of news related to one's job, an examination, or a financial concern.

....
Page of Pentacles Reversed

When reversed, the Page of Pentacles may bring disappointing news about an exam, a job offer, or some other financial matter. Rather than put in the required effort, this reversed Page tries to manage by doing the least amount of work necessary. Often this leads to failure or less than stellar results. He tends to be lax about the care of his body and would rather go out to a bar with friends than spend time at the gym.

KNIGHT OF PENTACLES: DEPENDABLE AND USEFUL

Etteilla (1791): Usefulness, profit, advantage; (R) peace, repose, inactivity, sleep, laziness, discouragement.

Mathers (1888): A useful man, trustworthy, wisdom, economy, order, regulation; (R) a brave man, but out of employment, idle, unemployed, negligent.

Waite (1911): He rides a slow, enduring, heavy horse, to which his own aspect corresponds. He exhibits his symbol, but does not look therein. *Divinatory Meanings:* Utility, serviceableness, interest, responsibility, rectitude—all on the normal and external plane; (R) inertia, idleness, repose of that kind, stagnation; also placidity, discouragement, carelessness.

Crowley/GD: Lord of the Wide and Fertile Land. King of the Spirits of Earth. Preoccupied with material things, patient, heavy, plodding, dull, nonintellectual, strong instincts. The traits displayed depend on the dignity of the card.

Astrology: Fire of Earth.

Jungian Functions: Intuition (Fire) and sensation (Earth).

Decans/Timing: 20 Leo to 20 Virgo. Tropical, 12 August–12 September. Sidereal, 06 September–07 October.

Associated Trumps: The Sun and the Hermit.

Associated Pips: Seven of Wands, Eight and Nine of Pentacles.

Keywords (+): Patient, calm, dependable, orderly, reliable, steady, predictable, useful, hardworking, productive, economical, conservative, thorough, methodical, service-oriented, thoughtful, profitable, grounded, practical, well regulated; a hard worker, a good provider, a workhorse; a long-standing situation.

Keywords (-): Lazy, idle, careless, neglectful, materialistic, stubborn, boring, plodding, slow, uninspiring, dull, inactive, unemployed, discouraged, ineffectual, lacking in motivation, timid, rigid, inflexible, stagnating, overly cautious, emotionally obtuse; a Neanderthal, a ne'er-do-well, a workaholic.

Knight of Pentacles Upright

Knights correspond to the element Fire, suggesting that action, enterprise, excitement, and novelty are coming into your life. When upright, the Knight of Pentacles represents a patient and hardworking individual whose chief aim is in getting the job done right. His main focus is on financial and material well-being so that at times he may seem emotionally unavailable as he spends most of his time working. Nonetheless, he is dependable and trustworthy—a good provider—and he will offer the querent a strong sense of security.

Knight of Pentacles Reversed

When reversed, the Knight of Pentacles plods along in a dull and idle manner. He may be quite lazy and inflexible in his thinking, and he is almost certainly emotionally obtuse. His rigidity and lack of motivation may cause him to stagnate rather than move forward on his life course. Alternatively, he may be so focused on work and material security that he neglects his emotional commitments and other aspects of his life.

QUEEN OF PENTACLES: A HELPFUL WOMAN OF MEANS

Etteilla (1791): A dark lady, a woman of means, wealth, luxury, optimism, confidence, frankness; (R) doubt, indecision, disquiet, uncertainty, vacillation.

Mathers (1888): A dark woman, a generous woman, liberality, greatness of soul, generosity; (R) certain evil, a suspicious woman; a woman justly regarded with suspicion, doubt, mistrust.

Waite (1911): The face suggests that of a dark woman, whose qualities might be summed up in the idea of greatness of soul; she has also the serious cast of intelligence; she contemplates her symbol and may see worlds therein. *Divinatory Meanings*: Greatness of soul, a serious cast of intelligence; opulence, generosity, magnificence, security, liberty; (R) evil, suspicion, suspense, fear, mistrust.

Crowley/GD: Queen of the Thrones of Earth. Motherly, kind-hearted, intuitive, practical, sensible, industrious, quietly lustful. The traits displayed depend on the dignity of the card.

Astrology: Water of Earth. The Queen of Pentacles gives birth to winter at the December solstice in the Northern Hemisphere.

Jungian Functions: Feeling (Water) and sensation (Earth).

Decans/Timing: 20 Sagittarius to 20 Capricorn. Tropical, 13 December–10 January. Sidereal, 04 January–03 February.

Associated Trumps: Temperance and the Devil.

Associated Pips: Ten of Wands, Two and Three of Pentacles.

Keywords (+): Good-natured, benevolent, generous, helpful, warm, optimistic, confident, practical, shrewd, down-to-earth, patient, responsible, industrious, hardworking, steadfast, persistent, fertile (symbolized by the rabbit), fond of physical comfort, pregnant, domestic; luxury, material abundance, hospitality, security, wealth, business acumen, management skills, love of nature, enjoyment of sex, the good things in life, a woman of means.

Keywords (-): Phlegmatic, lazy, materialistic, greedy, profligate, hedonistic, lustful, suspicious, indecisive, fearful, insecure, distrustful, preoccupied with status and wealth; conspicuous consumption, irresponsibility, neglect of one's body, health problems.

....
Queen of Pentacles Upright

Queens are mature nurturing individuals (mother figures) who are responsive to the emotional climate surrounding the querent. They represent important women related to the current situation or significant personality traits needed by the querent to navigate the matter at hand. When upright, the Queen of Pentacles is skilled at taking care of material needs. She may be reminding you to get sufficient exercise, keep the doctor's appointment, or properly attend to your finances. Our natural resources are a gift with which we have been entrusted. This queen is especially fertile and may be pregnant with child or with creative ideas about a new business venture. She will come to your aid when you are in financial need.

....
Queen of Pentacles Reversed

When reversed, the Queen of Pentacles is cautioning you to take proper care of your body and your material well-being. Perhaps you have not been getting sufficient exercise or have not done sufficient financial planning to achieve financial security. Are you too focused on hedonistic pleasures that you are neglecting to prepare for a rainy day? Don't let greed and suspicion interfere with your advancement in life.

KING OF PENTACLES: STEWARD OF MATERIAL RESOURCES

Etteilla (1791): A dark gentleman, a businessman, a stock market speculator, negotiator, professor, scientist, mathematician; (R) defective, weak, deformed, wicked, corrupt.

Mathers (1888): A dark man, victory, bravery, courage, success; (R) an old and vicious man, a dangerous man, doubt, fear, peril, danger.

Waite (1911): The figure calls for no special description. The face is rather dark, suggesting also courage, but somewhat lethargic in tendency. The bull's head should be noted as a recurrent symbol on the throne. The sign of this suit is represented throughout as engraved or blazoned with the pentagram, typifying the correspondence of the four elements in human nature and that by which they may be governed. In many old tarot packs this suit stood for current coin, money, deniers. But the cards do not happen to deal especially with questions of money. *Divinatory Meanings*: Valor, realizing intelligence, business and normal intellectual aptitude, sometimes mathematical gifts and attainments of this kind; success in these paths; (R) vice, weakness, ugliness, perversity, corruption, peril.

Crowley/GD: Prince of the Chariot of Earth. A good manager, competent, thoughtful, practical, productive, energetic, persevering, steadfast, trustworthy. The traits displayed depend on the dignity of the card.

Astrology: Air of Earth. (Note the earthy scene, the garden and the presence of Taurus the Bull on his throne.)

Jungian Functions: Thinking (Air) and sensation (Earth).

Decans/Timing: 20 Aries to 20 Taurus. Tropical, 10 April–10 May. Sidereal, 04 May–04 June.

Associated Trumps: The Emperor and the High Priest.

Associated Pips: Four of Wands, Five and Six of Pentacles.

Keywords (+): Cautious, productive, steadfast, reliable, protective, organized, constructive, patient, capable, wise, methodical, steady, responsible, persistent, hard-working, prudent, traditional, security-conscious, good business sense, mathematical aptitude; stewardship, practicality, stability, a good provider, sound management, financial security, endurance, care of one's body, success in work-related activities.

Keywords (-): Imprudent, stubborn, impatient, greedy, workaholic, jealous, sexist, insensitive, materialistic, wasteful, opportunistic, fearful, dishonest.

....
Upright King of Pentacles

Kings are mature accomplished individuals (father figures) who are in charge of the matters related to their suit and element. They represent important men in the querent's life or significant personality traits needed by the querent to navigate the situation. When upright, the King of Pentacles represents a productive person of authority, skill, and practical wisdom in the material world. He may have an aptitude for science and mathematics. This card suggests that you are able to take charge of the situation and achieve success in business, science, or some other established field of endeavor. The upright King of Golden Coins often foreshadows an improvement in financial circumstances or an advancement related to career. This King knows how to achieve worldly success and status.

....
Reversed King of Pentacles

When reversed, this card may warn of financial risk, greed, jealousy, dishonesty, irresponsibility, or acting out of expediency rather than following a prudent course of action. The mythical King Midas, preoccupied with acquiring gold, is one incarnation of the King of Pentacles reversed. The inverted King of Coins is related thematically to the Four of Pentacles.

Conclusions

E ven after a book goes to press, an author never feels that his work is quite complete. There are always lingering doubts. Did I say enough about topic X? Was topic Y explained clearly? Will readers get confused by how I explained such and such? Should topic Z have been omitted and perhaps something else been discussed in its place? And so on. In this final chapter, I would like to outline what I hoped to accomplish in this text and conclude with a brief reflection on the psychological value of reading the tarot.

If you have reached this point in the book, you should have a sense of the origins and history of the tarot, how it developed as a card game in Renaissance Italy and how it spread to France where eventually it became popularized as a means of divination in the eighteenth century. You should also be familiar with the three most popular categories of tarot decks—the Marseille, Waite-Smith, and Crowley-Harris Thoth tarot—and how they differ from so-called oracle and fortune-telling decks.

Having experimented some with the cards, you should have a sense of where the information in a tarot reading comes from and how your presuppositions and attitudes influence your experience of the cards. On a technical level, you should have an understanding of the importance of shuffling and selecting cards with sincere intention, asking appropriately worded questions, endeavoring to empower the client, using various types of tarot spreads, making sense of tarot reversals and (if it suits your fancy) using elemental dignities. On a theoretical level, you should have some appreciation of the importance of the four elements (Fire, Water, Air, and Earth), number symbolism, tarot ethics, and (if such topics interest you) the role that Kabbalah, the Hebrew alphabet, and astrology played in generating modern meanings for the cards.

The discussions of the individual cards begin with the canonical divinatory meanings recorded by Etteilla in the eighteenth century and proceed to review how tarot giants such as Mathers in the nineteenth century and Waite and Crowley in the twentieth century conceptualized the same cards. In this way, the reader can get a sense of the historical development of the ideas linked to each card. There is also a listing of keywords for the potentially positive (+) and negative (-) uses of the energy embodied in each card. Finally, there is a brief delineation of the upright and reversed positions of the cards; these should not be regarded as mutually exclusive but rather as obverse sides of the same coin. Ultimately, you need to develop your own understanding of each card, regardless of what so-called "experts" think the card means.

The Psychological Value of Reading the Tarot

While reflecting on the material in this text, it dawned on me that reading the tarot serves much the same function as the imaginative play of childhood. In his work with children, British psychoanalyst D. W. Winnicott observed that child's play forms the basis for adult creativity and the search for self.[46]

The play of childhood (or of adulthood, for that matter) takes place in a "transitional" zone between the inner world of fantasy and imagination and the supposedly real world outside the individual. Playing imaginatively within this transitional space allows an independent sense of self to develop in relation to the world of other people. Through play, children are able to work with and thereby conquer their fears and anxieties without risking harm in the "real world." Winnicott regarded the function of play as so significant that he viewed all human cultural activity as forms of play.

What, then, is a tarot reading if not an excursion into the imaginative world of childhood play? By entering the transitional space of tarot reading, we create for ourselves a safe environment where we can play with our deepest fears and anxieties as well as our most cherished hopes and wishes. We then return to the "real" world to make our dreams a reality. The playful myth-making that emerges as we read the tarot links us to the mythic imagination of past generations and moves us forward in our search for self.

---

46.   D. W. Winnicott, *Playing and Reality* (London: Tavistock, 1971).

Appendix

The Two Zodiacs

Western astrologers generally use the tropical zodiac calculated on the basis of the seasons of the year. They indicate the first day of spring in the Northern Hemisphere by saying that the sun has entered the sign Aries. This method is called the tropical or season-based zodiac.

Vedic astrology follows a different convention. Astrologers in India start the zodiac at the beginning of the *constellation* of stars called Aries: the so-called sidereal or star-based zodiac. A problem with the sidereal zodiac is that astrologers differ in their opinions about exactly where the group of stars called Aries begins.

Because the Golden Dawn preferred the sidereal zodiac, I have included both the tropical and sidereal dates for the zodiac signs. The accompanying table lists the thirty-six decans of the zodiac with their corresponding start dates in both the tropical and sidereal zodiacs. These dates are calculated for the period from 0 Aries in 2014 to 0 Aries in 2015 and will vary slightly depending on the location and particular year. The table is set for London in honor of the Golden Dawn.

To use the table for timing, determine which decan the tarot card in question belongs to (this is indicated in the section describing each card) and look up the date in the table. For example, if you asked when a new relationship was likely to come into your life and you drew the Seven of Pentacles, you would look up that card in the chapter on pip cards and find that it corresponds to the third decan of Taurus, whose start dates are May 10 in the tropical zodiac and June 4 in the sidereal zodiac. Since each decan lasts for roughly ten days, your answer (depending on which zodiac you prefer) would be either May 10–May 20, or June 4–June 14. As mentioned previously, the Golden Dawn preferred the sidereal zodiac and would give June 4–June 14 as the answer.

Tropical Date (season-based) of zodiac position	Zodiac Position	Sidereal Date (star-based Lahiri zodiac) of zodiac position
March 20	0 Aries	April 14
March 30	10 Aries	April 24
April 9	20 Aries	May 4
April 20	0 Taurus	May 14
April 30	10 Taurus	May 25
May 10	20 Taurus	June 4
May 21	0 Gemini	June 15
May 31	10 Gemini	June 25
June 10	20 Gemini	July 6
June 21	0 Cancer	July 16
July 1	10 Cancer	July 27
July 12	20 Cancer	August 6
July 22	0 Leo	August 18
August 2	10 Leo	August 27
August 12	20 Leo	September 6
August 23	0 Virgo	September 17
September 2	10 Virgo	September 27
September 12	20 Virgo	October 7
September 23	0 Libra	October 17
October 3	10 Libra	October 27
October 13	20 Libra	November 6
October 23	0 Scorpio	November 16

Tropical Date (season-based) of zodiac position	Zodiac Position	Sidereal Date (star-based Lahiri zodiac) of zodiac position
November 2	10 Scorpio	November 26
November 12	20 Scorpio	December 6
November 22	0 Sagittarius	December 16
December 2	10 Sagittarius	December 25
December 12	20 Sagittarius	January 4
December 21	0 Capricorn	January 14
December 31	10 Capricorn	January 24
January 10	20 Capricorn	February 3
January 20	0 Aquarius	February 13
January 30	10 Aquarius	February 23
February 9	20 Aquarius	March 4
February 18	0 Pisces	March 14
February 28	10 Pisces	March 24
March 10	20 Pisces	April 3
March 20	0 Aries	April 14

Recommended Reading

Hundreds of books have been written about the tarot, most of them during the last century. Included in this bibliography are but a handful of representative texts I have found particularly useful. The list is not intended to be exhaustive, and there are no doubt many excellent books that have not been mentioned due to lack of space or simple oversight on my part.

Tarot Books for Beginners

Almond, Jocelyn, and Keith Seddon. *Understanding Tarot: A Practical Guide to Tarot Card Reading.* San Francisco: Thorsons, 1991. This is a thoughtful text that presents the cards in an understandable way.

Bunning, Joan. *Learning the Tarot: A Tarot Book for Beginners.* San Francisco: Weiser, 1998. This text has become one of the staples for newcomers to the tarot.

Ellershaw, Josephine. *Easy Tarot Handbook.* Woodbury, MN: Llewellyn Worldwide, 2009. This is an extremely helpful and practical book, written as a guide to the Gilded Tarot but applicable to any deck in the Waite-Smith tradition.

Gray, Eden. *The Complete Guide to the Tarot.* New York: Bantam, new edition, 1982. This classic text spurred much of the modern interest in the tarot.

Greer, Mary K. *Tarot for Your Self: A Workbook for Personal Transformation*. Franklin Lakes, NJ: New Page Books, 2002.

———. *21 Ways to Read a Tarot Card*. Woodbury, MN: Llewellyn Worldwide, 2006. Mary K. Greer is one of the grand masters of modern tarot, and anything she writes about the cards is worth reading.

Jayanti, Amber. *Tarot for Dummies*. Hoboken, NJ: Wiley Publishing, 2001. The author has a uniquely helpful way of viewing each card as a set of questions being posed by the tarot to the person who consults the cards.

Junjulas, Craig. *Psychic Tarot*. Stamford, CT: U.S. Games Systems, 1985. This brief text, illustrated with the Aquarian Tarot, contains excellent pithy delineations of the cards.

Katz, Marcus, and Tali Goodwin. *Around the Tarot in 78 Days: A Personal Journey Through the Cards*. Woodbury, MN: Llewellyn Worldwide, 2012. This is a card-per-day workbook for getting to know the cards.

Kenner, Corrine. *Simple Fortunetelling with Tarot Cards*. Woodbury, MN: Llewellyn Worldwide, 2007. The author writes with a clear and understandable style that enables the reader to rapidly grasp the meanings of the cards.

Louis, Anthony. *Tarot Plain and Simple*. St. Paul, MN: Llewellyn Worldwide, 2002. This book first appeared in 1996 and has become a highly popular beginner's guide to the tarot.

MacGregor, Trish, and Phyllis Vegas. *Power Tarot*. New York: Simon and Schuster, 1998. This book contains wonderfully accurate delineations of the cards and a large number of tarot spreads for just about any type of question.

McElroy, Mark. *A Guide to Tarot Card Meanings*. TarotTools.com Publishing, 2014. This is a clear and thoughtful compendium of tarot card meanings.

Moore, Barbara. *Tarot for Beginners: A Practical Guide to Reading the Cards*. Woodbury, MN: Llewellyn Worldwide, 2010. This is a down-to-earth and clearly written guide for those who are completely new to the tarot.

———. *Llewellyn's Classic Tarot Companion*. Woodbury, MN: Llewellyn Worldwide, 2014. A guide by Barbara Moore makes use of the tarot deck featured in this book.

Nasios, Angelo. *Tarot: Unlocking the Arcana*. Atglen, PA: Schiffer Publishing, 2016. Angelo is the author of informative YouTube videos on tarot. His first book is a clearly written and informative introduction to the tarot.

Pollock, Rachel. *Seventy-Eight Degrees of Wisdom*. Wellingborough, UK: Aquarian Press, 2 vols. 1980 and 1983. This is a tarot classic in which the author set the tarot free from the tradition of mere fortune-telling and established it as a valuable tool for self-understanding and personal development. A must read.

Zerner, Amy, and Monte Farber. *The Enchanted Tarot*. New York: St. Martin's Press, 1990. In this beautifully illustrated introduction to the tarot, the author takes a novel approach of presenting a dream, awakening, and enchantment for each card.

Intermediate to Advanced Tarot Books

Ben-Dov, Yoav. *Tarot: The Open Reading*. CreateSpace Independent Publishing, 2013. This book focuses on interpreting the Tarot of Marseille.

Huggens, Kim. *Tarot 101: Mastering the Art of Reading the Cards*. Woodbury, MN: Llewellyn Worldwide, 2013.

Jodorowsky, Alejandro, and Marianne Costa. *The Way of Tarot: The Spiritual Teacher in the Cards*. Rochester, VT: Destiny Books, 2009.

Louis, Anthony. *Tarot Beyond the Basics*. Woodbury, MN: Llewellyn Worldwide, 2014.

Moore, Barbara. *Tarot Spreads: Layouts & Techniques to Empower Your Readings*. Woodbury, MN: Llewellyn Worldwide, 2012.

Rickleff, James. *Tarot Tells the Tale: Explore Three-Card Readings Through Familiar Stories*. St. Paul, MN: Llewellyn Worldwide, 2004.

Stern, Jane. *Confessions of a Tarot Reader*. Guilford, CT: skirt! (Globe Peguot Press), 2011.

Tyson, Donald. *1*2*3 Tarot*. St. Paul, MN: Llewellyn, 2005.

Waite, Arthur Edward. *The Pictorial Key to the Tarot*. Secaucus, NJ: Citadel Press, 1959.

Wen, Benebell, *Holistic Tarot, An Integrative Approach to Using Tarot for Personal Growth*. Berkeley, CA: North Atlantic Books, 2015.

Special Topics

Akron (C. F. Frey) and Hajo Banzhaf. *The Crowley Tarot*. Stamford, CT: U.S. Games Systems, 1995.
Bunning, Joan. *Learning Tarot Reversals*. York Beach, ME: Weiser, 2003.

Crowley, Aleister. *The Book of Thoth*. York Beach, ME: Weiser, 1974.

Feibig, Johannes, and Evelin Burge. *The Ultimate Guide to the Rider-Waite Tarot.* Woodbury, MN: Llewellyn Worldwide, 2013. This book focuses on the symbols used by artist Pamela Colman Smith in designing the popular Rider-Waite-Smith deck.

Greer, Mary K. *The Complete Book of Tarot Reversals.* St. Paul, MN: Llewellyn Worldwide, 2002.

Kenner, Corrine. *Tarot and Astrology.* Woodbury, MN: Llewellyn Worldwide, 2011. This book focuses on the Golden Dawn associations between astrology and tarot.

McCormack, Kathleen. *Tarot Decoder.* London: Quantum Publishing, 2014. This book focuses specially on interpreting each of the seventy-eight cards in the context of the Celtic Cross Spread.

Nichols, Sallie. *Jung and Tarot, An Archetypal Journey.* York Beach, ME: Weiser, 1980.

Pollack, Rachel. *The Kabbalah Tree.* St. Paul, MN: Llewellyn Worldwide, 2004. One of the leading figures in modern tarot explains her understanding of the Kabbalah, which is essential to the Golden Dawn approach to delineating the tarot.

Regardie, Israel. *The Golden Dawn: A Complete Course in Practical Ceremonial Magic,* sixth ed. St. Paul, MN: Llewellyn, 2002.

Wang, Robert. *The Qabalistic Tarot: A Textbook of Mystical Philosophy.* San Francisco: Weiser, 2004. Known for his knowledge of Kabbalah and Jungian psychology, Robert Wang explains his approach to combining Kabbalah and tarot.

Wanless, James. *Strategic Intuition for the 21st Century: Tarot for Business.* New York: Three Rivers Press, 1998. This book is written for managers and executives about how to use the tarot to generate creative ideas and solutions in the world of business.

Winnicott, D. W. *Playing and Reality.* London: Tavistock, 1971. This psychoanalytic text presents a theory about the importance of play in human development. Since the tarot is a type of play, the lessons of the analyst's couch also apply to reading with the tarot.

History and Origins of Tarot

Decker, Ronald. *Art and Arcana: Commentary on the Medieval Scapini Tarot.* Stamford, CT: U.S. Games Systems, 2004.

———. *The Esoteric Tarot.* Wheaton, IL: Theosophical Publishing House, 2013.

Dummett, Michael. *The Game of Tarot.* London: Duckworth, 1980.

Etteilla. *Dictionnaire synonymique du Livre de Thot ou Synonymes de significations primitives tracées sur Feuillets du Livre de Thot. (Thesaurus of the Book of Thoth, or Synonyms of primitive meanings drawn on sheets of the Book of Thoth).* Paris, 1791.

Huson, Paul. *Mystical Origins of the Tarot.* Rochester, VT: Destiny, 2004.

Kaplan, Stuart. *The Encyclopedia of Tarot.* New York: U.S. Games Systems, Vol. 1, 1978; Vol. 2, 1986.

Place, Robert. *The Tarot: History, Symbolism, and Divination.* New York: Tarcher, 2005.

A Few Internet Resources

Listed below is a very small sampling of the many useful websites about tarot. A Google search will reveal a host of other valuable offerings.

Aeclectic Tarot (the oldest and largest tarot forum community on the Internet). www.tarotforum.net

Ancient Hebrew Research Center at www.ancient-hebrew.org/

Angelo Nasios YouTube Site. Videos about tarot. www.youtube.com/user/AngeloNasios

Art of Change Tarot website by Carolyn Cushing. artofchangetarot.com/

Barbara Moore. Articles about tarot. www.llewellyn.com/blog/author/barbara_moore/

Birth Card Calculator. The Tarot School. www.tarotschool.com/Calculator.html

Donnaleigh's Tarot. donnaleigh.com/

Free On-Line Readings. Tarot Journey with Leisa ReFalo. tarotjourney.net/free-on-line-readings/

Free Tarot Reading. Llewellyn website. www.llewellyn.com/tarot_reading.php

Learning the Tarot by Joan Bunning. www.learntarot.com/

Mary K. Greer's Tarot Blog. marygreer.wordpress.com/

S. L. MacGregor Mathers. *The Tarot (1888).* At sacred-texts.com: www.sacred-texts.com /tarot/mathers/

Psychic Revelation. Tarot Card Interpretation and Meanings. www.psychic-revelation .com/reference/q_t/tarot/tarot_cards/index.html

Super Tarot website by Paul Hughes Barlow. supertarot.co.uk/

Tarot Elements website by Catherine Chapman. tarotelements.com/

Waite, Arthur Edward. *The Pictorial Key to the Tarot (1911).* At sacred-texts.com: www .sacred-texts.com/tarot/pkt/index.htm

Bibliography

Akron (C. F. Frey) and Hajo Banzhaf. *The Crowley Tarot*. Stamford, CT: U.S. Games Systems, 1995.

Almond, Jocelyn, and Keith Seddon. *Tarot for Relationships*. Northamptonshire, UK: The Aquarian Press, 1990.

———. *Understanding Tarot. A Practical Guide to Tarot Card Reading*. San Francisco: Thorsons, 1991.

Amberstone, Ruth Ann, and Wald Amberstone. *Tarot Tips*. St. Paul, MN: Llewellyn Publications, 2003.

———. *The Secret Language of Tarot*. San Francisco: Weiser Books, 2008.

Aristotle. *De Generatione et Corruptione,* trans. C. J. F. Williams. Oxford, UK: Clarendon Press, 1982.

Arroyo, Stephen. *Astrology, Psychology, and the Four Elements*. Sebastopol, CA: CRCS Publications, 1978.

Avelar, Helena, and Luis Ribeiro. *On the Heavenly Spheres, a Treatise on Traditional Astrology*. Tempe, AZ: American Federation of Astrologers, 2010.

Banzhaf, Hajo. *The Tarot Handbook*. Stamford, CT: U.S. Games Systems, 1993.

Beitchman, Philip. *Alchemy of the Word: Cabala of the Renaissance*. Albany, NY: State University of New York Press, 1998.

Ben-Dov, Yoav. *Tarot: The Open Reading*. CreateSpace Independent Publishing, 2013.

Bing, Gertrud, ed. *"Picatrix" Das Ziel des Weisen von Pseudo-Magriti, Studien der Bihliothek Warburg,* Vol. 27, translated into German from the original Arabic text by Hellmut Ritter and Martin Plessner in 1933. London: The Warburg Institute, 1962. Online at warburg.sas.ac.uk/pdf/fbh295b2205454.pdf.

Brumbaugh, Robert S. *The Philosophers of Greece.* Albany, NY: State University of New York Press, 1982.

Bunning, Joan. *Learning Tarot Reversals.* York Beach, ME: Weiser, 2003.

———. *Learning the Tarot: A Tarot Book for Beginners.* San Francisco: Weiser, 1998.

Bursten, Lee. *Universal Tarot of Marseille,* illustrated by Claude Burdel. Torino, Italy: Lo Scarabeo, 2006.

Carroll, Wilma. *The 2-Hour Tarot Tutor.* New York: Berkley Books, 2004.

Carter, Charles E.O. *The Principles of Astrology.* London: Quest Books, 1963.

Crowley, Aleister. *The Book of Thoth.* San Francisco: Weiser Books, 2008.

De Angeles, Ly. *Tarot, Theory and Practice.* Woodbury, MN: Llewellyn Publications, 2007.

Decker, Ronald. *Art and Arcana, Commentary on the Medieval Scapini Tarot.* Stamford, CT: U.S. Games Systems, 2004.

———. *The Esoteric Tarot.* Wheaton, IL: Theosophical Publishing House, 2013.

Dowson, Godfrey. *The Hermetic Tarot.* Stamford, CT: U.S. Games Systems, 2006.

Drury, Nevill. *The Tarot Workbook.* San Diego, CA: Thunder Bay Press, 2004.

Dummett, Michael. *The Game of Tarot.* London: Duckworth, 1980.

Duquette, Lon Milo. *Understanding Aleister Crowley's Thoth Tarot.* San Francisco: Weiser Books, 2003.

Ellershaw, Josephine. *Easy Tarot Reading.* Woodbury, MN: Llewellyn Publications, 2011.

Etteilla. *Dictionnaire synonymique du Livre de Thot ou Synonymes de significations primitives tracées sur Feuillets du Livre de Thot. (Thesaurus of the Book of Thoth, or Synonyms of primitive meanings drawn on sheets of the Book of Thoth).* Paris, 1791.

———. *l'Astrologie du Livre de Thot.* Paris, 1785. Edition published by Guy Trédaniel (ed.) with commentary by Jacques Halbronn. Paris, 1990.

Fairfield, Gail. *Choice Centered Tarot.* Smithville, IN: Ramp Creek Publishing, 1984.

Farley, Helen. *A Cultural History of Tarot: From Entertainment to Esotericism.* London: I.B. Tauris, 2009.

Feibig, Johannes, and Evelin Burger. *The Ultimate Guide to the Rider-Waite Tarot.* Woodbury, MN: Llewellyn Worldwide, 2013.

Fenton-Smith, Paul. *Tarot Masterclass.* Crow's Nest NSW, Australia: Allen & Unwin, 2007.

Filipczak, Zirka Z. *Hot Dry Men, Cold Wet Women: The Theory of Humors in Western European Art.* New York: American Federation of Arts, 1997.

Forrest, Steven. *The Inner Sky: The Dynamic New Astrology for Everyone.* New York: Bantam, 1984.

Fortune, Dion. *Practical Occultism in Daily Life.* Northamptonshire, UK: The Aquarian Press, 1976.

Frankl, Viktor E. *Man's Search for Meaning.* New York: Washington Square Press, Simon and Schuster, 1963.

Gibb, Douglas. Tarot Eon at taroteon.com.

Graves, Robert. *The Greek Myths.* London: Penguin Books, 1992.

Gray, Eden. *A Complete Guide to the Tarot.* New York: Bantam Books, 1972.

Greer, Mary K. *21 Ways to Read a Tarot Card.* Woodbury, MN: Llewellyn Worldwide, 2006.

———. *Tarot for Your Self.* Franklin Lakes, NJ: New Page Books, 2002. Originally published 1984 by Newcastle Publishing.

———. *The Complete Book of Tarot Reversals.* St. Paul, MN: Llewellyn, 2002.

Hall, Manly P. *The Secret Teachings of All Ages.* San Francisco: H.S. Crocker, 1928. Available at www.sacred-texts.com/eso/sta/index.htm.

Harris, Roy. *Language, Saussure and Wittgenstein.* London: Routledge, 1988.

Heisenberg, Werner. *Physics and Philosophy: The Revolution in Modern Science.* New York: Harper & Row, 1958.

Hughes-Barlow, Paul, and Catherine Chapman. *Beyond the Celtic Cross.* London: Aeon Books, 2009.

Huson, Paul. *Dame Fortune's Wheel Tarot.* Torino, Italy: Lo Scarabeo, 2008.

———. *Mystical Origins of the Tarot.* Rochester, VT: Destiny Books, 2004.

Jayanti, Amber. *Tarot for Dummies.* Hoboken, NJ: Wiley Publishing, 2001.

Jodorowsky, Alejandro and Marianne Costa. *The Way of Tarot: The Spiritual Teacher in the Cards.* Rochester, VT: Destiny Books, 2009.

Jung, Carl. *The Portable Jung*. New York: Penguin Books/Portable Library, 1976.

———. "Synchronicity: An Acausal Connecting Principle" from *The Collected Works of C. G. Jung, Vol 8.: Jung Extracts*. Princeton, NJ: Princeton University Press, 2010.

Junjulas, Craig. *Psychic Tarot*. Stamford, CT: U.S. Games Systems, 1985.

Kaczynski, Richard. *Perdurabo, The Life of Aleister Crowley*. Berkeley, CA: North Atlantic Books, 2010.

Kaplan, Stuart R. *The Encyclopedia of Tarot,* vols. 1 and 2. New York: U.S. Games Systems, 1978, 1986.

———. *Tarot Classic*. Stamford, CT: U.S. Games Systems, 2003.

———. *The Artwork & Times of Pamela Colman Smith*. Stamford, CT: U.S. Games Systems, 2003.

Katz, Marcus, and Tali Goodwin. *Around the Tarot in 78 Days: A Personal Journey Through the Cards*. Woodbury, MN: Llewellyn Worldwide, 2012.

Kenner, Corrine. *Simple Fortunetelling with Tarot Cards*. Woodbury, MN: Llewellyn Worldwide, 2007.

———. *Tarot and Astrology*. Woodbury, MN: Llewellyn Publications, 2011.

———. *Tarot for Writers*. Woodbury, MN: Llewellyn Publications, 2009.

Knight, Gareth. *The Magical World of the Tarot*. San Francisco: Weiser, 1996.

Louis, Anthony. *Tarot Plain and Simple*. St. Paul, MN: Llewellyn Publications, 1996.

———. *Tarot Beyond the Basics*. St. Paul, MN: Llewellyn Publications, 2014.

MacGregor, Trish, and Phyllis Vega. *Power Tarot*. New York: Fireside, 1998.

Marteau, Paul. *Le Tarot de Marseille*. Paris: Arts et Metiers Graphiques, first ed. 1949.

———. *El Tarot de Marsella*. Madrid: Editorial EDAF, S.L.U, 2011.

Mathers, S. L. MacGregor. *The Tarot: Its Occult Significance, Use in Fortune-telling, and Method of Play*. London: The Houseshop, 1888. In the public domain and available as a Kindle e-book from Amazon Digital Services (ASIN: B004IE9Z14) and at www.sacred-texts.com/tarot /mathers/.

Mayer, Elizabeth Lloyd. *Extraordinary Knowing: Science, Skepticism, and the Inexplicable Powers of the Human Mind*. New York: Bantam Books, 2007.

McCormack, Kathleen. *Tarot Decoder*. London: Quantum Publishing, 2014.

McElroy, Mark. *A Guide to Tarot Card Meanings.* TarotTools.com Publishing, 2014.

———. *What's in the Cards for You?* St. Paul, MN: Llewellyn Publications, 2005.

Michelson, Teresa C. *The Complete Tarot Reader.* St. Paul, MN: Llewellyn Publications, 2005.

Moakley, Gertrude. *The Tarot Cards Painted by Bonifacio Bembo for the Visconti-Sforza Family: An Iconographic and Historical Study.* New York: New York Public Library, 1966.

Montgomery, Stephen. *People Patterns: A Modern Guide to the Four Temperaments.* Del Mar, CA: Archer Publications, 2002.

Moore, Barbara. *Tarot for Beginners: A Practical Guide to Reading the Cards.* Woodbury, MN: Llewellyn Worldwide, 2010.

———. *Tarot Spreads: Layouts & Techniques to Empower Your Readings.* Woodbury, MN: Llewellyn Worldwide, 2012.

———. *Llewellyn's Classic Tarot Companion.* Woodbury, MN: Llewellyn Worldwide, 2014.

Morgan, Michele. *A Magical Course in Tarot.* Berkeley, CA: Conari Press, 2002.

Morin, Jean-Baptiste. *Astrologia Gallica, Book 22, Directions,* trans. James Herschel Holden. Tempe, AZ: American Federation of Astrologers, 1994.

Naparstek, Belleruth. *Your Sixth Sense.* San Francisco: HarperSanFrancisco, 1997.

Nasios, Angelo. *Tarot: Unlocking the Arcana.* Atglen, PA: Schiffer Publishing, 2016.

Nichols, Sallie. *Jung and Tarot, An Archetypal Journey.* York Beach, ME: Samuel Weiser, 1980.

O'Connor, Peter A. *Understanding Jung, Understanding Yourself.* New York: Paulist Press, 1985.

Osho. *Osho Zen Tarot: The Transcendental Game of Zen.* New York: St. Martin's Press, 1995.

Pennebaker, James, and John Evans. *Expressive Writing: Words That Heal.* Enumclaw, WA: Idyll Arbor, 2014.

Place, Robert M. *Alchemy and the Tarot: An Examination of the Historical Connection with a Guide to the Alchemical Tarot.* Saugerties, NY: Robert M. Place, 2012.

———. *The Tarot: History, Symbolism, and Divination.* New York: Penguin, 2005.

Pollock, Rachel. *Seventy-Eight Degrees of Wisdom.* Wellingborough, UK: Aquarian Press, 1980, 1983.

———. *Tarot Wisdom: Spiritual Teachings and Deeper Meanings.* Woodbury, MN: Llewellyn Publications, 2008.

———. *The Kabbalah Tree.* St. Paul, MN: Llewellyn, 2004.

———. *The New Tarot Handbook*. Woodbury, MN: Llewellyn, 2011.

Regardie, Israel. *The Golden Dawn: The Original Account of the Teaching, Rites & Ceremonies of the Hermetic Order, Sixth Ed.* St. Paul, MN: Llewellyn, 1989.

Renée, Janina. *Tarot for a New Generation*. St. Paul, MN: Llewellyn, 2001.

———. *Tarot Spells*. St. Paul, MN: Llewellyn, 2000.

Rickleff, James. *Tarot Tells the Tale: Explore Three-Card Readings Through Familiar Stories*. St. Paul, MN: Llewellyn, 2004.

Roberts, Richard. *The Original Tarot & You*. Berwick, ME: Ibis Press, 2005.

Rosengarten, Arthur. *Tarot and Psychology*. St. Paul, MN: Paragon House, 2000.

Rowson, Everett K. "Homoerotic Liaisons among the Mamluk Elite in Late Medieval Egypt and Syria" in *Islamicate Sexualities: Translations Across Temporal Geographies of Desire*. Eds. Kathryn Babayan and Afsaneh Nahmabadi. Cambridge, MA: Harvard University Center for Middle Eastern Studies, 2008.

Saunders, Thomas. *The Authentic Tarot*. London: Watkins Publishing, 2007.

Schwickert, Friedrick, and Adolf Weiss. *Cornerstones of Astrology*. Dallas, TX: Sangreal Foundation, 1972.

Shapiro, Rami M. *Hasidic Tales*. Woodstock, VT: SkyLight Paths Publishing, 2003.

Sharman-Burke, Juliet, and Liz Greene. *The New Mythic Tarot*. New York: St. Martin's Press, 2008.

Shavick, Nancy. *Traveling the Royal Road: Mastering the Tarot*. New York: Berkley Books, 1992.

Stern, Jane. *Confessions of a Tarot Reader*. Guilford, CT: skirt! (Globe Pequot Press), 2011.

Stewart, Rowenna. *Collins Gem Tarot*. Glasgow, UK: Harper Collins Publishers, 1998.

The Holy Bible. King James Version (1611). New York: Barnes & Nobles, 2012.

Tyson, Donald. *1*2*3 Tarot*. St. Paul, MN: Llewellyn, 2004.

Waite, Arthur Edward. *The Pictorial Key to the Tarot,* London: W. Rider, 1911. Waite's original text is in the public domain and available online at www.sacred-texts.com/tarot/pkt/pkttp.htm and at en.wikisource.org/wiki/The_Pictorial_Key_to_the_Tarot, and also as a Kindle e-book from Amazon Digital Services (**ASIN:** B00L18UZG4).

———. *The Pictorial Key to the Tarot (1911),* with an introduction by Gertrude Moakley (1959). Secaucus, NJ: Citadel Press, 1959.

Wang, Robert. *The Qabalistic Tarot*. San Francisco: Weiser Books, 1987.

Wanless, James. *Strategic Intuition for the 21st Century, Tarot for Business.* Carmel, CA: Merrill-West Publishing, 1996.

Wasserman, James. *Instructions for Aleister Crowley's Thoth Tarot Deck.* Stamford, CT: U. S. Games Systems, 1978.

Watters, Joanna. *Tarot for Today.* Pleasantville, NY: Readers Digest, 2003.

Wen, Benebell, *Holistic Tarot, An Integrative Approach to Using Tarot for Personal Growth.* Berkeley, CA: North Atlantic Books, 2015.

White, Dusty. *The Easiest Way to Learn Tarot—Ever!* Charleston, SC: BookSurge Publishing, 2009.

Willowmagic, Raven. *Tarot Tips of the Trade.* Amazon.com: Kindle edition, 2010.

Winnicott, D.W. *Playing and Reality.* London: Tavistock, 1971.

Zerner, Amy, and Monte Farber. *The Enchanted Tarot* (book). New York: St. Martin's Press, 1990.

Ziegler, Gerd. *Tarot, Mirror of the Soul.* San Francisco: Weiser, 1998.

ANTHONY
LOUIS

HORARY
ASTROLOGY
PLAIN
&
SIMPLE

FAST
&
ACCURATE
ANSWERS
TO
REAL
WORLD
QUESTIONS

INCLUDING UNDERSTANDING EVENT CHARTS

Horary Astrology: Plain and Simple
Fast & Accurate Answers to Real World Questions
ANTHONY LOUIS

Here is the best how-to guide for the intermediate astrologer on the art of astrological divination. Horary astrology is the best method for getting answers to questions of pressing personal concern: Will I ever have children? Should I buy that lakefront property? What happened to my car keys? When used wisely, horary acts like a trusted advisor to whom you can turn in times of trouble.

978-1-56718-401-3, 288 pp., 7 x 10   **$22.99**

ANTHONY LOUIS

TAROT
Plain and Simple

with illustrations by
Robin Wood

Tarot Plain and Simple
Anthony Louis

The tarot is an excellent method for turning experience into wisdom. At its essence the Tarot deals with archetypal symbols of the human situation. By studying the Tarot, we connect ourselves with the mythical underpinnings of our lives; we contact the gods within. As a tool, the Tarot helps to awaken our intuitive self. This book presents a thoroughly tested, reliable and user-friendly self-study program for those who want to do readings for themselves and others. It is written by a psychiatrist who brings a profound understanding of human nature and psychological conflict to the study of the Tarot. Tarot enthusiasts will find that his Jungian approach to the card descriptions will transport them to an even deeper level of personal transformation.

978-1-56718-400-6, 336 pp., 6 x 9   **$16.95**

To order, call 1-877-NEW-WRLD
Prices subject to change without notice
Order at Llewellyn.com 24 hours a day, 7 days a week

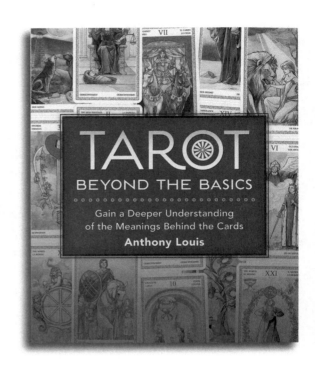

TAROT
BEYOND THE BASICS

Gain a Deeper Understanding
of the Meanings Behind the Cards

Anthony Louis

Tarot Beyond the Basics
Gain a Deeper Understanding of the Meanings Behind the Cards
Anthony Louis

Take your tarot reading to a higher level. With an emphasis on tarot's astrological influences and a number of detailed sample readings, *Tarot Beyond the Basics* shows the way to becoming an advanced practitioner. Here, Anthony Louis shares how-to instructions for working with reversals, number symbolism, intuition, the four elements, and the philosophical roots of tarot.

Explaining astrology for tarot readers clearly and in a way that makes sense, Louis shows how to use the tarot to give powerful readings that change people's lives. The "real" tarot exists in the mind of each reader and is interlaced with his or her stories and experiences. The abundance of knowledge presented in *Tarot Beyond the Basics* is sure to make your readings come alive with meaning and significance.

978-0-7387-3944-1, 408 pp., 7½ x 9⅛   **$19.99**